The Consolations of
HUMOR

The Consolations of
HUMOR
and Other Folklore Essays

Elliott Oring

UTAH STATE UNIVERSITY PRESS

Logan

© 2023 by University Press of Colorado

Published by Utah State University Press
An imprint of University Press of Colorado
1580 North Logan Street, Suite 660
PMB 39883
Denver, Colorado 80203-1942

ASSOCIATION
of UNIVERSITY
PRESSES
The University Press of Colorado is a proud member of
Association of University Presses.

The University Press of Colorado is a cooperative publishing enterprise supported, in part, by Adams State University, Colorado State University, Fort Lewis College, Metropolitan State University of Denver, University of Alaska Fairbanks, University of Colorado, University of Denver, University of Northern Colorado, University of Wyoming, Utah State University, and Western Colorado University.

ISBN: 978-1-64642-517-4 (hardcover)
ISBN: 978-1-64642-518-1 (paperback)
ISBN: 978-1-64642-519-8 (ebook)
https://doi.org/10.7330/9781646425198

Cataloging-in-Publication data for this title is available online at the Library of Congress

Cover after *Le Radeau de la Méduse* (The Raft of the Medusa), Théodor Géricault, 1818–1819. Public domain image from Wikimedia Commons. Jester hat © MG SG/Shutterstock.

For Barbara Kirshenblatt-Gimblett,
who doesn't do jokes,

and
Victor Raskin,
who does,

and
Inta Carpenter,
who would like to

Contents

Preface

Life is the art of drawing sufficient conclusions from insufficient premises
—Samuel Butler, *The Notebooks*

Folklore might be defined as the study of the arts and traditions of everyday life. The rest is commentary. That commentary, however, is likely to prove extensive. It will have linguistic, historical, philosophical, psychological, and sociological dimensions. Folklorists have also directed their attention to certain forms of art and tradition, what are called the *genres* of folklore. Some of these genres can be concisely (although not unambiguously) defined—joke, proverb, riddle, folktale, ballad, game—others less so. Folklorists have also directed their attention largely to the arts and traditions that are sustained in certain kinds of social groups: rural, occupational, ethnic, religious, and age-based (children or elderly). The stuff of folklore is most often a communication within a particular face-to-face social network.

Over the years, I have contributed slightly to the scholarly literature on folksong (Oring 1971), superstition (Oring 1977), legend (Oring 1990, 2008), and game (Oring 1997) but primarily to the study of jokes (Oring 1981, 1984, 1992, 2003, 2016, 2018). To the extent that essays in this volume focus on a particular genre, that focus is on jokes. Jokes, and humor more generally, continue to challenge scholars. What is a joke, and what is it about a joke that provokes amusement and ofttimes laughter? I have my own theoretical allegiance with respect to the first of these questions, which is eminently clear in my previous publications as well as in the essays included in this volume. I hold no theory with respect to the second

https://doi.org/10.7330/9781646425198.c000   ix

question. Although some have attempted to address it (e.g., Freud 1960 [1905], 8:146–151), laughter remains something of a mystery.

The first three chapters of the volume are concerned with joke content. Chapter 1, "The Consolations of Humor," examines a series of jokes and anecdotes that circulate almost exclusively among the members of the Church of Jesus Christ of Latter-Day Saints, otherwise known as the Mormons. They revolve around the figure of J. Golden Kimball, once a member of the church hierarchy. Chapter 2, "Three *Jewish* Jokes," raises questions about how Jewish jokes should be defined and interpreted within the context of an international jokelore. Chapter 3, "Whatever Became of the Dirty Joke?," looks back at some of the research on the "dirty joke," what we think we know about it, and how folklorists might contribute to its understanding.

Chapter 4, "Incongruous, Appropriate, Spurious," and chapter 5, "Overlaps, Oppositions, and Ontologies," address the structure of humor rather than its content. The chapters advance the notion that humor depends upon the perception of an *appropriate incongruity* but develop some critical refinements. Chapter 4 then endeavors to demonstrate the usefulness of these concepts in the analysis of an extended series of joke texts. Though the grasping of a joke may often prove to be easy, the analysis of what is grasped is not always simple or obvious. Chapter 5 extends the discussion by questioning the efforts by a group of computational linguists to reduce the recognition of a humorous text to a computer algorithm. The task they have assumed is daunting, and I am not sure that their program can be accomplished in the absence of formal definitions of the concepts discussed in chapter 4.

The remaining chapters do not address jokes but matters more generally theoretical. Chapter 6, "Memetics and Folkloristics: The Theory," critically examines the concept of the *meme* first proposed by Richard Dawkins. The meme was intended to denote a unit of culture that, like the gene, was a replicator and consequently was subject to the very same set of processes: replication, variation, and selection. Chapter 7, "Memetics and Folkloristics: The Applications," examines attempts to apply Dawkins's conceptualization to specific folklore materials. Chapter 8, "Four Laws of Folklore," highlights previous attempts by folklorists to identify laws that govern the operation of their subject matter and challenges the reluctance of folklorists to examine these laws critically or to propose and test new ones. The final chapter, chapter 9, "To Explain Tradition," raises an old question: how it is that certain beliefs and practices are marginalized and abandoned while others are not. Despite the longevity and centrality of this question to the field, it is not one that has been rigorously engaged when it has been engaged at all. The chapter lays out the problem and suggests some of the means that might be marshalled in responding to it. The Afterword is not a summary but identifies a theme underlying the various chapters, although the chapters were not consciously composed with this unity in mind. Furthermore, the Afterword links the materials in the chapters to related questions, issues, and concerns. The Afterword should not be skipped, although this recommendation will prove of little value to readers who have already skipped the Preface.

Scholarship proceeds through a series of questions and answers that in turn generate new questions. Questions prove more durable than answers. Answers often disappear, not least because they fail to adequately resolve the question they address. Questions, however, often persist. They may fade from view for a period of time as fashions change, but they can and often do return. It is by its questions that a discipline is defined. These essays constitute a series of questions about the materials, methods, and theories of folklore. Hopefully, they will stimulate others to address these questions, propose their own answers, and ask new questions of their own.

***

No book is published without help. First and foremost are the numerous scholars whose names and works are cited throughout the text and endnotes of the various chapters. In the absence of their efforts, I would have had little to say. Useful comments, criticisms, corrections, translations, and bibliographic references were offered by Salvatore Attardo, Michael J. Bell, Simon Bronner, Ray Cashman, Scott Clarkson, Bill C. Ellis, Michael Dylan Foster, Christian Hempelmann, Michael Owen Jones, Robert Mankoff, Olivier Morin, David Pavot, Julia Rayz, Tsafi Sebba-Elran, Timothy Tangherlini, Hrag Varjabedian, Tony Veale, and two anonymous reviewers.

Over the years, I have had many fruitful conversations and/or arguments (for me they are the same) with Anastasiya Astapova, Haya Bar-Itzhak, Władisław Chłopicki, Christie Davies, Charles Clay Doyle, Henry Glassie, Terry Gunnell, Valdimar Hafstein, Bill Ivey, Paul Jordan-Smith, Greg Kelley, Barbara Kirshenblatt-Gimblett, Jay Mechling, Moira Marsh, Wolfgang Mieder, John Morreall, Tom Mould, Victor Raskin, and Gregory Schrempp. All have contributed to this book even if they probably don't know how. My friends and relatives continue to serve as sources of inspiration and amusement: Victor Astapov, Inta Carpenter, Larry Danielson, Benjamin Fass, Genevieve Giuliano, Jess Hordes, Naomi Hordes, Rosan Jordan, Judit Katona-Apte, Norman Klein, Barbara Lloyd, Tim Lloyd, Alejandro Omidsalar, Mahmoud Omidsalar, Teresa Omidsalar, Claire Oring, Katie Oring, Mark Oring, Nathan Power, Fred Reinman, Gloria Reinman, and Kathleen Stocks. Many thanks to Inta Carpenter for her close initial reading and editing of the chapters of this book and to Norman Klein and Kathleen Stocks for their attentive proofreading. Of course, all the errors and oversights somehow remain my responsibility. It's a funny world.

***

"The Consolations of Humor" was first presented as a Folklore Archives Founder's Lecture at Brigham Young University on January 25, 2017. It was published in the *European Journal of Humour Research* (2017, 56–66). "Three *Jewish* Jokes" is a significantly expanded version of "On Account of a Joke" that appeared in *Masoret Haya: Essays in Folklore in Honor of Professor Haya Bar-Itzhak* (Haifa: Pardes, 2020, xxii–xxxvi). "Overlaps, Oppositions, and Ontologies" appeared in *Humor: International Journal of Humor Research* (2019, 151–170). "Memetics and Folkloristics: The Theory" appeared in *Western Folklore* (2014, 432–454), and "Memetics and Folkloristics: The Applications" in *Western Folklore* (2014, 455–492). "Four Laws of Folklore" was published in *Western Folklore* (2022, 51–73). A much-abbreviated version of "To Explain Tradition" was presented at the 10th International Conference of Young Folklorists hosted by Tartu Ülikool (University of Tartu), Estonia, on May 20, 2021. That lecture was published in *Journal of Ethnology and Folkloristics* (2021, 1–18). Permission to republish these essays is greatly appreciated.

The Consolations of
HUMOR

CHAPTER ONE

The Consolations of Humor

Life does not cease to be funny when people die any more than it ceases to be serious when people laugh.
 —George Bernard Shaw, *The Doctor's Dilemma*

I have long regarded aggression as an explanation for jokes as seriously misguided. Whenever and wherever it has been proposed, there have existed alternate hypotheses that could explain—indeed, better explain—the data and address its particular characteristics (Oring 1973, 1975, 1984, 1981, 1987, 1992).[1] The presumption of aggression as the motive for jokes derives primarily from the work of Sigmund Freud, although what Freud had to say about jokes has routinely been misconstrued (Freud 1960, 8:96–102). All in all, Freud did not maintain that jokes were like dreams that are produced by sexual and aggressive impulses welling up from the unconscious. Even when an aggressive motive might be identified in a joke, that aggression was likely to be both conscious and obvious (Oring 2016, 3–15). Finally, as I noted over forty years ago, "Aggressive impulses, may, on occasion, utilize forms of intellectual play (i.e., jokes) as weapons, but impulses of play, mediated by the intellect, can similarly manipulate aggression in the construction of jokes" (Oring 1975, 159). In other words, one may on occasion use a joke as a means of assault, but one might as easily manipulate forms of assault to craft jokes.

Linked to the hypothesis of aggression is the idea that jokes serve the purposes of release and relief. Jokes are compensatory and serve to reestablish equilibrium in the psyches of joke tellers and their audiences (e.g., Keith-Spiegel 1972, 20–21; Goldstein, Suls, and Anthony 1972, 160; Rothbart 1977, 90; Dundes 1987,

44; Morreall 2008, 222–224; Kuipers 2008, 362). They serve as a "safety valve" that allow for "letting off steam" so that the system does not self-destruct. The presumption is that without the means that jokes provide to express pent-up sexual or aggressive impulses, the integrity of the psychophysiological system is ever in jeopardy.[2]

In the examination of the corpus of jokes—anecdotes, actually—that follows, two points should emerge. The first point is that there seems to be no substantive grounds for imputing aggressive motives to their tellers or their audiences. In fact, the central character of the corpus of anecdotes that is to follow was a much beloved figure in his lifetime, and the character is still regarded with affection by many who know him only through these anecdotes. Of course, one might always argue that aggression is unconscious and that the jokes are a reaction formation to some underlying hostile impulse. Anything, of course, is possible, but one should ask for solid evidence—ethnographic evidence—and not just the assertion of the psychoanalytic principle that underneath every expression of love is a deep reservoir of hate. The second point is that these jokes might offer compensations, but compensations unrelated to the release of and relief from libidinal forces. They instead can be understood as compensations of a different kind—the consolations of philosophy.

J. Golden Kimball was a Mormon who became a general authority in the Church of Jesus Christ of Latter-Day Saints. Born in 1853, he became a muleskinner (a mule driver) at the age of fifteen following the death of his father, and he adopted the rough manners and lifestyle of his occupation. His life changed in the early 1880s when he became seriously interested in his Mormon faith. He was sent to be a missionary in the southern United States, an area in which Mormon missionaries were deeply resented and where missionary work could be life-threatening. His missionary work, however, was so successful that he was appointed president of the Southern States Mission and later was called to serve as one of the Seven Presidents of the First Council of the Seventy. Between missions, he returned to ranching, married, and fathered six children. As a general authority, he was often called upon to travel to various church wards throughout the West to solve problems and address congregations. It was through these visits and his public speaking that he became widely known for his dedication to the church, his honesty, and his humor (Eliason 2007, 1–7). The jokes and anecdotes about J. Golden Kimball revolve around these traits and the incompatibility of the habits of his muleskinner way of life—swearing, drinking coffee, lacking deference to authority—and his position in the church hierarchy.

William A. Wilson, a dean of Mormon folklore scholarship, actually argued that neither J. Golden Kimball nor any high church authority was the central figure of Mormon humor. It was rather the "beleaguered bishop . . . the Relief Society president, and occasionally a high councilor or the stake president" who were the targets of jokes (2006a [1985], 224). Wilson also claimed that there was no single meaning for such jokes. A number of different—even contradictory—meanings were possible, which depended largely on the tellers and listeners and the particular circumstances in which the jokes were told—what folklorists call the "social context" of the humor (2006a, 234–235).

Undoubtedly, there is truth in this view, and yet it would impose a definite limitation on the interpretation of Mormon humor, the interpretation of humor in general, and the interpretation of any kind of folklore. The limitation lies in the fact that folklorists would have nothing to say about the corpus of J. Golden Kimball stories or any other body of Mormon lore. They could only speak about individual expressions that erupt in an array of idiosyncratic circumstances. Folklore studies would then become an interminable journey from social interaction to social interaction without ever being able to make any credible generalizations.

This problem is not one that arises from Wilson's perspective alone. Others have made similar arguments (e.g., Ellis 2003a, 89), and it is, to some extent, a consequence of the performance approach to folklore that first crystallized in the early 1970s and which has had a following in folklore studies ever since. A performance is a unique event with a particular set of participants, a specific physical location, and a particular interactional dynamic (Bauman 1977). It is not really comparable to any other event except in the broadest sense that events have actors, settings, and social structures and proceed from within a basic set of broadly recognized symbolic forms.

Wilson does modify his perspective somewhat when he suggests that jokes remain "as clear markers of central issues in the society, as a barometer of those concerns engaging the minds of the people at any particular moment" (2006a, 235). And this also has a measure of truth. But what exactly is a central marker? Do we find out what concerns people by scrutinizing the topics of the jokes they tell? If so, why not simply listen to their conversations; study their letters to editors in newspapers; or sample their emails, Internet forums, tweets, and Facebook pages? Surely these would give a better picture of their concerns than their jokes, *unless* there is something to be found in jokes that might not necessarily emerge in these other kinds of communications.

If jokes and other forms of folklore are important, it could only be because there is something in them that is *unconscious* such that their disseminators are to some degree unaware of the implications of what they are saying and doing. This does not mean unconscious in the psychoanalytic sense of the term: primitive sexual and aggressive impulses repressed in some particular portion of the psyche that disguise themselves in various symbolic formations and that can only be discerned through close psychological analysis. Many aspects of thought and behavior are unconscious simply because people cannot entirely know their sources or histories and cannot be fully aware of their organization, associations, presuppositions, or implicatures.

Consequently, we often do not know precisely what we are doing or exactly how we are doing it (Spiro 1974, xiii). A few quick examples should suffice as illustrations. Most obvious is the example of language. We speak with only the most rudimentary sense of how to form a grammatical utterance. We engage in various grammatical transformations, unaware that we are doing so. If we were called upon to give an account of the rules governing our utterances, we would likely fail—spectacularly fail. The four maxims identified by H. Paul Grice that govern cooperative conversation—quantity, quality, relevance, and manner—are largely unconscious in the same sense. Recently, I tried to explain to a foreign colleague the use of the definite and indefinite article in English. I thought it would be simple, but I found that I could not do it. The best I could do was point out where in her essay the usage was awkward or was wrong.

Also consider what I would call a rule of eating behavior in the United States. Food that is picked up with a utensil must be placed in the mouth and not returned to the plate or bowl in the absence of some kind of excuse (e.g., "Boy, that's hot!"). The presumption is that food being picked up with a utensil should be of the right size to be placed in the mouth and consumed. Food that can be returned to the plate is food that can be picked up with the hands. While there may be regional differences concerning which foods fall in the categories of what might be called "utensil food" and "hand food," the rule seems to be a broad one. And although most would recognize this rule to be generally true once it has been stated, no one ever explicitly formulated or formally taught this rule even though it is followed rather conscientiously.

Much of what we do as social beings in social settings and social interactions is unconscious in this sense. We act according to rules of which we are largely unaware and register things automatically without subjecting them to deliberate scrutiny. The same is particularly true in processing a joke and other forms of folklore. We unreflectively survey an extensive body of acquired knowledge and select those bits from that archive relevant to the situation at hand. Sometimes we are aware of what we are doing and how we do it, most often we are not.

I regard jokes, and humor more generally, as dependent upon the perception of an *appropriate incongruity*. To get a joke and be amused by it, one must perceive a structure of ideas in which two conceptual domains that are regarded as incongruous are simultaneously recognized as appropriately related. Furthermore, that appropriate relationship is recognized as spurious, specious, or illegitimate by standards of logic, practicality, or tradition (see chapter 4). A children's riddle can serve as a simple illustration:

> When is a door not a door?
> When it's ajar.

The riddle question presents an incongruity—indeed, a logical contradiction. Something is a door and not a door; that is, it is both *A* and *not A*. The riddle answer makes the incongruity appropriate by suggesting the door is ajar, that is, *ajar*, partially opened. But it also suggests that the door is not a door but a storage container, *a jar*. To grasp the humor of this riddle one must recognize the incongruity, the appropriateness established by the word *ajar*, and the spuriousness of this appropriateness since it depends upon a pun that is recognized as illegitimate since a word or phrase must have a constant meaning in a communicative situation. If words can change their meaning in the course of an argument, there is no hope for ever reaching a valid conclusion. Were puns or double meanings allowed, then the syllogism

> All philosophers are men.
> All men are mortal.
> Socrates is a philosopher whose ideas endure,
> Socrates is immortal.

might be permitted if "immortal" is allowed to mean that Socrates's ideas and reputation live on long after the death of his body. "Immortal" is being used in both a literal and figurative sense. It is not the man Socrates who physically endures but his ideas, his philosophy, his reputation, and his influence. Actually, this elision in the move between the literal and figurative (the physical and ideational) sense of "immortal" was the basis of Woody Allen's quip, "I hope to achieve immortality by not dying." This, of course, is a joke in that the initial sense of the word *immortality* is taken figuratively only to be replaced—incongruously—by its literal, corporeal meaning.

The deciphering of a joke is an intellectual process. A joke is "complexly cognitive" (Davies 1991, 59). I do not hold with those who believe that humor is at root an emotional process, although humor is able to *arouse* emotion—usually because of its contents.[3] It is true that an individual's emotional relation to the contents of a joke may inhibit or enhance the perception and appreciation of its humor, but a joke needs to be intellectually comprehended as an appropriate incongruity to be understood. The amusement engendered by a joke may itself be an emotional response to it, but that emotion is the *result* of a cognitive process, not an emotional one (Oring 2016, 57–80).

As for the riddle about the door that is not a door or the quip by Woody Allen, it is important to note that we recognize the appropriate incongruity and the spuriousness intuitively, automatically, without reflection or deliberation. If we must stop to deliberate and reflect, we might *see* why the expression in question is a joke, but we are unlikely to *appreciate* it as a joke. If we must puzzle over it, if we must analyze it, if we must try to explain it, the joke will lose its value as a source of amusement.

Consider a more complicated example:

What were the last words spoken at the Last Supper?
  Everyone who wants to be in the picture, get on this side of the table. (Keillor 2005, 109)

This is an interesting specimen for a number of reasons. Whatever one's religious affiliation or level of religious knowledge, one should recognize that "Everyone who wants to be in the picture, get on this side of the table" were not words spoken either early or late at the Last Supper. The answer is both logically and scripturally incongruous. "From now on I tell you, I shall not drink wine until the day I drink the new wine with you in the kingdom of my Father" (Matt. 26:29) might prove a more accurate answer to the question. But that would hardly be funny. In humor, you do not get points for getting things right.

So, the incongruity is clear—we might say even jarring. Matters of posing for pictures were an unlikely subject of discussion at the Last Supper. The appropriateness of the incongruity lies in the reflexive accession of the image of Leonardo da Vinci's depiction of the Last Supper painted on the wall of the convent of Santa Maria delle Grazie in Milan. Although few have seen the original, which has almost completely deteriorated, the image has proliferated in painted copies and has been reproduced in magazines, books, films, and on the Internet. It is the go-to image of the Last Supper in Western society. But da Vinci's painting depicts Jesus and the disciples sitting only on one side of a table. When one comes to think about it, it is a strange arrangement of people around a table for a meal, a meal that is often characterized as part of a Passover seder. The figures are sitting as though at a dais set before a room of spectators. What are Jesus and his disciples doing sitting in an arrangement in which it would be difficult to talk, to hear, to interact, or even to see one another, let alone conduct a complex and lengthy religious ritual? This is the idea to which the joke calls attention; an idea which, for the most part, we have reflexively registered but never consciously considered. The joke claims that the peculiar arrangement is for the benefit of creating a picture—perhaps Leonardo's painting—but it would seem more an allusion to the kind of commemorative photography that regularly takes place at social gatherings. So, the appropriateness of the incongruity lies in recognizing an anomaly in Leonardo's depiction and recognizing that the idea of posing for a picture might appropriately account for the strange arrangement of people, while simultaneously recognizing this justification to be totally spurious.

It is sobering to think that had Leonardo not painted *The Last Supper* and had we only to rely on the images of Duccio di Buoninsegna (1308–11), Hans Holbein the Younger (1524–25), Juan de Juanes (1562), Tintoretto (1594), Peter Paul Rubens (1632), or Fritz von Uhde (1886), there would have been no joke. These painters placed disciples at the Last Supper on *both* sides of the table. We should be thankful to Leonardo, for without his painting, we would have been deprived of an otherwise decent joke. (This last comment is itself meant to be humorous, and the reader is given the assignment of explaining why by using the concepts and categories outlined above.)

This last joke example shows how much of what we see, say, and do is unreflective and might properly be called *unconscious*. We do not consciously think our way through a joke, we do not consciously work out the appropriate incongruity (which is why it often proves difficult for people to explain what exactly amused them about a joke), and we do not consciously register the anomalies of things we have repeatedly observed—such as the odd arrangement of people in a painting—until a joke, or something else, calls our attention to them. I would also add that often we do not consciously register why we find particular jokes or kinds of jokes striking, agreeable, or seemingly meaningful.

This is the sense in which I propose that the study of jokes and other forms of folklore might provide insights into what people might be perceiving, thinking, and feeling—insights different from those that might be obtained from listening in on their conversations or reading their email correspondence; insights that come because aspects of folklore expressions are unconscious and because the effects of and the responses to these expressions—aside from amusement and laughter—may be unconscious as well.

Wilson did not believe that J. Golden Kimball stories were "the heart and center of Mormon humor," and he suggested that these stories showed every indication of having moved from oral folk culture into Mormon popular culture (Wilson 2006a, 224). What Wilson was probably referring to was the reprising of J. Golden anecdotes in books, in live one-man shows, and even on phonograph recordings and DVDs.[4] Wilson first published these views in 1985. In 1999, however, Eric Eliason showed that J. Golden stories were actually fairly easy to collect. Although Kimball died in 1938, Eliason's students collected ninety-four

J. Golden Kimball stories comprising forty-one different story types (Eliason 2007, 44). Even if Wilson were correct and J. Golden stories in the 1980s were on the wane as oral forms of communication, they would still constitute a set of facts that needed to be examined, analyzed, and explained. Eliason has amassed and published what seems, for the time being at least, the definitive collection of these stories which he has supplemented with explanatory notes and commentaries (2007). It is only with such annotated collections that scholars from outside a culture are able to access, understand, and comment on these materials and incorporate them into more general discussions of the structures, meanings, and functions of humor.

One of the great incongruities upon which a substantial number of J. Golden Kimball jokes turn is that between the ideal and the real. One encounters the ideal—that is, the correct, proper, respected, decorous, elevated—which is suddenly transformed in a joke into something ordinary, mean, contemptible, unseemly, or low (see Raskin 1985a, 127). This is particularly true in what is often termed "religious humor." Instances demonstrating this opposition at work are almost too numerous to recount.

> One time he [J. Golden Kimball] went out to feed the calf on Sunday morning. He was all dressed in his satins and Sunday best. The darned calf wouldn't drink. In order to get the calf to drink he had to stick his fingers in the milk and put them in the calf's mouth, then stick the calf's nose in the milk. He did that and the calf snorted or sneezed and sprayed milk and mucus all over Brother Kimball. He said, "If I weren't a Mormon, if I wasn't trying not to swear, and I wasn't a priesthood holder, I'd push your _____ damned head in the bottom of the bucket." (Eliason 2007, 86; expletive deleted in published text)

J. Golden swears in the course of emphasizing his status as a Mormon, a priesthood holder, and someone who has abjured swearing. The incongruity is appropriate because J. Golden is not only a habitual swearer, but someone who swears so automatically that he often seems unaware that he is doing so. The playing out of a joke based on the opposition between the ideal and real is not necessarily unidirectional. The path is not always from high to low (although I would venture that the preponderance of religious jokes based on this opposition do follow this path). The movement can sometimes be from low to high.

> Supposedly, J. Golden Kimball stood in General Conference and said, "I would never have the courage to stand before this great congregation in this historic building without being under the influence . . . of the Holy Ghost of course." (Eliason 2007, 67)

Given J. Golden Kimball's tendency to stray from the Word of Wisdom (and a suggestion that on occasion he did imbibe [Stegner 2013, 400]), along with the conventional meaning of the phrase "under the influence," one might expect that J. Golden's courage in General Conference stems from his having had a good stiff drink. But, in fact, the joke creates an expectation of a disdained and censured influence to ultimately settle upon a lofty and revered one.

If one peruses the corpus of J. Golden Kimball anecdotes, one will find that the anecdotes repeatedly turn on his personal behaviors and traits of character. J. Golden is honest, direct, hard-working, chastising but compassionate, impatient, practical, humble, wise, and funny. By this last characteristic, I do not merely mean that the anecdotes about him are funny but that a good number of anecdotes depict him as being deliberately funny in his asides and retorts. Furthermore, he is totally committed to the doctrines and institutions of the Church of Jesus Christ of Latter-Day Saints even if he seems incapable of curbing his swearing, his coffee drinking, and his speaking what he sees to be the truth to both ordinary church members and higher church authorities. Yet he is also aware of and owns up to his failings, even if in the very course of repenting he transgresses yet again. For he is not merely repentant, but, as he says, "*damned* repentant." His cursing seems to be the highlighted element of his behavior even for those not familiar with any substantial portion of the joke corpus. As Eliason points out, those who had heard J. Golden Kimball's name but were unfamiliar with the story tradition would ask, "Wasn't he the cussing apostle?" (Eliason 2007, 16). A "damn" or a "hell" could be inserted into stories even when the expressions seem gratuitous and not essential to the creation of the anecdote's humor (Eliason 2007, 9). Eliason reckons that some swear word—usually "hell" or "damn"—shows up in 71 percent of the corpus of J. Golden anecdotes so that swearing constitutes an important speech register of these stories (45). (Stories that Eliason includes in a chapter of his book that he sees as most closely resembling J. Golden anecdotes [115–122] do not employ any swear words, except in one instance where there is a specific reference to J. Golden Kimball in the text [viz. 120].)[5] Perhaps the prominence of swearing in the repertoire owes something to the fact that it is a public transgression—and J. Golden is depicted as swearing on the radio or at conference—whereas something like coffee drinking, which is less prominent in the corpus, is a behavior more likely to be done in private or with a small group of friends.

It could be argued, however, that J. Golden's swearing is simply another facet of his honesty. Swearing is meant to convey and arouse emotion. That is why swearing invariably draws on the vocabularies of sex, scatology, and religion for its figures of speech. Such words come precharged with emotion. To swear then is to convey the emotional content of a message; it marks for oneself and for others that what is being said is not merely cerebral but passionate. When one feels emotion but does not express it, one is, to some extent, being dishonest. One is suppressing an essential aspect of a message. Since Mormons are socialized to be polite, helpful, and dutiful, they are asked to suppress this emotional dimension in their expressions, but in the act of doing so, they also suppress an authentic aspect of their selves. The J. Golden Kimball of the stories does not allow his honest feelings to be overruled by social convention or religious injunction. When he has some truth to speak, whether about a practical project, a backsliding congregation, or the dullness of a sermon delivered by a church authority, he speaks directly and to the point. His swearing is meant to convey the emotional dimension of his message. Consequently, J. Golden's swearing is not merely a survival of his muleskinning days, nor can it be dismissed as just a moral failing. It is an expression of sincerity and part and parcel of his honest persona. In this respect, the stories provide an arena for the display of a basic conflict in Mormon values, that between politeness and emotion; or, perhaps more generally, between piety and truthfulness.

So why did (and do) Mormons tell stories about J. Golden Kimball? This question marks the move from analysis to interpretation. Perhaps the most common hypothesis is that the stories serve as a safety valve for letting off steam in a programmed and closely monitored social and religious environment (Wilson 1977, 54–55; Eliason and Mould 2013, 355, 359; Brunvand 2013, 363; Siporin 2013, 395). Wilson felt that Mormon missionary jokes contribute to survival: "A missionary who can laugh . . . is likely to be more effective . . . [and] is likely to better survive the battle" (2006b, 211). The idea that humor relieves tensions is usually attributed to Sigmund Freud (Eliason 2007, 35), although, as noted above, this is not what Freud actually claimed (Oring 2016, 3–15). Certainly, this is a possibility, although the experimental confirmation of the tension-relief thesis is equivocal (see chapter 3). A number of hypotheses advanced to explain political jokes told behind the Iron Curtain were all found to be wanting. The idea that the jokes relieved tensions was one of those hypotheses, but it seemed that people "survived" whether they told jokes or not. In fact, it could be argued that there was probably a slightly smaller chance of survival for those who told jokes since a joke teller could lose a job, be sent to the gulag, or, at one time, be shot for engaging in what was regarded as "anti-Soviet conversation" (Oring 2016, 109–128).

I have always thought of jokes more as philosophy than therapy—as commentary rather than catharsis (e.g., Oring 1992, 16–80; 2003, 58–70). In the case of the J. Golden Kimball materials, we have a cycle of jokes about a general authority whose commitment to the church is rock solid. J. Golden was a man who dedicated himself to fulfilling all the tasks that had been set for him by that church. He was hardworking and determined to get results. He would have given his life for the church. He was so honest that he would not even tolerate "nice falsehoods" to be said about him at his funeral (Eliason 2007, 76). His sense of justice can even be favorably compared with that of God's.

> J. Golden Kimball was sent out to call a missionary from an outlying stake [parish] in the valley. He told the stake president to find a list of eligible men, then he and the stake president sat down and eliminated all but one. This one was a poor farmer saving up to buy a wagon. J. Golden says to call on him anyway. When they told him what they wanted, the man says, "I want to buy my wagon, I don't want to go on a mission." J. Golden tells him, "If you go, you'll be able to buy a better one when you get back." So the man accepted the call and went but had to sell his horses and use his savings in order to go. The man goes and comes back and goes to work to buy back his horses. Then he goes to see J. Golden Kimball and tells him, "It's been a year and I still can't buy my horses, let alone the wagon." J. Golden takes him out to the stable and picks out his best horses and wagon and gives them to the man. The guy doesn't want to accept them and has to be persuaded to take them. He finally takes them and leaves. Elder Kimball goes inside, and his wife is waiting for him to scold him for being so dumb as to give away their best horses. She really lays into him, and J. Golden tells her, "Be quiet woman, if the Lord won't keep his promises, by hell, I will." (Eliason 2007, 98)

Of course, J. Golden was in no position to make promises on God's behalf. Nevertheless, J. Golden seems irritated when God fails to reward his righteous own. A promise was made to the farmer, and even though the farmer does not regard it as J. Golden's obligation to fulfill, J. Golden nevertheless fulfills it. He is that honest. (Although he may have overlooked the possibility that he was being used as an instrument of divine justice.) Incidentally, this is one of those texts where the use of *hell* is somewhat gratuitous. The joke would work well even if the word were omitted.

Despite J. Golden's many virtues, he had failings. In one anecdote, J. Golden is even portrayed as harboring doubts.

> In his last years, he [J. Golden] met a friend in the street who said to him, "how are you Golden? How are you getting along?" "Well, to tell you the truth, I'm not doing so good. Getting old and tired. You know Seth, I've been preaching this gospel nigh into sixty years now, and I think it's time for me to get over to the other side to find out how much of what I've been saying is true." (Eliason 2007, 70)

This last anecdote would seem to be a migratory one as a similar text can be found in a collection of Jewish jokes (Mendelsohn 1941, 68). In any event, in this text there is the suggestion that even a general authority, someone who has risked his life for the church and has devoted his days to furthering its mission, could still entertain uncertainties as to the reality of it all.

It would be hard to believe that someone who would recount J. Golden anecdotes would consider that they depict the life of a sinner who had no place in the world to come. As one anecdote about J. Golden states, "He had as big a funeral as there was for President [Brigham] Young" (Eliason 2007, 113). So, what in these anecdotes do people find so attractive? Of course, many of them are funny, but there are myriads of jokes that are probably funnier than the ones told about J. Golden Kimball.

These anecdotes paint the picture of someone who is faithful but not rigidly or mindlessly faithful. He strays—not in fundamentals, but he strays, nevertheless. He even has doubts and seems to question God's justice. He resorts to swearing, can never seem to fully control his addiction to coffee, and has never acquired the talent for tact over an unwelcome and pointed truth. The stories are about someone who is fundamentally faithful and good, but not *too* faithful or *too* good.

> Uncle Golden used to say, "I have heard so much about goodness that sometimes I get unhappy, even at conference, and I feel like a little girl I heard of who did wrong." Her mother importuned her and labored with her so much that she said, "Mother, don't try and make me good; just shoot me." (Eliason 2007, 109)

In these respects, J. Golden is like most people. Religious institutions—regardless of denomination—invariably make enormous demands on their followers. They are asked to censor what they say, control what they do, and inhibit what they desire. Poverty, sickness, and death are represented as being part of a plan that is ultimately for their benefit. In other words, religions set a godly metric for human behavior. And since humans are not gods, they are bound, at least to some degree, to fail in living according to it. J. Golden likewise fails, but there is little doubt as to his genuine and significant merits. J. Golden Kimball is something more than a saint in the colloquial sense of that word in Mormon culture, and his failings serve only to highlight those merits. Because the J. Golden of the anecdotes is a human being in every sense of the term, he can serve as an exemplar to all those who must work out their salvation on earth as human beings. I think it is in this sense that the J. Golden Kimball jokes might constitute a philosophy; a philosophy that injects a note of realism into the struggle for salvation and describes a terrain of action for those who strive but who cannot entirely succeed. It shows them the possibility of salvation despite numerous and inevitable lapses. Perhaps that is why J. Golden Kimball is often promoted in the traditional anecdotes from a president of the Seventy to the rank of apostle (Eliason 2007, 46). The higher his status within the church, the more certainly his salvation can be assumed even if he thoughtlessly—and sometimes deliberately—acts and strays pretty much like everyone else.

Anthropologist Melford Spiro did fieldwork in a number of societies in different parts of the world: Micronesia, Israel, and Burma, currently Myanmar. At this last research site, Spiro devoted considerable effort to studying the beliefs and behaviors that focused on *nats*, which were spirits the Burmese propitiated in order to gain health, wealth, and prestige, or to avoid danger (Spiro 1974, 4, 266). The nats, however, were only approached to achieve goals in this world. They were never approached to achieve results in the otherworld. The otherworld was strictly the province of Buddhism, and charity, morality, and meditation were the sole means to be reborn into a higher life and eventually to achieve nirvana—the extinction of existence when all suffering comes to an end (269). To a great extent, the two modalities—the nat cults and Theravada Buddhism—are incommensurate, but Spiro argues that they are symbiotic in the sense that it is only because the nat cults deal with the exigencies of this world that Buddhism can maintain its rarified and uncompromising regime about achieving the next. Without the nat cults, Buddhism would have to compromise its doctrines, because people live in and have to deal with this world even if all they are supposed to be doing is preparing for a world to come (279–280).

Perhaps J. Golden Kimball stories do something similar. After all, Latter-Day Saints are human beings living in this world even if they are in a constant state of preparation for the next. The stories express a necessarily human scale of operation even for actors who hold they are actually participating in a vast cosmic drama. The two scales are necessarily incommensurable. But the jokes are able to highlight something of this incongruity of the human and godly and find some measure of appropriateness in it, even if that appropriateness ultimately proves specious. J. Golden Kimball stories—and perhaps religious humor more generally—point to the necessarily human dimensions of activity even when it is ostensibly directed toward the sacred and eternal.

CHAPTER   TWO

Three *Jewish* Jokes

But beware of arriving at conclusions without comparison.

—George Eliot, *Daniel Deronda*

1

A salesman who was traveling to Petrograd was unable to continue his journey because of a severe snowstorm. The stationmaster told him that the trains would surely
be running again at six o'clock the next morning, as the tracks would be cleared by
that hour. The traveler had no alternative but to go to the local hotel.

By the time he arrived at the small-town hostelry all the rooms had been taken
by the other passengers of the delayed train. However, the desk clerk was a kindly
soul who could not bear to put a weary stranger out in such a blizzard, and he hit
upon an idea.

"Listen, my friend, all of the rooms here have a single bed each, so I can't very
well ask the occupants to put you up for the night. But there is one room here with
two beds in it."

"Thank God!" breathed the salesman. "I was afraid I might have to sleep out in
the cold tonight."

"Wait a minute, I must tell you something," said the clerk hurriedly. "The guest
in that room is a General in the Czar's army. But I'll ask him if he will share his
room with you."

"Don't bother," sighed the other resignedly. "A General would never share his
room with a Jew." He thought about it for a moment and then his face brightened.
"Look, I have an idea!" he said excitedly. "Maybe I can sleep in that extra bed after

   https://doi.org/10.7330/9781646425198.c002

all. It is very late now, so the General must be fast asleep. Tomorrow I must rise early to catch the six o'clock train. At that hour of the morning he'll still be sound asleep, and he'll never know that I was in the other bed. Just be sure to wake me up on time."

The hotel clerk agreed. Quietly the traveler tip-toed into the room of the Czarist officer, and without a sound—almost afraid to breathe—the intruder undressed and went to sleep. In the morning the clerk awakened the General's clandestine roommate at the appointed hour.

But in the predawn darkness the Jewish guest unwittingly donned the General's uniform and hurried off to meet his train. On the way, he could not help but notice that everyone he met bowed and greeted him in a most respectful manner. "How do they know that I shared the same room with a General?" he wondered.

He met a Captain and then a Major, and both saluted him smartly. At the ticket office the agent handed him a first-class ticket and assigned him to a private compartment.

"How is it that a Jew is treated so magnificently?" he asked himself, bewildered by the unaccustomed courtesy.

Inside the compartment he speculated on the probability that his single night's association with a great Czarist officer might have given him a kind of aristocratic aura—one of reflected glory. He stood before a mirror and stared at his reflection and examined his features for any possible change in his appearance, and as he did, a look of utter shock spread over his face as he recognized the General's uniform.

"Oy vay" he groaned. "That shlemiel of a desk clerk! I ask him to wake me up and instead he wakes up the General. Now, how will I ever catch this six o'clock train when I'm still sleeping back at the hotel?" (Spalding 1969, 52–53)

A very similar joke appears in Jacob Richman's *Laughs from Jewish Lore,* first published in 1926, although there is no snowstorm, no reference to Petrograd or anywhere else, and there is the addition that the idea of sharing the room with a general disturbed the Jew but also "tickled his vanity" (1954, 184–187).

Anyone familiar with Jewish folklore and literature will recognize this joke as the basis of Sholem Aleichem's 1913 story "Iber a Hitl," although the action in the short story takes place in a train station, where the protagonist falls asleep on a bench next to a uniformed official. In his sleep, he loses his hat, and when he is awakened and rushes to catch the train home, he accidentally dons the official's hat in its place (Howe and Wisse 1979, 129–138). The English translation, "On Account of a Hat," first achieved a measure of prominence in the United States when Irving Howe and Eliezer Greenberg featured it in their *Treasury of Yiddish Stories* in 1954 (Roskies 2001, 39). It has since been anthologized on a number of occasions (Sholom Aleichem 1956; Bellow 1963; Howe and Greenberg 1974; Howe and Wisse 1979; Ostrom 1991), and it is the first literary piece included in the enormously successful *The Big Book of Jewish Humor*, edited by William Novak and Moshe Waldoks (1981, 8–14). Although Sholem Aleichem's story is based on a joke, it is a piece of literature. Consequently, it introduces matters of setting, character, motivation, and voice that would likely be absent from any oral joke. The story also continues beyond what might be called the punchline, which is a structural characteristic that differentiates a joke from a comic tale (see Oring 1992, 84–88). The story has been interpreted by literary critics as an expression of the Jews of the Pale's relationship to authority, their paranoia, wish-fulfillment, loss of identity, and even their annihilation of self (Roskies 2001, 45; Adler 1998, 20; Butwin and Butwin 1977, 75–78).

To my knowledge, no one has identified a joke that is set in a train station and is based solely on an exchange of hats. One might presume that the version that inspired Sholem Aleichem resembled Spalding's text as it concerns a czarist general and his uniform.[1] Nevertheless, the kernel of the joke in which some aspect of an individual is changed so that he fails to recognize himself—Motif J2012: *Person does not know himself*—is the basis of a great variety of tales and jokes (Thompson 1955–1958). A man fails to recognize himself because his beard has been cut off or altered (J2012.1); his clothes are new (J2012.4); he is dressed like others (J2012.5); or he is naked and without clothes (J2012.6). A woman may not know herself because her clothes have been cut off (J2012.2) or she has been tarred and feathered (J2012.3). ATU 1284: *Person Does Not Know Himself* would be the closest tale type to Spalding's joke and Sholem Aleichem's tale. The type revolves around someone's appearance being altered while asleep and who upon waking does not recognize himself or mistakes himself for someone else (Uther 2011). The type is also known in Oriental Jewish tradition (Jason 1988, Type 1531A), but it can be found throughout Europe, in North Africa, the Middle East, the Americas, and Asia. Stith Thompson originally included Type 1531A: *Man Shaved and with Hair Cut Does Not Recognize Self* as separate from Type 1284, but Hans-Jörg Uther eliminated it in his revision of the index.[2]

Perhaps the earliest version of the story is the one found in the Greek joke book *Philogelos*, which is believed to date back to the fourth or fifth centuries CE, although extant manuscripts are considerably later (Beard 2014, 185; Baldwin 1983, iv).

> An egghead [*skolastikos*] and a bald man and a barber were on a trip together.
> Having camped in a remote spot, they agreed that they would each keep watch
> over their belongings in shifts of four hours. The barber happened to draw the first

watch. Wanting to have a bit of fun, he shaved the egghead's dome as he slept, then woke him up when his own shift was done. Rubbing his head as he came to, the egghead found that he was bald.

"What a big fool that barber is," he grumbled. "He's woken up Baldy instead of me!" (Baldwin 1983, 11)

Alter Druyanow includes a version of Type 1284 in *Sefer ha-bedichah ve-ha-hidud* (The Book of the Joke and the Witticism):

A Jew and a priest happened to share a room together at an inn. Before going to sleep, the Jew asked the servant: "Please wake me before morning for the first train." The servant did as requested, and the Jew got up, and without lighting a candle, in order not to disturb the sleep of the priest, dressed in the clothes that came to hand in the dark and hurried to the train. When he entered the station and glanced at a mirror on the wall, he froze on the spot: a man in priest's clothes looked back at him from the mirror. He scratched his head and groaned: "Curses on that stupid servant! I told him to wake me, and he woke the priest." (Druyanow 1963, 2:44)

It might be felt that the Jew's exchange of clothes with a priest would make the joke a Jewish one because the scene captures the essence of the Jew's position in Eastern Europe; a figure distanced from the religion and culture of the dominant society who, perhaps unconsciously, yearns for it. But there is a similar joke in which a yeshiva student accidently dons the cloak of a rabbi with whom he is sharing a room (Mendelsohn 1935, 64), and there is a Chinese tale in which a convicted Buddhist monk dresses his drunken jailer in his own clothes and shaves his jailer's head so that when the jailer wakes up and sees his garments and feels his head, he says, "The monk is still here but where am I?" (Ting 1978, 190; Ikeda 1971, 248). A joke about a Jew exchanging items of clothing with a czarist general or a priest should not make the joke a Jewish one although such jokes will probably *resonate* differently for Jews than for non-Jews.[3] But then jokes about Buddhist monks will likely resonate differently for Buddhists than for anyone else.[4]

I do not know how many literary critics would be willing to claim that the joke in the *Philogelos* would necessarily reflect an identity crisis on the part of the *skolastikoi* of the era, or that tales of Hodja Nasrredine, Chinese jailers, traveling salesmen in the Ozarks (Randolph 1965, 114), or the many other protagonists of ATU Type 1284 speak to the identity crises of these individuals or their social groups. My concern, however, is less with interpretations of Sholem Aleichem's tale than with the question of what makes a "Jewish joke" and the implications of recognizing a Jewish joke as one with close analogues in other languages and cultures.

2

Once there was a wicked bishop who wished to drive the Jews out of his local area. And so he decided to challenge a representative of the Jewish community to a debate, with the result that if the bishop won, he would be able to do with the Jewish community what he would. The Jewish community, naturally, was very frightened of the prospect, and no one wanted to be the one who would bear the burden of what might happen if they lost. And so they were about to forfeit until one simple man, Yankel, stepped forward and agreed to take on the challenge. The problem was that neither Yankel nor the bishop spoke a common language, and so it was decided that the disputation would take place in pantomime.

The bishop strode proudly to the center of the town square and held up three fingers. Yankel, for his part, held up a single finger in return. Then the bishop, looking slightly flustered, pointed into the distance; Yankel responded with a finger stabbed sharply toward the earth. The bishop, now entirely discombobulated, produced an apple from inside his cassock; Yankel took out a loaf of bread. And with that, the bishop stalked away, shouting, "Enough! The Jews have triumphed."

His fellow churchmen gathered about him, asking what happened. He said, "The brilliant Jew had a response for everything. First, I held up three fingers to indicate the power and the majesty of the Holy Trinity; in return the Jew held up a single finger to retort that majestic power is more fully embodied in a singular form like the one God of the Hebrews, and what is more perfect in essence is finer. In return, I suggested to him that our Son of God would return from afar, from where he is now, to show the Jews the error of their ways: the Jew replied, in turn, that faith must be judged not by some abstract happening in the distant future but by what occurs in the present, at the present moment, and where was our Messiah now? I had one more possibility: I produced Eve's apple, sign of original sin that scourges us all; but when he produced wheat, the staff of life, showing Divine mercy, rather than prejudgment, I fell silent. I had nothing more to say." The churchmen shook their heads.

Back on the other side of the square, at the synagogue, there was great and festive rejoicing: and the rabbis said to Yankel, "Yankel! How did you do it? How did you best the brightest mind of the Church in theological disputation?" Yankel frowned. "Well, to be honest, I don't quite know," he said. "First, he told me that he wanted three debates, and I suggested that one would be plenty. And then he thought we should do them over there, and I said that here would be fine with me; and then we had lunch." (Dauber 2017, 13–15)

This joke is probably better known than the one about the traveler who mistook himself for a czarist general. Versions of this joke appear in a number of popular collections of Jewish jokes (e.g., Richman 1954, 67–70; Gross 1955, 57–59; Druyanow 1963, 2:326–327; Spalding 1969, 12–14; Novak and Waldoks 1981, 88–89).

The setting for the joke is a public disputation between Christians and Jews, dialogues and disputations that have a long history. Some were in writing (e.g., Justin Martyr's dialogue with Tryphon in the second century CE), and others were in public arenas (e.g., the Disputation of Paris in 1240, the Disputation of Barcelona in 1263) and some persisted into early modern times (Roth 1972, 79–103). Disputation did not automatically connote interfaith conflict. Disputation was central to Christian theological training in the Middle Ages and early modern times (Mintzker 2017, 117–122). Nevertheless, when disputations with Jews took place—whether with Catholics, Protestants, or Muslims—they were imposed on the Jewish community, and the outcomes were usually preordained. When Nachmanides was summoned to debate the Franciscans and Dominicans in Barcelona in 1263, the king awarded him a monetary prize for his conduct and opinions, but the disputation was terminated before its conclusion, and Nachmanides was forced to leave Spain (Roth 1972, 4:213–215; 12:775–776). Disputations might end with the emendation of or confiscation and burning of thousands of copies of the Talmud.[5]

The joke of Yankel and the bishop is old and widespread. It appears as AT Type 924A: *Discussion between Priest and Jew Carried on by Symbols* in *The Types of the Folktale* (Aarne and Thompson 1964, 323), although it might revolve around a Greek and a Roman (Ruiz 1972 [ca. 1330], 22–28), a monk and a dervish (Gibb 1836, 115–118), a Christian and a Moor (Oriol and Pujol 2008, 186), or a professor and a miller disguised as a student (Wright 1879, 173–176; Šmits 1962, 12:266–267 [Motif H607.2.1]). AT Type 924B: *Sign Language Misunderstood* concerns two men (often a king and a shepherd) that have a similar dispute in gestures. The difference between the two subtypes depends largely on the characters involved and the meanings attributed to the symbols. In Type 924A, the characters represent different religions or religious statuses, and the pointing of a finger, for example, is likely to be interpreted by one party in theological terms. In Type 924B, the difference between the characters tends to be social and economic, and the gestures are likely to be understood in political or economic terms. Thus, the shepherd thinks, for example, that the gestures of the king refer to the number of sheep he is requesting. In Hans-Jörg Uther's revision of the Aarne-Thompson index, these types were combined in the single ATU Type 924: *Discussion in Sign Language* (Uther 2011, 557–558).

The type has a broad distribution. It is found in England, Europe, North Africa, the Middle East, as well as in Anatolia, India, China, and Japan. It has found its way to the Americas. In a Chinese version of the religious subtype, the contest is conducted between a wandering Buddhist monk and a cobbler, butcher, or pastry maker who is standing in for the local temple priest. Thinking that he is communicating with another monk, the wandering monk's gestures are directed to Buddhist doctrine. The substitute's gestures are directed to matters of business. The monk, for example, raises one finger to indicate one Buddha, and the cobbler raises two fingers to indicate two shoes to a pair, which the monk in turn interprets as referring to two arhats, and so on. In the Asian versions, there are often more than three sets of gestures in the exchange (Ting 1978, 146–147).

A Japanese version of the type appears in *Konjaku Monogatarishū*. The tale is somewhat different, however. A bodhisattva from one part of India comes to visit a bodhisattva in another part and sits by the gate of his compound. When informed of his presence, the sage sends his disciple to him with a box of water. The sage at the gate sends it back with a needle in it. A room is hastily prepared, and the disciple is told to quickly admit the visitor to the compound. The two sages understand the signs that are exchanged; it is only the disciple who fails to understand them until they are explained to him (Mills 1970, 356–357). This tale would not seem to be comic—at least, by Western standards. This Japanese version was published in the eleventh or twelfth century CE but is supposed to be a translation from a seventh-century Chinese collection, a significant portion of which is a translation or adaptation of earlier Hindu sources (Ikeda 1971, 206–207).

The East Asian versions might seem to be older than Western versions, but Haim Schwarzbaum (1968, 117–118) points to the following Aggadah in the Babylonian Talmud:

> Rabbi Joshua b. Hananiah was before the Emperor (Cæsar). A *Min* [an apostate, a Judeo-Christian] who stood by showed him with his hand a people from whom God had turned away His face. R. Joshua ben Hananiah showed him with his hand that "His hand is still over us." Asked the Emperor of R. Joshua: Do you know what the Min has shown you with his hand? He replied: Yes, he showed me a people from whom God had turned away His face. He asked him: What have you shown him with your hand? He answered: I showed him that God's hand is still inclined over us. The Emperor then asked the Min: What have you shown to R. Joshua ben Hananiah? He said the same. And he asked him: What did he show you? He replied: I do not know. Then the Emperor said: A man that does not know what is shown to him by a sign, should he dare to raise his hand in the presence of an emperor? He ordered, and the Min was killed. (*Hagigah* 5b; Jewish Virtual Library)

Joshua ben Hananiah was a Tana (an authority quoted in the Mishnah, which was compiled circa 200 CE) who lived from the middle of the first into the early decades of the second century. A number of tales in the Talmud tell of his clever answers to impossible questions, answers that are motifs in world folklore and literature. For example, when asked where the middle of the world is, Rabbi Joshua points to the place he is standing and declares it to be the middle of the world and challenges his interlocutors to measure it and convince themselves (Motif H681.3, *Where is the center of the earth? Here; if you don't believe it measure it for yourself*). When asked to move a well in the desert to the city (Motif H1023.25. *Task: bringing a well [pond, lake] to the king*), he asks for a rope of bran because that is the only rope used for moving wells (Motif H1021.2. *Task: making a rope of chaff*). When asked to patch up a torn millstone (Motif 1023.7. *Task: sewing together a broken mill stone*), Hananiah asks for a thread of sand with which to patch it (Motif 1021.1. *Task: making a rope of sand*) (Kolatch 1964, 148–150).

Although he is a historical figure of the first and second century, the tales of Joshua ben Hananiah are recorded in the Gemara of the Babylonian Talmud, which was compiled in writing only in the sixth or seventh century CE (Goldenberg 1984, 136).[6] The stories of his encounters with the Roman emperor are not contemporary records. In fact, there are any number of Talmudic stories of rabbis (R. Gamliel, R. Tarfon, R. Judah ha-Nasi, R. Tanhum, for example) in exchanges with or before an emperor—even with Alexander the Great—which involve metaphorical communications or debates about philosophical and legal questions. Nevertheless, what is presented in the tale of Joshua ben Hananiah is an early tale of a disputation that is conducted in a language of signs.

In some sense, these tales can be seen as a subset of an extremely widespread set of tales in which riddles or symbolic questions are exchanged (Motifs H530–H886). The earliest instance of a misunderstanding of a symbolic exchange would seem to be recorded in *The Persian Wars* of Herodotus (c. 484–425 BCE), where the significance of the gifts sent by Gobryas of the Scythians to Darius of the Persians is misunderstood (Schwarzbaum 1968, 117).

This Talmudic tale about Rabbi Joshua, however, differs from the contemporary joke in significant ways: (1) in the tale, only a single gesture is exchanged; (2) there is no mutual misunderstanding of gestures—Rabbi Joshua understands the gesture of the apostate, although the apostate does not understand that of the rabbi; (3) in the Talmudic tale, it is wisdom, not blockheadedness, that is triumphant; and (4) perhaps most important, the Talmudic tale is decidedly serious; it is not a joke. Despite the existence of this early tale of Rabbi Joshua and the apostate, it is still not certain that the comic tale began in the west and moved east rather than the other way around.

Alter Druyanow, Dov Noy, Haim Schwarzbaum, Jacob Richman, Irving Kristol, and Ed Cray all recognize that what were characterized as Jewish jokes were often related to or derived from jokes and tales of non-Jewish origin (Druyanow 2010, 125; Noy 1962, 48; Schwarzbaum 1968, 27–36; Richman 1952, 8–10; Kristol 1951, 433; Cray 1964, 342–343). But they did not address, or even seem to notice, the problems that fact might create for the definition and interpretation of the Jewish joke. For example, if a Jewish joke is held to be one that is "produced by Jews," according to Jeremy Dauber (2017, xii), what does it mean if a joke is adapted from a comic tale that has global distribution? Dauber (who provides the text of Yankel and the bishop quoted above) allows that Jewish humor may be "crafted in concert with non-Jews" (2017, xii), but what exactly does that mean? Is it sufficient that a joke produced by non-Jews need only be populated with Jewish characters and relocated to a Jewish setting to become a Jewish joke? If the Jewish joke is, as defined by Cray, "one which intrinsically deals with the Jew and would be point-less if the Jewishness of a character were removed" (1964, 344n5), the question arises about those versions of ATU Type 924, which include no Jewish characters and may not even involve a religious disputation. At the same time, one could not dismiss these tales as "pointless," as their plots and motifs are similar to those in versions with Jewish characters and meaningful enough to have been repeatedly communicated across great expanses of time and space.[7]

Taking a cue from Freud (1960, 8:111–112), Hillel Halkin defines the Jewish joke as one that is self-denigrating while simultaneously conveying a degree of self-praise (2006, 48). It could be argued that the joke about Yankel and the bishop is self-denigrating because of the community's timorousness in dealing with the threat of expulsion, its reluctance to send their wisest and most knowledgeable representative to the disputation, and its wit's-end choice of the simpleton Yankel instead. Yet, the self-praise is there as well. As the story turns out, even the least of Jews proves capable of defeating an oppressor.[8] But many of the versions of ATU 924 that do not involve Jewish characters might be read in terms of self-denigration and praise as well. The lowly know they are lowly, but they triumph over the mighty whether by cunning or a fluke. In fact, this is a theme of many a folktale and joke, not of just those of ATU Type 924. So, what makes a joke Jewish? Is it simply the presence of Jewish characters operating in a Jewish cultural setting?

The problem of joke interpretation is perhaps even more acute than that of joke definition. If the Jewish joke is to be understood as a response to persecution and anti-Semitism (Dauber 2017, xiv), what is to be made of the numerous versions of the comic tale that have nothing to do with anti-Semitism or, for that matter, with Jews at all? And what of the view that the joke be read as a critique of Jewish theological certainty (Dauber 2017, 16). In the joke, Yankel triumphs over his Christian adversary. But according to Dauber, the joke cuts two ways. On the one hand, it suggests there is something stupid about anti-Semitism. The attacks by the church on Judaism self-implode as the bishop's overly intellectualized interpretations of Yankel's gestures bring about his own defeat. Yet as Dauber also notes, Yankel is a fool. He wins the contest not by theological acumen or even native cleverness but by dumb luck. Dauber argues that the joke imparts the message that the confidence of the Jews in their own theological position as God's chosen is severely misplaced (2017, 15–16).[9]

Jokes that appear after the Jewish Enlightenment sometimes do reflect criticism of, and sometimes even an assault on, the confidence of those Jews who believed they belonged to a nation chosen by God (Altman 1971, 134). According to Irving Kristol, given the tribulations of the Jewish people, the Jewish joke highlighted, and punctured, their "God-forsaken religiosity" (1951, 434–435). The jokes recognized, as many observant Jews seemingly did not, that God had let them down (Halkin 2006, 51). But how well does ATU Type 924 evidence this theme? Are Japanese and Chinese versions of the type equally indicative of Buddhist theological uncertainties? When a peasant unwittingly bests a king in a symbolic exchange, should it be read as an assault on the oppressive feudal order as well as simultaneously undermining the certainty of the peasant's position? All in all, what happens to the interpretation of the Jewish joke when it is compelled to be conducted in a comparative context, in the light of the numerous jokes and tales about non-Jewish characters with which it is clearly allied?

On one occasion, what are characterized as "Jewish jokes" have been subjected to scientific investigation. A psychologist performed an experiment to see how jokes whose contents have been altered were likely to be perceived as Jewish ones (Nevo 1991). The more elements of a joke that are Judaized—the name of the protagonist, the secondary characters, the roles, subgroups, culture, location, language, and stereotypes—the more likely the joke is to be perceived as Jewish. No particular element of a joke proved to be more important in the perception of a joke as Jewish than any other. The perception was a function of the quantity of elements rather than the quality of any particular one. The experiment focused solely on matters of content. Matters of logic (e.g., Cohen 1999, 45–68), self-directed aggression (e.g., Freud 1960, 8:111–112), philosophical import (e.g., Ausubel 1948, xx), and rhetorical style (e.g., Stora-Sandor 1991, 213) were not addressed in the experiment.[10] But the significance of the experiment is clear: if a non-Jewish joke can be Judaized simply by a change of characters and setting, is there anything necessarily "Jewish" about it in its outlook, structure, sensibility, or spirit?

The Judaizing of jokes has largely been ignored by folklorists and literary scholars.[11] To be fair, it is extremely difficult to catch a joke in the act of being Judaized. I have documented only two cases where it was clear to me that a Jewish character was inserted into a joke that previously had lacked one (Oring 2011a, 371–372; 2012b, 196–197, 204). When a joke is suspected of having been Judaized, the suspicion is usually based upon comparative textual analysis as in the cases of ATU Types 1284 and 924 discussed above. Sometimes, however, something in the text itself can arouse suspicions as to the text's origins.

3

A Jewish businessman was in a great deal of trouble. His business was failing, he had put everything he had into the business, he owed everybody, it was so bad he was even contemplating suicide. As a last resort he went to a Rabbi and poured out his story of tears and woe.

When he had finished, the Rabbi said, "Here's what I want you to do:

Put a beach chair and your Bible in your car and drive down to the beach. Take the beach chair and the Bible to the water's edge, sit down in the beach chair, and put the Bible in your lap.

Open the Bible; the wind will rifle [sic] the pages, but finally the open Bible will come to rest on a page. Look down at the page and read the first thing you see. That will be your answer; that will tell you what to do."

A year later the businessman went back to the Rabbi and brought his wife and children with him. The man was in a new custom-tailored suit, his wife in a mink coat, the children shining. The businessman pulled an envelope stuffed with money out of his pocket, gave it to the Rabbi as a donation in thanks for his advice.

The Rabbi recognized the benefactor and was curious. "You did as I suggested?" he asked.

"Absolutely," replied the businessman.

"You went to the beach?"

"Absolutely."

"You sat in a beach chair with the Bible in your lap?"

"Absolutely."

"You let the pages rifle until they stopped?"

"Absolutely."

"And what were the first words you saw?"

"Chapter 11." ("Woes" n.d.)

Chapter 11 is a subdivision of the United States Bankruptcy Code, which allows for the reorganization of a business while giving the business owner protection from creditors and litigation. In other words, this is a joke that can only make sense for someone who holds that bit of knowledge of the American legal system. Many non-Americans would not understand the joke, and not a few Americans might fail to get it. Whatever else it may be, it is not a transplanted Old World joke.

It must have arisen in the United States. In fact, the joke could not have existed before 1978 when the revision of the United States Bankruptcy Code included the law on business reorganization under Title 11, Chapter 11.

The only Jewish elements in the joke are the figure of the rabbi, the presumably Jewish member of his congregation, and, perhaps, the stereotype of the Jew as someone who identifies and seeks out any and all advantages in business matters. The reference to the "Bible" rather than to a *Chumash* (Pentateuch) or *Tanach* (acronym for Torah, Prophets, and Writings, i.e., The Hebrew Bible), however, strikes a false note. Even the idea of looking randomly through the Bible for guidance would seem to have more of a Christian than a Jewish flavor. One text titled "The Chumash" (n.d.) nevertheless uses the word *Bible* throughout the text. Another text does use the word *Torah* ("Businessman" 2007) instead of *Bible* and another "torah commentaries"—an odd choice ("This I Believe" 2007).[12]

I am not alone in sensing the dissonance of the word *Bible* in the joke. On one website, two responses registered discomfort with the word: "Surely a Rabbi would suggest the Torah not the bible?" and "Rabbis give out Torah's dont [*sic*] they?" indicating that the term *Bible* struck these readers as awkward in a Jewish joke. The tentative nature of these comments, and the notion that Torah refers to a book rather than a scroll (except when contrasted with *Neviim* [Prophets] and *Ketuvim* [Writings]) suggests they were made by non-Jews. Indeed, one of the commenters went by the name of Omarhussain ("Chapter 11" 2008). On the message board of another site: "I don't know why they say 'Jews' in the joke, and then say 'Bible' . . . I guess the original joke wasn't about Jews" ("Turkishclass" n.d.).

I examined nine texts of this "Jewish joke" on the Internet.[13] Eight of the nine texts are of the same basic type, which I will call Type 1A: (1) A man despondent over his failing business seeks help from a rabbi; (2) the rabbi advises that he go to the beach with a Bible and allow the wind to leaf through the pages until they lead him to a page with an inspirational text; (3) the man returns to the rabbi accompanied by his family in very much improved financial circumstances and offers a donation to the synagogue; (4) the rabbi interrogates the man as to whether his instructions had been dutifully followed; and (5) the inspirational text is revealed. Some of these texts are virtually word-for-word copies of one another (e.g., "Woes" n.d.; Brenner 2010, 99–100; "Businessman" 2007; "This I Believe" 2007). What I call Type 1B texts strongly resemble Type 1A texts but lack the protracted questioning by the rabbi. There is only a straightforward question about what guidance the man found in the Bible ("Read Your Bible" n.d.; "Chapter 11" 2008; and "Chumash" n.d.). There are only very minor variations in phraseology within each type. The Type 1A texts start, "A Jewish businessman was in a great deal of trouble." Type 1B texts tend to start, "A man has been in business for many, many years, and the business is going down the drain." It is likely that most of the texts within the two subtypes are digital copies of one another.[14] The wardrobes of the families who come to see the rabbi are different in the two types but are quite similar within type. One text ("Fresh Start" n.d.) might be categorized as Type 1C. It resembles Type 1B but going to the beach does not figure in it at all. The man is told by the rabbi to go home, open the Bible, and point randomly to a page. The man does not bring his family with him but simply tells the rabbi he is remarried. In fact, the rabbi at first does not remember the man or the advice he gave him. This particular text assigns all the characters names—Benjamin, Rabbi Levy, Ruth. Only one of the texts with Jewish content varies radically from those of Type 1: "A clever rabbi tried to help several of his congregants who went into bankruptcy by reading Chapter 11 in the Bible" (Rabeeya 2004, 23). This is practically a distillation of a joke to its punchline, but the book in which it appears seems to reduce all its jokes to this format, so this version would seem to be idiosyncratic to this author and this book.

In addition to the nine texts about a rabbi and his congregant, I found seventeen texts with non-Jewish characters.[15] Most involve a pastor, priest, preacher, or minister and his congregant. Five texts ("Lay Advice" 2003; "Divine Advice" n.d.; "Financial Advice" n.d.; "Jokes" n.d.; "Little Sister" n.d.) are Type 1A jokes and are almost identical word-for-word to the "Jewish" texts of this type. Type 1B lacks the prolonged interrogation by the clergyman. There are two texts that are almost identical to the Jewish Type 1B texts and that are identical to one another except that one involves a priest and the other a minister ("Prairie Home" 1999; "Overslept" 2005). The beach excursion, the accompaniment of wife and family, and the prolonged interrogation by the clergyman are absent in the Type 1C texts. The parishioner is merely instructed to "meditate," go "somewhere peaceful," or just look in the Bible for guidance ("Funny Bankruptcy" n.d.; "Yuksrus" n.d.; "Jesus Site" n.d.; "Morganking" n.d.; "Tokarska" n.d.; "Clean Joke" n.d.). The parishioner later returns exhibiting a degree of wealth, thanks the clergyman, and reveals what he found in the Bible either directly or in response to a single question by the clergyman. Two of these texts ("Morganking" n.d.; "Tokarska" n.d.) are identical but include an important difference: The man whose business is failing is named Matthew. When he returns in improved circumstances, he reveals that the first phrase he saw in the Bible was "Matthew Chapter 11." The incorporation of the name of the protagonist in the punchline is peculiar to these texts. Such a device could not work in a Jewish version since books in the Pentateuch are not named after people but after the first words of the book.[16]

Four texts do not involve members of the clergy at all. We might categorize these as Type 2 texts. One begins with a frame story about Bob teaching a scripture class and warning about the dangers of looking for messages in randomly chosen verses. He illustrates his point with an account of Fred, who ran into his old classmate Tom, who looked very prosperous. When asked how he became prosperous, Tom said that he opened the Bible and pointed to a word, which was "oil," so he invested in an oil well and made money. He did it again and wound up pointing to "gold," so he bought gold and was again successful. Tom then hurries home to try the procedure himself and winds up pointing to "Chapter 11" ("Biblical Interpretation" n.d.). The other three texts are identical copies of one another and describe two friends meeting and the prosperous friend describing to his unambitious friend how randomly pointing to a word in the Bible led to his success. When the other friend tries the method, he winds up pointing to "Chapter 11." What is significant about these texts is that they do not depend upon a businessman who discovers a way to escape his creditors and reestablish his fortune. Rather they suggest prosperity in life is a matter of fate or that divination will simply confirm differences in ambition that already exist ("Chapter 11" n.d.; "Oil" n.d.; "Two Friends" n.d.). Structurally, these texts differ from all the others, although they make use of the same punchline. While these three texts do not include mention of a church or a clergyman, they all are categorized as religious humor on the websites in which they appear. It is worth noting that one text of Type 1B ("Yuksrus" n.d.) involves a preacher going into a roadhouse when his truck breaks down and meeting his drunken and shabby friend who at one time had been rich. The joke then proceeds as Type 1B, but the opening reflects something of a transitional text between Type 1B and Type 2. Two friends meet, but in this case, one is a clergyman and the other is down on his luck.

All in all, there is nothing to indicate that the joke about the rabbi and his congregant began its life as a Jewish joke. The fact that the word *Bible* is so awkward in the Jewish texts strongly suggests—although it does not demonstrate—that the Jewish versions ultimately derive from a non-Jewish source. Furthermore, the greater variation in the non-Jewish texts might indicate that the joke has a longer tradition in a non-Jewish setting.

"Jewish humor at its best interprets the incongruities of the Jewish condition" (Wisse 2013, 33). A Jewish joke "must express a Jewish sensibility. Merely giving characters in a joke Jewish names or ascribing the joke to Jewish characters, does not a Jewish joke make" (Telushkin 1992, 16). "In nothing is Jewish psychology so vividly revealed as in the Jewish joke" (Rosten 1968, xxiii). But if the Jewish joke is to be understood as providing some insight into the psyche of Jews and the hidden concerns of the community, then those jokes must in some sense be singular. They should not reproduce the jokes told in other communities. It would seem that one or more of three conditions should obtain: (1) The joke can be shown to be created within the Jewish community and is a distinctive product of that community; (2) a joke that has originated outside the Jewish community reveals that it has been transformed in some *significant and consistent* way in the course of its adoption into the community's repertoire; and (3) a joke in the repertoire of a Jewish community, even if it has non-Jewish analogs, forms part of a distinct constellation of jokes in relation to constellations of jokes in other communities (see Oring 1992, 41–52). None of these conditions would seem to obtain in the case of the "Chapter 11" joke. Every aspect of the joke except for the identification of the rabbi and the very occasional insertion of a Hebrew word (*torah, shul*) can be found in jokes with non-Jewish protagonists and settings. Even the idea that Jews seek to exploit every business advantage is an after-the-fact interpretation of the joke. The idea is a characteristic of the majority of the jokes—Jewish and non-Jewish—and would pertain to businessmen rather than to Jews per se.

Because Jews regard themselves—rightly or wrongly—as having a distinctive and superior repertoire of jokes and are so regarded—again, rightly or wrongly—by others, I suspect that Jews tend to Judaize every good joke that they encounter, in the first stage at least, by injecting it with Jewish content. But Jewish content should not in itself a Jewish joke make. If we do not come to understand how particular jokes are Judaized and what relation they bear to jokes in the repertoires of other peoples, we will never come to know what, *if anything*, is Jewish about Jewish jokes. A Jewish joke must rest on more than a mere claim; a broader investigation of the joke is needed. After all, a joke about a rabbi and a synagogue may prove to be no more Jewish than a Jew in a military cap proves to be a czarist general.[17]

Whatever Became of the Dirty Joke?

Everything is about sex except sex. Sex is about power.
—Oscar Wilde (attributed)

If one conducts an online search in academic databases for titles that contain the words *dirty joke*, *obscene joke*, or even *sexual joke*, the results prove surprisingly meager. JSTOR coughs up only one title in a folklore journal. The pickings from psychological, sociological, and linguistic databases are almost as thin.[1] A small cluster of articles shows up in the work of classicists exploring the appearance of such material in the works of Aristophanes, Sappho, or Archestratus of Gela (Syracuse). What does show up in JSTOR is a bundle of seven reviews of Gershon Legman's two-volume opus *Rationale of the Dirty Joke*.[2]

The dearth of references is perhaps not as strange as it might at first seem. Dealing with dirty or obscene jokes is somewhat polluting. Consequently, scholars have tended to keep away. Two names prominently associated with such materials—Gershon Legman and Reinhold Aman—had rather checkered careers on both professional and personal levels (Davis 2019; Miller 2020).

Then there is the critique of such jokes, which are viewed as contributing to the objectivization of women and as instruments of sexual harassment. On a folklore listserv back in the early 1990s, the response to the posting of a collection of sorority girl jokes (which would not normally be considered dirty jokes) was: "These jokes offend me"; "Thinking of folklore as items for collection enables the illusion of scholarly objectivity . . . and to deny that they mean to offend women"; "I too [want to express] what I felt about the nasty misogynist insults masquerading as

https://doi.org/10.7330/9781646425198.c003   31

jokes. . . . I think one can objectively describe their tone as vicious" (Folklore Log 9202). One might think that a list of jokes posted by scholars for scholars might provoke some trenchant analysis that might precede or accompany such reaction (e.g., Oring 2003, 58–70). But these jokes were met almost uniformly and reflexively with indignation, condemnation, and rejection.

Perhaps a third reason for the absence of a sustained body of research articles on dirty jokes is that there is the belief that they have been successfully theorized and are well understood. That understanding proceeds from Sigmund Freud's *Jokes and Their Relation to the Unconscious* first published in 1905. In that work, Freud likened the mechanisms of jokes—condensation, displacement, indirect representations—to those of dreams. Dreams, in Freud's view, allowed otherwise repressed sexual and aggressive thoughts in the unconscious to find expression. Consequently, most scholarly and popular commentators on jokes have regarded them in precisely this way, as the expressions of repressed, unconscious thoughts.

Freud's theory of jokes has consequently been largely regarded as a "release" or "relief" theory. That is to say, jokes are regarded as releases of and relief from repressed sexual impulses welling up from the unconscious. "Wit is a camouflage which functions to deceive the superego temporarily as repressions are being suddenly released" (Keith-Spiegel 1972, 13, 20). "Joking, like dreaming, serves as a safety valve for forbidden feelings and thoughts" (Morreall 1987, 111).[3] "Repressed impulses find relief in a disguised form in jokes as well as in dreams" (Ruch and Hehl 1988, 983). "A joke allows the id's impulses to thread their way through the ego's defenses" (Holland 1982, 52). "One element of emotional maturity is the ability to accept restrictions on pleasure-seeking (id) drives and to redirect the energies into secondary gratifications (sublimation). These energies must find some secondary outlet. One of the most effective substitute gratifications is wit" (Dundes 1987, 42). This list of citations could easily be extended.

Given this understanding of Freud's theory, it would follow that the nature of the dirty joke is fundamentally explained. We know of Freud's topography of the unconscious and his outline of the development and transformation of sexual impulses and their objects. Sexual impulses begin with birth and its zones and objects change in the course of individual development. These erotic zones and sexual objects must eventually be repressed. Consequently, sexual jokes are releases of repressed sexual impulses from the unconscious. *Quod erat demonstrandum.* There is nothing left to say. Dirty jokes should be understood completely.

This easy explanation is the result of merging some of Freud's comments on jokes with his more general ideas of individual sexual development and repression. It does not emerge directly from what Freud had to say about obscene jokes in *Jokes and Their Relation to the Unconscious*. Freud's discussion of sexual joking in that book is considerably more delimited:

> Where a joke is not an aim in itself—that is, where it is not an innocent one—there are only two purposes that it may serve, and these two can be subsumed under a single heading. It is either a *hostile* joke (serving the purpose of aggressiveness, satire or defense) or an *obscene* [*obszöner*] joke (serving the purpose of exposure). (Freud 1960, 8:96–97, emphasis in original)

Freud reckons the obscene joke as an instrument of exposure, *not* as the satisfaction of an unconscious sexual impulse. The obscene joke would really seem to be a subcategory of the hostile joke. Freud's basis for this characterization of the purposes of obscene jokes is their relation to smut (*Zote*), the deliberate bringing forth of sexual matters in coarse speech. Smut, he claims, is directed by a male at a female by whom he is sexually excited. It is intended to convey this excitement in the hope of exciting that person in turn. In other words, it is a *strategy of seduction* (Freud 1960, 8:97). Smut, according to Freud, causes the hearer to imagine the sexual parts and acts that are mentioned and communicates that the speaker is imagining them as well (98). If a woman is open to the sexual suggestion and yields to it, smut rapidly disappears and resolves itself in sexual behavior. If, however, the attempt at seduction is blocked, the sexual language will become hostile. Usually, according to Freud, the source of the interference is the presence of another man. But rather than direct hostility at the source of that interference, the seducer turns that person into an *ally* in his aggression. This listener becomes the person to whom the smut is addressed, and who laughs because his own libido has been effortlessly satisfied by the smutty speech (99). It is the entrance of the barmaid or innkeeper's wife in a country tavern that provokes smut on the part of the customers according to Freud.

In higher levels of society, however, a woman's presence brings smut to an end, and men address it only to one another. Among those of "refined education, smut becomes a joke and is only tolerated when it has the character of a joke." The greater the distance between blatantly sexual matters and the allusion to such matters that a hearer can reconstruct in his imagination, the higher a joke is likely to rise in civilized society (Freud 1960, 8:100).

Freud's theory that jokes are transformations of smutty talk creates serious problems for regarding obscene jokes as simple releases of unconscious libidinal energy. First, the sexual is very much present in consciousness in smut. It is nether repressed nor suppressed. A person who tells a sexual joke also knows quite well what he or she is doing. Unlike a dream, there is nothing unconscious about the thoughts that are expressed in a joke. They are conscious and deliberate. It is only the hearers of a joke who may be tricked into recognizing a sexual motif or theme when they had no reason to expect one (and often, even this is not the case). Second, the energy that is released in laughter following the telling of a joke is not the energy of a repressed impulse. According to Freud, it is the energy that has been devoted to the *inhibition* of sexual impulses that is released. In other words, what is released is not libidinal energy at all. Finally, Freud's own theory of the sexual joke is not about what should not be *thought*. It is about what can and cannot be *said* in certain social situations. Freud regards the obscene joke more a matter of rhetoric than depth psychology (Oring 2016, 12).

If we take Freud's theory at face value, questions remain. What is going on in the exchange of sexual jokes in a group of men? If the aim is exposure, whose exposure, and why are they doing so? If sexual jokes are simply a more "civilized" instrument than coarse smut, what then is their utility in the absence of women? What barriers have been erected between these men and their sexual objects that precipitate the hostility underlying such exposures in that particular time and place?

I am not sure where Freud acquired his ethnographic knowledge of smut in country taverns, although he did take summer vacations in the country with his family, and there were, in his early years (1887–1902), the occasional meetings and travels with his friend and intellectual confidante Wilhelm Fliess. It could be that Freud's knowledge of smutty speech came only from reading rather than any in-tavern experience. What Freud does not provide, however, is a complementary description and analysis of obscene joke telling in a group of bourgeois males. Freud had been a medical student from 1873 to 1881—three years longer than the usual medical course—and then continued to work in the Physiological Institute of Ernst Brücke and at the Chemical Institute of Carl Ludwig before moving on to the General Hospital of Vienna (Clark 1980, 49). It is not as though Freud never found himself in exclusively male company. It seems odd that he can so confidently characterize the use of smut in country taverns but totally avoid describing obscene joking among his peers.

Perhaps folklorists should not criticize Freud's ethnographic lapse too severely. After all, folklorists have not done much better. Folklorists have collected plenty of sexual jokes over the years (e.g., Legman 1968, 1975; Mitchell 1976; Randolph 1976), but beyond a few reports of sexual jokes told by individuals (e.g., Green 1977; Sacks 1978; Leary 1984, 5–6; Mitchell 1985; Mulkay 1988, 120–125; Oring 2011a, 367–376), the description of such jokes in natural face-to-face exchanges is almost nonexistent.

The most significant published work on the dirty joke by someone who might be considered a folklorist is the two-volume *Rationale of the Dirty Joke* by Gershon Legman, published in 1968 and 1975.[4] I reviewed this work in *Western Folklore* in

1977, and I was not very sympathetic to Legman's commentary on the thousands of jokes in the collection. Legman's approach to the dirty joke was passionately psychoanalytic—in a way that even Sigmund Freud might not have recognized. According to Legman, dirty jokes are a verbal expression of a wished-for sexual relationship with a desired object (1968, 13). Furthermore, Legman claims that joke tellers have their own favorite styles and joke subjects—usually a single taboo theme such as castration or homosexuality (14). A person's favorite joke, he declares, is a key to their character (16)—a thesis, incidentally, that Legman illustrates with only two examples, one of which was not the person's favorite joke but rather the only joke the teller could remember at the time (16–17). It is, by the way, a notion that Freud explicitly discounted (1960, 142). According to Legman, the sexual joke represents the neurotic situation of its *original* teller, and as it is made light of, it thereby renders it understandable and endurable (1968, 17–18).[5] Subsequent tellers are themselves neurotic, and the jokes allow them and their hearers to "slough off . . . the great anxiety . . . [they] feel in connection with certain culturally determined themes" (1975, 420).[6]

Curiously, Legman is conflicted over his collection of jokes. On the one hand, he bemoans the loss of the original folk materials, as they had been expurgated, distorted, submerged, or destroyed by the inferior vehicles and products of the culture industry: men's magazines, joke books, and columns in the popular press (Legman 1968, 26–27). "The folk nerve has almost been completely cut. . . . These publications shoot out their hopeless puns and 'one-liners' with less and less emphasis on the art of telling" (1968, 27). On the other hand, as he holds all these materials—folk or fabricated—in utter contempt for the aggressions they express (1968, 1), it is difficult to apprehend entirely the reason for his regrets. And, of course, the "art of telling" is of necessity completely obliterated in his compendium.

It is worth a glance at a couple of examples of Legman's analyses of dirty jokes to grasp his perspective. The very first joke in the first volume of *Rationale*, which he analyzes is:

> Little Johnny Jones, age 7, is in love with Mary Smith, the little girl next door, and comes to confide in his father that they plan to get married. Mr. Jones is amused. "What are you going to do about money?" he asks with pretended gravity. "I have my allowance, and Mary has nearly a dollar in the piggy bank." "That's all right for now," says his father, "but what will you do when the children come?" "Well, we've had pretty good luck so far." (1968, 49–50)

Legman relates this joke to the child's discovery of the sexual act of the parents and the hypocrisy of parents who condemn or even punish any sexual behaviors on the part of the child. The child's retribution is a joke in which the child exposes this hypocrisy and, in some examples, actually exposes the parents or parent surrogates themselves. The immediate problem this poses, as Legman well recognizes, is that children do not tell such jokes. Adults tell them. Legman, however, purports to solve this problem by noting that the adults who tell them were once children themselves and that it is "clearly an indigestible memento of childhood that the child-voyeuristic joke attempts to resolve" (1968, 51). Thus, the adult who makes up such stories wishes that he had been such a knowing child in relation to his parents (63). That this joke might be a relic of a child's psychological distress from parental hypocrisy seems a stretch. He provides no clear evidence for this residual upset. Furthermore, the adults who tell such jokes probably have children of their own from whom they also knowingly withhold sexual information. Legman goes on to claim that even seemingly innocent expressions by children—like the ones that used to occur on the TV show *Art Linkletter's House Party*—that suggest sexual knowledge and meaning are intentional and, in fact, retaliatory (50–52). Incidentally, Freud, in recounting an anecdote about the innocent expression of a sexual idea by a child, does not employ that anecdote to evidence the child's sexual knowledge, let alone its use as a retaliatory tactic directed against parents (Freud 1960, 8:183–184).

The discussion of the precocious Little Johnny joke is actually one of Legman's more restrained efforts of psychological analysis. An area where one might have more reason to presume deep-seated anxiety persisting into adulthood—the fear of castration—Legman sees underlying the following joke:

> Two farmers are talking. One says, "I can't understand all those crows I keep finding dead in my corn-field every morning. Can somebody be poisoning 'em?"
> The other farmer laughs. "It's that hired man of mine," he says. "He's been screwing your daughter up in the corn-field every afternoon, and those crows are nacherally laughin' theirselves to death" (1975, 584).

Legman comments that this joke is more likely an example of "castratory death than of mere sex-linked sadism as is true of almost all *stories* of killing animals, even for food" (1975, 584, emphasis in original). He then goes on to state that it is a "toss-up" whether it is the farmer's discomfiture over his daughter's sexual activity or the crows' death that is the real joke. Does Legman's analytic perspective even keep him from being able to discern wherein the *joke* lies?

Legman is frequently ambivalent about his own claims concerning the motives and functions of dirty jokes. On the one hand, he regards the jokes as cathartic, and they allow joke tellers to relieve the guilt for their own neurotic impulses (1975, 20). On the other hand, he holds that such anxieties are never really relieved, hence the compulsion to tell and retell the jokes to any and every possible audience (31). Legman asserts that it is the audience that is really the butt of the joke (1968, 1; 1975, 20)—dirty jokes are really "hostilities disguised as amenities" (1975, 24, 29). Yet he also claims that audiences must share a teller's neurotic anxieties if a joke is to succeed, that is, if it is to be greeted with laughter (21). Audience laughter, he claims, is less the result of amusement than a relief from the ordeal of listening (38). All these propositions are strictly assertions, and some would appear to be contradictory. Legman provides no evidence for any of these claims, nor would there be any obvious or easy way to produce it.

Legman not only makes assertions about the psychology of jokes; he also makes claims about their situation and operation in performance—their sociology. For example, most of a teller's dirty jokes revolve about a single taboo theme (1968, 14, 16; 1975, 16). A compulsive joke teller must go on endlessly (1975, 29). (The use of the word *compulsive* undermines his principle, as it becomes a matter of definition.) More laughter emanates from the tellers of dirty jokes than from the audience (13), although elsewhere he claims that the teller seldom laughs (33), which was Freud's view (1960, 8:100, 148–149). According to Legman, no one ever says, "That reminds me of a joke" and goes on to tell a clean joke (1975, 24–25). Most of these claims should be easily amenable to ethnographic verification or refutation. I suspect they would not withstand even casual scrutiny.

While I believe that Legman's commentaries on dirty jokes severely reduce the value of his two volumes, *Rationale of the Dirty Joke* nevertheless constitutes a major compendium of the kinds of materials that are under discussion. The jokes were gathered over decades, and despite the opacity of Legman's criteria for selection and inclusion, the volumes might be used to make some statements about the character—if not the psychology—of the dirty joke. In other words, the collection might prove useful in affirming something about dirty jokes simply on the basis of their contents.

What follows are five theses that derive from Legman, from Freud, and from Michael Mulkay, a sociologist who based his observations on his perusal of Legman's collection. The importance of these theses is that they address aspects of jokes whose truth might be decided without any presuppositions about the workings of the unconscious mind.

1. CREATION. Dirty jokes are created by men, and there is no place for women in the joke except as their butt (Legman 1968, 217).

2. EXPOSURE. The dirty joke serves as a substitution for smut when the possibility of smut is socially inhibited. The purpose of the joke is the exposure of that object to whom sexual access has been impeded (Freud 1960, 8:96–100; Legman 1968, 12).

3. AVAILABILITY. The assumption in the joke is that women are available as partners for any man at all times even if they seem reluctant (Legman 1968, 221–222, 236).

4. OBJECTIFICATION. Women in the joke can be adequately represented by the sexual, domestic, and other services which they can provide to men (Legman 1968, 236; Mulkay 1988, 136).

5. DOMINANCE. The male voice is ever dominant over that of the female (Mulkay 1988, 137). Sometimes the woman does not speak at all (Legman 1968, 225–226). A female character's remark will be reinterpreted in sexual terms, presumably to the woman's discomfiture (Mulkay 1988, 137).

Each of these theses can, in fact, be supported by examples in Legman's volumes. The question is whether these theses represent what is going on in the collection as a whole. To test their applicability, I chose a one-hundred joke sample from the collection. Legman in one place estimated the number of jokes printed in *Rationale* at about sixteen hundred and in another place at two thousand (1968, 34; 1975, 48), so my sample constitutes 5 percent of the jokes in the volumes based on Legman's higher estimate. To ensure that my own biases did not influence my choice of jokes, I used a random number list to make the selection.[7]

While the claim of Thesis 1, that the creation of sexual jokes might be a male occupation, does not seem unreasonable, there is virtually no data on the creation of jokes, dirty or otherwise.[8] We have many assumptions but little knowledge. Furthermore, we have only scant knowledge of the extent of such joking by females. In the thousands of jokes that Legman included in his work, he does not usually identify the gender of the tellers, although it is information that should have been very easy for him to provide. Even though such identifications might only have informed us about whom Legman solicited for his texts, rather than offer a representative distribution of tellers by gender, it still might have proven helpful data.[9]

As far as the female always being the butt of the joke, this is decidedly false. There are ten jokes that revolve around the stupidity—most often the sexual stupidity—of the male (1968, 9, 37, 93, 129, 361; 1975, 216, 276, 554 [?], 790, 830), and there are six other jokes in which a husband is cuckolded (1968, 129, 716, 718, 733, 763, 789 [?]). Combined, these comprise the largest single theme in the sample, some 16 percent of the whole (also see Johnson 1973, 213). This accords well with Carol Mitchell's observation that almost 22 percent of her collection could be considered "fool" jokes—an analytic, not an ethnic category—and the fool in jokes, and in folklore more generally I might add, is almost invariably a male (1976, 32, 45).

A few jokes in the sample could be said to focus on the female body and, in that sense, could be said to expose the female body as maintained in Thesis 2. There is a joke about a female circus acrobat who finishes her spectacular act with three back somersaults, landing split-legged on the floor. She takes several curtain-calls in that position until the stage manager tells her to get up. She tells him to rock her back and forth to break the suction (1975, 406). A couple of jokes in the sample revolve around men being able to notice and discern vaginal odors (1968, 406). But then there are also three jokes that focus on the size of the male penis (1968, 293, 461; 1975, 587). One joke might be said to focus on a disgusting aspect of a female body, but it is male behavior that proves the most disgusting (1975, 388). If the exposure of females by males is the raison d'être of the dirty joke, then the great majority of these jokes remain to be explained. Five jokes concern male masturbation and the satisfaction that it provides, which hardly evidences this thesis (1968, 87, 88, 90, 310; 1975, 193).

Thesis 3, the expectation that women are available to men at any time is evidenced by only two jokes in the sample (1968, 100, 350). Another joke, however, has a dapper playboy go up to a beautiful woman sitting at the bar and whisper in her ear, "Whaddya say to a little fuck," to which she replies, "Hello, little fuck" (1975, 718). The expectation that a woman is always available is decisively thwarted in this text.

Thesis 4, the woman as object, is problematic as it is formulated. As the texts in question are jokes, more particularly sexual jokes, there should be very little room for women in any other role than that of sexual object. Nevertheless, there would seem to be exceptions even to this thesis. There are a number of jokes about homosexuals and homosexual sex (1975, 72, 80, 166), but as the homosexual characters in the jokes are often feminized (as in the use of the term *fairy* or by their lack of assertiveness [1968, 733; 1975, 72]), it might be argued that the female remains an object even in jokes about male homosexuality. There are a couple of jokes that seem motivated by female desire (1968, 674; 1975, 196). Perhaps the most interesting joke with respect to this thesis is one in which a handsome new waiter in Nick the Greek's Restaurant is invited to Nick's home for dinner with Nick and his wife. When Nick leaves the room, Nick's wife seduces the waiter, and when they have their clothes off, she wraps her arms around his neck and her legs around his waist and screams "Nick, come and get it" (1975, 154). This joke trades on the script of Greek men preferring homosexual intercourse. But it is the woman who is the active agent in the joke, and it is she who restrains the waiter to facilitate the fulfillment of the sexual inclinations of her husband.

Thesis 5, the dominance of the male voice, is belied by a great number of jokes—twenty-five, to be exact—in the sample. Females definitely speak and often speak to the discomfiture of men (1968, 100, 130, 340, 355, 361, 422, 501, 609, 671, 672, 674, 768, 790, 830; 1975, 80, 154, 196, 411, 691, 718, 721, 748, 830, 870, 962). There are four jokes in the sample in which the words of a female are reinterpreted, suppressed, or controlled by a male (1968, 254, 261; 1975, 140, 306). But there are four jokes as well in which a seemingly innocent statement by a male is given a sexual meaning by a female (1968, 100, 340; 1975, 691).

To put all these numbers in perspective, only seven jokes in the sample might be said to unambiguously speak to the triumph of male sexuality (1968, 273, 276, 310, 568, 774; 1975, 79, 771); four speak to the size of the penis or of an erection, whether in fact or in boast (1968, 230, 268, 293; 1975, 587). Yet four jokes refer to male impotence or sexual inability (1968, 509, 552, 674; 1975, 648, 651), two to male cowardice (1968, 737, 747), one to self-castration (1975, 605), and two are about drunken men who piss themselves when they go to urinate because they can't tell whether their penises are inside or outside their pants (1975, 65, 105). (It should be pointed out that four jokes in the sample have nothing to do with sex at all [1968, 42; 1975, 613, 903, 963].)[10] All in all, when dealing with theses that are clearly stated, and which do not presume the existence of unconscious motivations informing the jokes, what has been claimed about dirty jokes, if not false outright, should at the very least arouse deep suspicions. To put the case more straightforwardly, we do not seem to know very much about dirty jokes.

If we do not know very much about the overall character of dirty jokes, I am even more dubious about our knowledge of their psychology. I have never been particularly enamored of the idea that sexual jokes, or jokes in general, serve to alleviate built-up tensions originating in the unconscious, what has sometimes been called the cathartic hypothesis (Berkowitz 1970; Schafer 1970). To me, jokes have always seemed closer to philosophy than to plumbing. My first discomfort with the cathartic hypothesis is that the thoughts expressed in dirty jokes are typically conscious ones. Joke tellers are quite aware of what they are joking about. My second discomfort, as noted above, is that Freud did not regard jokes and dreams as the same sort of expressions. He only noted that dreams employed the same *techniques* as jokes in their construction. He did not propose that jokes and dreams fulfilled the same functions (see Oring 2016, 1–15). While this would not invalidate a hypothesis that sexual jokes serve to relieve sexual impulses, it should serve to dampen the hypothesis' legitimation through its attribution to the founder of psychoanalysis. Third, if sexual "arousal," or "anxiety," "drive discharge," or "sexual tension," (Doris and Fierman 1956; Strickland 1959, 287; Rosenwald 1964, 682; Schafer 1970, 13; Mitchell 1977, 324) are constants in the human condition, the fact that dirty joke telling is only intermittent needs to be explained. As of yet, no one has correlated the telling of such jokes with increases in levels of sexual tension.[11]

And if tension is relieved, for how long does the relief last before there is a necessity to tell or hear another joke? Is the hypothesis unfalsifiable? Fourth, when one comes to think about it, the notion that the telling of a joke allows for the release of pent-up sexual energy from the unconscious—as many people seem to think Freud was arguing—is, at some level, odd. Admittedly, there may be instances in which our sexual impulses direct our behaviors in ways of which we are not fully cognizant. But we are usually quite aware of our sexual desires, and there are numerous ways that we can potentially satisfy them. Dreaming, fantasy, erotica, and pornography, with or without accompanying physical stimulation, have the potential, one would think, of providing greater sexual relief. What, compared to these, might a canned joke or off-the-cuff salacious witticism offer? Has anyone ever achieved orgasm listening to or telling a dirty joke? Perhaps someone has; after all, anything is possible, but it would beggar belief to argue this was the usual response to either the telling or hearing of dirty jokes.

Finally, the myriad of psychological experiments directed to the cathartic hypothesis have not resolved the question. Usually, such experiments approach two hypotheses; the catharsis of sexual and the catharsis of aggressive impulses. The general proposition is that those who are more *repressed* with respect to sex and aggression will respond to sexual and aggressive jokes more positively as they serve to relieve their aroused impulses. An alternate formulation is that aggressive humor produces amusement in those with elevated levels of hostility (KIine 1976, 10; Ferguson and Ford 2008, 286–287). Experimental set-ups often attempt to either arouse hostility in subjects (often by treating them brusquely or leaving them alone for a considerable period before the start of the experiment) or stir up sexual impulses by exposing subjects to various kinds of sexual materials (erotic photographs or literary passages). Then groups of aroused and non-aroused subjects are asked to rate the degree of funniness of various jokes or cartoons that have been previously rated for their sexual, aggressive, or "nonsense" character.[12] The behavioral responses (e.g., smiling, laughing, or frowning) of the subjects may be noted as well and rated by the experimenter. In some cases, psychological aspects of the subject are assessed before and/or after exposure to the humorous stimuli (e.g., Redlich, Levine, and Sohler 1951; Doris and Fierman 1956; O'Connell 1960; Singer 1968).

The results of such experiments have been equivocal (see Martin 2007, 36–43). Occasionally, the results are in the predicted direction (e.g., Strickland 1959, 279–280; Dworkin and Efran 1967, 235); other times, the data do not support the hypothesis (e.g., O'Connell 1960, 265–266; Byrne 1961; Singer 1968, 6). Sometimes, the results are unexpected; for example, sexual arousal decreases subsequent aggressive tendencies (e.g., Baron and Ball 1974); sexual cartoons are preferred both by those who are and are not previously aroused (Strickland 1959, 279); maladjusted individuals prefer aggressive jokes more than well-adjusted individuals unless there is a stressor, in which case, the opposite obtains (O'Connell 1960, 267–268); nonhostile cartoons reduce levels of aggression in aroused subjects (Baron and Ball 1974, 30; Singer 1968, 8); the checklist administered to assess the mood of the subjects after the arousal of aggressive impulses itself has the effect of lowering the levels of aggression independently of exposure to humor (Singer 1968, 7); the more positive the attitude to sex and the greater their sexual experience, the higher the subjects' appreciation of sexual humor (Ruch and Hehl 1988, 10).

The cathartic hypothesis has been questioned by a number of investigators on theoretical grounds. Leonard Berkowitz (1970, 4) argued that fantasy aggression without guilt was likely to provoke more aggression. Even sexual arousal could energize aggressive responses. Experiments suggest that aggressive feelings are not purged in witnessing or fantasizing aggression but intensified and enhanced. Exposure to aggression can reinforce rather than reduce these impulses. When one attacks those who are believed to deserve attack, that aggression is gratifying, and aggression is reinforced. When a group of subjects were rewarded for acting nonaggressively to attacks made on them, their physiological condition showed "cathartic-like" decreases. In other words, aggression is learned, and aggression reinforces aggressive behavior (1970, 6).

Jeffrey H. Goldstein, Jerry M. Suls, and Susan Anthony (1972) thought that the relation between arousal and humor appreciation was unclear. Those aroused by sexual or aggressive stimuli might find sexual or aggressive humor more amusing because of the salience of particular stimuli. The exposure of a subject to aggressive photographs may facilitate the processing of subsequent aggressive jokes; sexual stimuli may facilitate the processing of sexual jokes, and so on. Subjects exposed to aggressive scenes of physical violence rated aggressive cartoons higher than those that did not. But those exposed to automobile photographs rated cartoons about automobiles higher than those exposed to aggressive photographs (164–165). Another experiment using musical and medical themes supported the salience hypothesis. Here two verbal jokes were used as arousal stimuli and subjects were then asked to rate a group of seven jokes. The prediction was that those who first rated music jokes would tend to rate later music jokes higher than medically themed jokes, and vice versa. The results of the experiment were in the predicted direction although not highly significant (168–169). So, the rating of jokes in terms of their funniness may not necessarily reflect an underlying psychological motivation but a cognitive disposition.

As a folklorist, my concerns about these experiments are directed more to the test materials—the jokes—than the experimental designs. Psychological articles only sometimes include a reproduction or a description of their test materials. At best, some articles may provide an example or two of the jokes employed in the experiment. If this material should not be grasped because some subjects do not have adequate knowledge resources to understand it—whether it is a sex joke, aggressive joke, or a "nonsense" joke—it is unlikely to receive a positive rating from subjects. If such opaque jokes or cartoons should be included in one category of the test materials, it would be capable of throwing off the statistical analysis because what subjects are responding to is not aggressive, sexual, or neutral content but an indecipherable joke.

A cartoon, for example, employed by Redlich, Levine, and Sohler (1951, 729) depicts a daughter and her babe-in-arms being driven out of a New York apartment building by an irate father while the doorman whistles for a taxi. This cartoon is unlikely to be funny for those who are unfamiliar with the Victorian conceit of a daughter and her baby born out of wedlock being driven by a father from the parental home into a driving snow.[13] A cartoon showing a sign on a busy freeway stating "Keep Right" with an arrow pointing left might have proved merely perplexing to some rather than amusing. And the humor in the cartoon of a farmer in an Asian rice field who says to another farmer, "I wonder what Rice Krispies taste like?" (Baron and Ball 1974, 27) might be so thin as to almost predispose a low subject evaluation.

Since subjects are evaluating cartoons or jokes in aggressive, sexual, and "nonsense" categories, the cartoons and jokes have to be selected with care to ensure that they are similar in terms of what Freud called their joking "envelope" [*Einkleidung*], the technique that creates the joke (Freud 1960, 8:92). Consequently, jokes that are being employed to assess motivations must be held as constant as possible with regard to their technique. If all the jokes with good technique found their way into the sexual or aggressive category and all the ones with poor technique into the "nonsense" category or vice versa, the effort to assess motivation by rating jokes for their funniness would be hopelessly compromised. As one researcher noted early on, "The present findings suggest that the hostile cartoons employed in this study were on average somewhat funnier than the neutral ones. In future investigations, *it might be preferable* to control for this factor" (Rosenwald 1964, 694; my emphasis).[14] It is not clear, however, that this advice was ever heeded.

The jokes used in such experiments have to be of similar length and type and employ similar techniques. Thus, if there is a joke-riddle in one category, there should be a joke-riddle in the others. If a joke in one category is based on a pun, a joke based on a pun should appear in the other categories as well. The same should hold for jokes based on displacement or reversal or change in point of view. Even the prosody of the texts might matter. Cartoons by a single cartoonist should be distributed in the different categories. It would be problematic for more of Gahan Wilson's cartoons to be in one category and more of Chris Browne's (creator of *Hagar the Horrible*) in another. The jokes and cartoons also should be equally sophisticated; that is, the number and difficulty of the inferences necessary to get the joke should be approximately the same. It seems problematic to include the joke about the emperor who asks a man who looks strikingly similar to himself, "Did your mother work at the palace," who answers, "No, but my father did" (a joke example also employed by Freud [1960, 8:68–69]) in the hostile joke category while including the joke that a cow followed by a couple of ducks could be described as "milk and quackers" in the "nonsense" category (O'Connell 1960, 265). These are not comparable jokes. Such an experiment is off to a bad start.[15]

Given the current state of knowledge, it would be difficult to confidently affirm any hypothesis about sexual joking. What should folklorists be doing? Perhaps they should be advising experimentalists on the structures and styles of joke texts (assuming they would be open to suggestions). Otherwise, folklorists need to turn to ethnography. While there are numerous published books of dirty jokes—primarily for entertainment purposes (e.g., Mr. J. n.d.; Mr. P. 1984; "*Filthy*" 2005)—there is next to nothing on individual or group repertoires and precious little on dirty jokes as communications in real social situations (but see Abrahams 1964; Leary 1980a; 1980b).[16] Accurate and thick descriptions of dirty joke telling might significantly bear on the various psychological hypotheses that have been proposed to date.

Laboratory experiments are worthwhile enterprises. They can illuminate mightily when they are creatively designed, carefully executed, and faithfully repeated. Experiments presume to model processes in the real world. At present, however, there is little in the way of concrete knowledge of how dirty jokes are performed and exchanged in the real world. Serious ethnography is needed. The point is not merely to accumulate detailed descriptions, however. The descriptions need to speak to matters of theory. To explain the nature of the dirty joke, ethnography must lead to generalization. If each joke-telling occasion is regarded as an exceptional communicative event, uniquely defined in terms of personnel, setting, social structure, and the dynamics of interaction, ethnography will have no contribution to make. It will ever be unable to validate or refute a psychological or sociological proposition. Folklorists need to be able to move from their encounters with particulars to the formulation of generalizations, from the idiographic to the nomothetic (Harris 1979, 78–79).

There needs to be equal attention to female dirty joke telling to gauge the extent to which it takes place and under what circumstances. There is only a little in the way of description of sexual jokes told by females (Randolph 1976; Burns with Burns 1976; Green 1977; Mitchell 1976, 1977, 1978, 1985) and even less on such joke telling in context (but see Johnson 1973). As important is the description of such joking in mixed-gender groupings. There should be an attempt to describe the nature of the jokes, the character of their performance, as well as the dynamics of the interaction. A comparison of male and female sexual jokes and joke telling would naturally follow.[17]

The dirty joke is ancient (Baldwin 1983). It might be universal (Fine 1976; Senft 1985). Almost all are traditional. They are not internal fantasies but public performances. Dirty jokes are not meant to arouse but amuse. They are less sex than art (Collins 1970, 153; Oring 2016, 182–198).[18] Understanding the dirty joke should fall heavily in the province of folklore. Folklorists once showed some interest in these matters. That interest needs to be revived. The subject, it would seem, is too important to be left solely in the hands of psychoanalysts and psychologists.

CHAPTER FOUR

Incongruous, Appropriate, Spurious

A sense of humor is just common sense dancing.
—William James (attributed)

Jokes and other forms of humor are dependent on the perception of an *appropriate incongruity*. Simply put, a joke will involve some relation of words, ideas, or behaviors that are perceived as incongruous, which are nevertheless regarded, in some measure, as appropriately related. Perhaps the most transparent means of creating an appropriate incongruity is the pun—an identical or similar phonological relationship between words of phrases with different meanings:

Many a blonde dyes by her own hand. (Esar 1952, 77)

Teacher: Where do we find mangoes?
Student: Where woman goes. (78)

There is an incongruity in the first joke. Why should blondes, more than other people, die by their own hand? The incongruity is appropriate if the verb is recognized in its two senses: to lose life and to artificially color. The knowledge that many women color their hair blonde, that is, that many blondes are not natural blondes, makes the initial incongruity appropriate. (This joke probably works best in written form since the pun is more readily apparent than were it spoken.) The second joke also relies on a pun. The teacher seems to ask about where mangoes are grown, where they are a native product. This is a typical kind of question that a teacher might ask in primary school where students learn—or once

   https://doi.org/10.7330/9781646425198.c004

learned—about different countries and their agricultural products and manufactures. The student answer at first seems incongruous—a non sequitur—but when "mangoes" is quickly reinterpreted as "man goes," the answer, "where woman goes," becomes appropriate because men are attracted to women.

A more elaborate example:

> There's a nudist colony for communists. Two old men are sitting on the front
> porch. One turns to the other and says, "Have you read Marx?" And the other says,
> "Yes . . . I believe it's these wicker chairs." (Keillor 2005, 25)

This joke might be more difficult to process when read rather than when heard since spelling leaves less room for ambiguity. In any event, the appropriate incongruity should still be obvious. One communist asks another whether he has read Marx. The other answers in the affirmative but attributes it to the wicker chairs that they are sitting on, which would seem to have nothing at all to do with the question. There are two alternatives: let the incongruity stand and dismiss the response as a non sequitur with no connection whatsoever to the initial question or press for some other interpretation. There is such an interpretation that depends upon recognizing two puns in the joke: read = red and Marx = marks. Red marks are then understood to be the result of sitting naked on wicker chairs. The incongruity is appropriate.

In modern societies, phonic resemblances are usually not regarded as a basis for establishing valid connections between things or concepts, (unless they are derived from a common linguistic root, and if that derivation is obvious, the joke is not funny [Oring 2003, 8]). We regard the relationship between signs and meanings, for the most part, as arbitrary, as established by fiat or the vicissitudes of language history. There are realms, however, in which what we call puns would seem to establish more substantive connections. In some societies, a name is considered the essence of the thing itself. Various forms of magical practice are established based on this premise (e.g., Frazer 1925, 244–262; Trachtenberg 1961, 78–103).[1] To invoke the name is to invoke and control the object or the person named.

The Ndembu of Zambia, as well as other Bantu societies, explain the meaning of their religious symbols by means of what Victor Turner terms "fictitious etymologizing"; that is, a phonic resemblance rooted in similarities of sound rather than in a derivation from a common term (Turner 1969, 11). Thus, the name of the Ndembu ritual *isoma* is believed to derive from the word *ku-somoka*, "to slip out of place," and the ritual is meant to address the problem of women who have suffered repeated miscarriages (fetuses that have slipped out of place) and is designed to remind a woman of and restore her attachments to her matrilineal group (from which she is believed to have slipped out of place [1969, 15–16]). Punning is rampant in the Old and New Testaments but not as a source of humor. The rabbis and the Church Fathers took such puns seriously as they did connections between words based on their numerical values (*gematria*), the recoding of letters (*temurah*), and acronymic constructions (*notarikon*) in their search for deeper religious truths. For them, phonic resemblances and the connections between the written forms and values of words were considered anything but arbitrary. Today, puns have been largely relegated to the creation of humor—thoroughly discountable forms of expression. Puns, it would seem, are only seriously entertained in etymology (folk and scholarly), the creation and interpretation of poetry, psychoanalysis, and French literary theory.

Puns are only one of the means by which incongruities are made appropriate in jokes. Although they are common, they are, perhaps, the most devalued. There is a tendency—in our society at least—to groan rather than laugh at puns (Sherzer 1985, 219). Some believe the groan registers the difference between essence and accident (Culler 1988, 4). I suspect the groan is a response meant to acknowledge the transparency of that joke mechanism. A pun reveals all to clearly how a joke does its work.

Not all jokes depend upon puns, and they must establish the appropriateness of their incongruities by other means:

> "I was depressed, Doctor, so I tried to kill myself by taking a thousand aspirins."
> "What happened?"
> "Well, after the first two I felt better." (Keillor 2005, 194)

It is incongruous that a depressed man swallows a substance to poison himself only to find his depression lifted and his will to live restored. Nevertheless, there is a measure of appropriateness to the man's recovery since aspirin is an analgesic and taking aspirin in small doses—usually two, as in "take two aspirin and call me in the morning"—often does make people feel better.

There are a number of things to note about the appropriate incongruity perspective on jokes. First, the perspective is quite old. One of its earliest intimations appears in John Locke's *An Essay Concerning Human Understanding*, first published in 1690, in which Locke differentiates between wit and judgment: "For *wit* lying most in the assemblage of *ideas*, and putting these together with quickness and variety, wherein can be found an resemblance or congruity, thereby to make up pleasant pictures, and agreeable visions in the fancy, *judgment*, on the contrary, has quite on the other side, in separating carefully one from another, *ideas* wherein can be found the least difference, thereby to avoid being misled by similitude, and by affinity to take one for the other" (Locke 1798 [1690], 128, emphasis in original).

Francis Hutcheson, in his *Reflections upon Laughter and Remarks on the Fable of the Bees* published in 1750, emphasized the incongruous nature of the conjoined ideas: "That which seems generally the cause of laughter," is "the bringing together of images which have contrary additional ideas, as well as some resemblance in the principal idea: this contrast between ideas of grandeur, dignity, sanctity, perfection, and ideas of meanness, baseness, profanity, seems to be the very spirit of burlesque; and the greatest part of our raillery and jest is founded upon it" (Hutcheson 1750, 18). Hutcheson may have overstated the case in regard to those ideas that must necessarily be contrasted to produce laughter, but that observation has nevertheless persisted in the works of later commentators on the subject (e.g., Spencer 1860, 400; Raskin 1985a, 114).

James Beattie clearly articulated the appropriate incongruity perspective in 1779: "Laughter arises from the view of two or more inconsistent, unsuitable or incongruous parts or circumstances, considered as united in one complex object or assemblage, or as acquiring a sort of mutual relation from the peculiar manner in which the mind takes notice of them" (1779, 347). This perspective on humor was revived in the last century under the term *incongruity-resolution theory* with which my *appropriate incongruity* perspective substantially aligns except for my discomfort with the term *resolution* (see Suls 1972, 84; Oring 2003, 2; 1992; Ritchie 2009); a point to which I will return.[2]

Second, as useful as I have found the appropriate incongruity perspective to the analysis of particular jokes and joke repertoires, there are difficulties resident in the approach. Perhaps the central problem of appropriate incongruity and all other incongruity-based approaches to humor is that *incongruity* has yet to be formally defined. How much and what kinds of disparities between objects, behaviors, ideas, or linguistic formulations are sufficient for the disparity to register as an incongruity? Why, for example, is the idea that a poison might prove therapeutic incongruous? Actually, most substances that have been employed as medicines are poisonous if ingested or applied in excessive amounts or under the wrong conditions. Conversely, many of the substances that were recognized as poisonous (e.g., curare, foxglove, belladonna) proved curative when prepared, applied, and consumed in measured doses and controlled situations. The same difficulty attends the term *appropriate*. What is the nature of the relation between objects, behaviors, ideas, or linguistic formulations such that that relation would be recognized as an appropriate one (Oring 2016, 215)? Beattie recognized this difficulty almost two hundred and fifty years ago.[3]

These observations point to the fact that the analysis of humor in terms of *appropriate incongruity*, or in terms of any incongruity-resolution framework for that matter, is necessarily *post hoc*. That is to say, one can identify the incongruity and appropriateness within any text *that we first recognize as a joke*, but we are unlikely to be able to construct a procedure that can reliably discriminate between joke and non-joke texts. In other words, the terms *incongruity* and *appropriateness* (or even *resolution*) are not sufficiently well-defined to serve as the basis for an algorithm that could reliably recognize or even generate (generation being the far easier task) jokes.

Over the past decades, I have had a running skirmish with a group of computational linguists who are trying to solve the problem of machine recognition of a joke (see chapter 5). I fully appreciate the difficulty of their task. Alongside the problem of how the structure of humor might be coded for a computer, there is the formidable problem of natural language processing. Before a computer can decide whether a text is a joke, it has to be able to decipher a text. Anyone who has had to interact with a computer when calling their cable television company knows that these computers react appropriately only within a very narrow verbal range. An ability to recognize humor presumes a knowledge not only of the denotations of words but their connotations and an ability to grasp the *relations* between terms. Only when this is achieved might it be possible to move to the computer recognition of humorous texts. This second task, however, will depend on understanding how humor is produced within a text, and I believe that without some operationalization of the notions of incongruity and appropriateness, the effort will fail.

To date, the computational linguists have tried to operationalize incongruity as *opposition* (Raskin 1985a, 99; Attardo and Raskin 1991, 307–309), but this is a notion that seems woefully insufficient for the task. In a text there are all kinds of oppositions: between an animal and a human; between a person and a thing; between a male and a female; between a child and an adult; between a subject and an object; between a noun and a verb; and between a noun and every other noun that is not identical to it. Many of these oppositions will be irrelevant to the incongruity on which the joke is based. Unless linguists can specify what kinds of oppositions qualify as incongruities, any algorithm they write will likely be doomed to failure.[4] Consequently, they will be unable to do any more than I am able to do using the notion of appropriate incongruity. That is, if they recognize some text as a joke, they will be able to identify the incongruity (or what they call an *opposition*), and they will be able to discern its appropriateness (or what they sometimes call *compatibility* or *overlap* of semantic domains, or the operation of what they call *logical mechanisms*). In other words, their approach to the problem is as post hoc as my own. The sense that their approach is a formal one amenable to computerization is belied by my own reanalysis of some of their joke specimens that shows that their grasp of these jokes—without the aid of a computer—sometimes seems amiss (Oring 2011b; 2011c).

If appropriate incongruity—and incongruity theories in general—cannot be operationalized and consequently proves to be a post hoc analysis of something previously identified as a joke, why not abandon it for one of the many other theories that have been proposed over the centuries: Sigmund Freud's release and relief theory (1960 [1905]), the superiority theory of Thomas Hobbes (1962 [1651], 52; Gruner 1978, 30), Henri Bergson's automatism theory (1956, 81, 84, 91–92), Matthew M. Hurley's, Daniel C. Dennett's, and Reginald B. Adams, Jr.'s false belief theory (2011), Thomas C. Veatch's (1998) and A. Peter McGraw and Joel Warner's benign violation theory (2014), or Seana Coulson's conceptual integration or blending theory (2005)?

There are several reasons not to abandon incongruity theory. First, some of these other theories seem wrong on evidentiary grounds. For example, there are far too many instances of humor that do not display any sense of superiority or suggest the operation of an aggressive impulse. Even Freud acknowledged the existence of "innocent jokes" (Freud 1960 [1905], 90–96). Furthermore, naked manifestations of superiority or aggression are rarely funny. Special techniques are required to make them funny. Second, some of these theories apply to a far greater range of materials than humor and therefore fail to specify what is unique about jokes. Conceptual integration or blending theory, for example, character-izes a far greater range of textual constructions than jokes and therefore cannot distinguish humorous from non-humorous stimuli. Third, some theories seem to be subcategories of incongruity theory. Bergson's idea that humor results from the mechanization of something living could be subsumed under incongruity theory with the organic versus the mechanical serving as the basic incongruity in one class of appropriately incongruous texts. Fourth, some theories require additional assumptions for an analysis of a joke. Benign violation theory requires a presump-tion about the emotional responses of hearers to the content of the joke. And finally, it should be recognized that all these theories are post hoc as well. None of them can serve as the basis for an algorithm that might instruct a machine on how to differentiate a joke from a non-joke text. Given that all the theories that have appeared thus far also would seem to be post hoc, I would argue for the advan-tages of incongruity theory.[5]

It is somewhat odd that in reading articles and books on humor theory, there is usually little in the way of a determined and consistent analysis of actual jokes. That is largely because many theories address the *functions* of jokes rather than their *form*. They presume to work from what they claim a joke does rather than what causes one to recognize a text, an utterance, or a behavior as humorous in the first place. I have tried in the past to analyze individual jokes in terms of appro-priate incongruity and to review the analyses by other theorists of particular joke texts (e.g., Oring 1973; 1981; 1992, 2–12, 16–28; 2003, 8–10, 13–25; 2011a, 204–219; 2011b; 2016, 39–41, 84–90; 2019a; 2019b). It is sometimes difficult to find close and persistent analyses of jokes in other works.

Although incongruity and appropriateness seem to me to be necessary for the joke, there would seem to be another essential factor as well—*spuriousness*. The appropriateness established by a pun in a joke, for example, is spurious: it has been established by means that are not considered legitimate or valid in everyday discourse. We do not permit sounds to stand for different concepts in a single bona fide communication. In other words, the appropriateness established by the pun is at once perceived as faulty, flawed, and illegitimate (Oring 1992, 2–3; 1995; 2003, 5–9, 14–15, 59; 2016, 48, 52, 59, 69, 85, 92, 225n30). While the pun proffers a measure of psychological legitimacy, the pun is not logically or even common-sensically acceptable. We recognize that a similarity of sound cannot authentically repair a conceptual incongruity.

The spuriousness that characterizes the appropriateness of a pun is also resident in jokes that do not depend upon puns. For example, in the joke about the attempted suicide-by-aspirin, while it is appropriate that taking a few aspirin might relieve a headache or reduce a fever and make someone feel better, no one would suggest that taking two aspirin would cure suicidal depression, nor would anyone propose that someone attempting suicide by ingesting a prodigious number of aspirin tablets would pause after taking the first two to await their therapeutic effect. The appropriateness of the patient's escape from depression and suicide is *conceptually* appropriate—it is recognized that aspirin does alleviate pain—but it cannot be considered logically valid, realistically probable, or practically effective. In fact, it is this notion of spuriousness, which seems to lurk in the appropriateness of an incongruity, that has set me at odds with the concept of incongruity *resolution* (Oring 2003, 2). In the joke, nothing is ever legitimately resolved. Something always seems improper even when it is otherwise "appropriate." All in all, what I am proposing is that there is a third component in the operation of jokes: they are rooted in the perception of something that is at once incongruous, appropriate, *and* spurious.

While there have been any number of efforts to sketch a history of humor theories, including incongruity theories (e.g., Piddington 1963, 152ff; Monro 1953; Keith-Spiegel 1972; Morreall 1987), a history of the concept of spuriousness does not as yet exist. The notion has been largely overlooked. When notice has been taken, it is usually very brief, in passing, undeveloped, and almost never is there a reference to previous formulations of the idea.[6] Francis Hutcheson mentions that in the resemblances of contrasting images that engender laughter (or in my terminology, the appropriateness of incongruous domains) there is "a forced straining of a likeness" (1750, 18). The idea that a likeness, an appropriateness, is *forced* strongly suggests that it is at some level unnatural, unreasonable, improper, faulty, or spurious. Hutcheson, unfortunately, does not develop the observation further. Norman R. F. Maier points to the "ridiculousness" in humor; that is, an illogic that is only permitted within confined limits. The humorous situation is "momentarily true" but is not true "pragmatically." Consequently, humor is inconsistent with reality as a whole and cannot be taken seriously (1932, 72–73). Maier also fails to develop his observation further.

The psychoanalyst Sandor Feldman, in what he labeled "a supplement to Freud's theory of wit," noted the faulty thinking at the root of jokes and "the attitude of the ego which allows the acceptance of this faulty thinking and permits its enjoyment" (1941, 203). In my terms, the appropriateness of the incongruity is spurious, but the construction is accepted and enjoyed despite—indeed, because of—its faultiness. Feldman goes on to root the whole process in ego and superego development and the response of the individual to the castration threat, which to my mind, probably served to isolate his observation from the broader realm of incongruity theory.

Elie Auboin sees humor as rooted in incongruity, but also recognized that the connection established between incongruous categories is, at some level, spurious: "When we write that a double meaning, a faulty assimilation, an error of judgment . . . are accepted or justified, it can, of course, only be a conditional and temporary acceptance, subject to immediate review; a superficial justification and in no way absolute which for a moment *veils the absurdity of the judgment, or the reasoning,* of the act, but leaves the essential double character of the comical contrast" (1948, 95, my emphasis).[7]

Michael Mulkay remarks, also in a single sentence, that "the sense-making processes of humour are often quite unlike those of the serious realm; the congruity achieved in the humorous realm is frequently incongruous when judged by ordinary standards" (Mulkay 1988, 35). The terminology can be confusing. What Mulkay is calling "congruity" is what I call "appropriateness"; what he is calling "incongruous" is what I call "spurious." What he is basically noting is that the appropriateness created in a joke is at some level illegitimate or spurious by ordinary standards of reason or practice.

Avner Ziv recognizes that an incongruity in a joke creates an absurdity and to accept the absurdity one must abandon Aristotelian logic. Ziv referred to a "local logic" that "is appropriate in a way" because it provides a kind of explanation of the incongruity if the listener is "willing to play along" (1984, 77, 90). His view seems similar to that of Maier, although Maier is nowhere cited. Again, to translate it to my own terminology, a joke is created when an incongruity is made appropriate, but that appropriateness is spurious. The joke listener "plays along" with the faulty connection and tolerates its invalidity. If the appropriateness of an incongruity were viewed as legitimate, were a seeming incongruity made *totally* appropriate—were it, in fact, *resolved*—there would be no joke to perceive.[8]

Salvatore Attardo and Victor Raskin remarked, again, in passing, that the logical mechanisms of humor must provide a "logical or pseudological justification of the absurdity or irreality it postulates" (1991, 307). That is to say, an incongruity must be somehow made appropriate by recourse to logical or pseudological means. I am arguing that appropriateness or justification is never strictly logical—if it were, there would be no joke—and if a justification is pseudological, it is spurious by definition. I maintain that the appropriateness in the joke is a matter of psychological validity, not logical validity (Oring 1992, 2–3; Ritchie 2014). Appropriateness can be rooted in a pun, an analogy, a historical connection, an idiosyncrasy of character, or a traditional behavior. Whatever the means by which the establishment of an appropriate relation is created between incongruous categories in the joke, something about it always seems to be improper.

Last (although not chronologically) and certainly not least is a technical report first published by David Navon in 1981, which was later reformulated and republished in 1988 in the journal *Poetics*. Navon's is the only extended discussion of what I am calling the spuriousness of the appropriate connection between incongruous categories. Somehow this paper managed to escape bibliographies dealing with the structure of humor, and I only discovered it by accident after this chapter was written.[9] Navon articulates a position that is very close to my own. There is incongruity and there is seeming appropriateness, but that appropriateness is, in his words, "virtually inappropriate."[10] Like most of the commentators on this important element of jokes, Navon makes no reference to those others who have previously noted or alluded to the matter.

I also pointed to the spuriousness of the appropriate relationship between the incongruous categories (Oring 1981, 129; 1992, 2–3) and elaborated on the matter when challenged by Gregory Schrempp (1995) to address the question of why certain appropriate incongruities did *not* produce humor. My response was that the appropriateness apprehended in appropriate incongruities of non-humorous texts was not spurious but substantively engaged (Oring 1995; 2003, 2, 5–8).

Metaphors, similes, and analogies, for example, have long presented a challenge to incongruity theory because, like jokes, they create incongruities by connecting otherwise distinct conceptual domains.[11] The interpretation of metaphors also depends upon discovering their appropriateness. But unlike jokes, they are—except in special circumstances—not funny.[12] The reason metaphors are generally not funny, I believe, has little to do with anything about the semantic distance between source and target domains (Morrissey 1990, 124–125) or the absence of tabooed ideas in the target domain (Dynel 2012, 34–35). These may be intensifying factors but not their principal distinction. The incongruities in metaphors are made appropriate by identifying what are perceived as substantive, legitimate connections between the two domains. In other words, the appropriateness of a metaphor is not perceived as spurious. Should it be perceived as spurious, it would be a humorous metaphor; that is, as a kind of joke (see Attardo 2007, 2015).

This notion that metaphors depend upon identifying substantive relations between domains has been translated into the notion that metaphors are "fully resolved," whereas humorous metaphors and jokes are only partially resolved (Hempelmann and Attardo 2011, 125; Attardo 2015, 95; Piata 2016, 41). This is not what I am suggesting. The distinction between full and partial resolution was introduced into the analysis of jokes over forty years ago (Rothbart 1977), but I have found the concept unhelpful (see Forabosco 1992, 59; Oring 2003, 13–26). While I can understand why someone might regard the spurious "resolution" of a joke as somehow "incomplete"—after all, it is not entirely legitimate—the resolution of a metaphor is not "complete" either. The linkages established between domains in a metaphor, though substantive, are necessarily partial and thus incomplete as well.

For example, the metaphor "conscience is a man's compass" asks its interpreter to grasp the ways in which a conscience and compass are substantively similar. As a compass is an instrument that can provide orientation in a geographical landscape; a conscience can provide orientation in a moral one. The appropriateness of the metaphor lies in the perception of this basic similarity. Both compass and conscience can point to a proper path in life. The metaphor is commonplace enough so that the phrase "moral compass" is often used without explicit acknowledgement of its metaphorical nature. The connection of the domains is regarded as substantive and legitimate. It is by no means total, however. The differences between a compass and a conscience are more numerous and perhaps more significant than the similarities. A prototypical compass is a mechanical instrument that includes a balanced or floating magnetized needle that points north. A conscience is not a mechanical instrument, and, for the most part, it cannot be precisely located or even described in material terms. A conscience arouses emotion; a compass generally does not. There is a tested theory of how a magnetic compass works, while the theoretical underpinnings of conscience are much less secure. Conscience has a strong social component in its formation and operation; a compass does not. These are the kinds of factors that are not "resolved" in the interpretation of the metaphor. In the use of the metaphor, they must be overlooked, ignored, or suppressed (Glucksberg, Newsome, and Goldvarg 2001).

Highlighting some of these ignored or suppressed factors and making them explicit creates, in fact, a potential for humor: "His conscience was usually a reliable compass unless there was some sexually magnetic influence in the vicinity"; "His conscience was his compass, and like his compass, it never made him feel guilty"; "His conscience was his compass, and he kept both in a drawer"; "His conscience was his compass, but it didn't keep him from getting lost in the woods"; "Like a compass, his conscience did not really point to true north." In other words, humor can arise precisely from those areas where the appropriateness of a metaphor betrays its inadequacy.

Both metaphors and jokes depend upon incongruities that are regarded as appropriate. Humor depends upon focusing on the incongruities between domains and registering—although not necessarily explicitly—the spuriousness of the linkages created between them. In metaphor, the incongruities are overlooked or suppressed (Oring 1995, 231; Pollio 1996, 248–250). What keeps the incongruities in plain sight in jokes is the transparent spuriousness of the means by which the relation between the domains—the appropriateness—is established. In metaphor, the unresolvable elements are concealed and the substantive connections foregrounded.

When an incongruity is completely and genuinely appropriate or "resolved," I would contend that one is dealing not with a joke but a real *problem* or *puzzle.* Paul Schiller saw jokes as structurally related to problems and puzzles. Schiller's example of a problem is a geometrical demonstration that the angles of a triangle necessarily add up to 180 degrees. The solution depends upon showing by constructions and previously proven theorems that the angles of any triangle are necessarily the same as those that make up a straight line—180 degrees (1938, 218). His example of a puzzle is how an architect can build a house in the shape of a cube such that the windows in each wall all face south. The solution is that the house needs to be built at the North Pole (220). Both problems and puzzles start with a "configuration" that requires a change in the "thought pattern" to produce "understanding or insight" (218, 221). The difference between a problem and a puzzle, however, is that configurations for solving puzzles are "artificial" or "arbitrary," whereas a problem has a final configuration that is "natural" (220–221). Jokes, in Schiller's view, are special cases of solving problems and puzzles. In the joke, he claims, the starting configuration is "strange" and the solving one "natural" with neither of them being fixed (224).

Schiller is correct to view jokes in the context of problems and puzzles. All these forms proffer intellectual challenges that invite efforts at solution. Schiller's characterization of the differences between them, however, strikes me as a bit more than inexact. The problem, as Schiller points out, has a natural construction and a natural solution. But it seems to me that the puzzle is not distinguished by the artificial, arbitrary, and inappropriate nature of its solution, as he suggests, but by the artificial, arbitrary, and inappropriate nature of its question. The question about the house with southern exposures on four sides is deliberately crafted to perplex. Unlike the scientific or mathematical problem, which is grounded in a search for something unknown, a puzzle is constructed on a basis of something that is already known. The point of the puzzle is to confound. The point of a problem is to lead to a satisfactory solution about something that has arisen in the course of an investigation of the real or conceptual world.[13] The solution of a problem is meant to serve as a possible foundation for resolving further problems. That is not the case with a puzzle. When solved, a puzzle, like a joke, is simply proposed to others who are not as yet in possession of the solution.[14]

The solution of a puzzle is not artificial, arbitrary, or inappropriate as Schiller proposes. The solution is completely appropriate *given the puzzle question*. The solution only appears artificial because of the artificiality of that question.[15] Puzzle solutions, unlike the jokes analyzed above, do not have what might be called "ragged edges." They are not spurious given the question. So, the puzzle differs from the problem in that the puzzle question may be artificial, but its solution is completely appropriate to the question.

One example of a puzzle presented by Schiller is: how can you make a figure of four equilateral triangles using six matchsticks without breaking or crossing any of them? The solution is impossible if sought exclusively within two-dimensional space. But if an equilateral triangle is formed with three of the matches, and the tips of the other three are placed at the points of intersection of that triangle so that they rise to form a pyramid, four equilateral triangles are created (1938, 219). A solution is possible in three dimensions that is not possible in two. That solution is also *entirely appropriate*, as it completely satisfies the conditions set out in the puzzle problem.

It is surprising that Schiller regards the situation of D. Katz's mouse as an instance of a puzzle (1938, 219). The mouse was found one day stuck in the bars of its cage with its abdomen on the outside of the cage and its head on the inside. No one had ever seen a mouse try to go backward. Perplexity ceased when it was realized that the mouse had escaped from the cage and only got stuck when it tried to get back through the bars into the cage. It seems to me that an experimenter had been confronted with a real world—a natural—problem about mouse behavior that admitted a real world and completely appropriate solution. Why consider this example a puzzle rather than a problem? It seems a real-world problem with a completely appropriate real-world resolution.

Schiller sees in jokes a "dynamic duality" (1938, 222). In a pun, the duality is bridged by a similarity in sound. In another situation, the duality is bridged by a habitual behavior that is enacted or a character trait that is expressed in a situation where such a behavior is unsuitable. Getting a joke involves seeing something from two different points of view (224). The experience of humor depends upon an easy shift between them (226).

In a cartoon of an industrial plant that Schiller cites, a bulge appears to be moving up a tall brick chimney until a fat chimney sweep emerges at the top, Schiller points to the "inappropriate" (i.e., incongruous) way the chimney behaves—like an esophagus. Schiller concludes that the humor resides in the entertaining of two absurd propositions: that a brick chimney could bulge and that a fat chimney sweep could make it bulge. In effect, Schiller is maintaining—to put it in my own terminology—that the incongruity of the bulging chimney is made appropriate by the revelation of the stout chimney sweep. Schiller's view of humor certainly aligns with the appropriate incongruity perspective, but it must be recognized that the appropriateness is spurious as the sweep's portliness could not actually make a brick chimney visibly bulge.[16]

A further difference between jokes on the one hand and problems and puzzles on the other hinges on the amount of time employed in finding a resolution. Problems and puzzles can stand for hours, days, years, or centuries before a satisfactory solution is reached. A joke needs to be grasped almost instantaneously in order to produce its effect. The appropriateness of the incongruity (or the incongruousness of what at first sight seems appropriate) requires almost immediate recognition. Deliberation—though fitting for problems and puzzles—is the enemy of the joke. If a joke has to be explained, the person needing the explanation may finally grasp why it is a joke and how it works, but the quotient of amusement is likely to be greatly reduced, if there is any at all. It is unlikely to elicit the spontaneous laughter that often accompanies jokes that are speedily apprehended. Even the riddle-joke becomes a puzzle if the poser leaves it to the devices of the listener to solve rather than offering an immediate solution.

If we want to change the puzzle about the house with all southern exposures into a joke, it might be reformulated as something like: "Why did the Polack build his house at the North Pole? Because he wanted only southern exposures." No one would build a house at the North Pole just to have southern exposures. A southern exposure may be a desirable feature for a house in many climes, but it would not prove desirable if built in the arctic. (In fact, at the North Pole during winter, the sun does not rise above the horizon.) The appropriateness, in other words, is spurious. (It is not necessary to have a Pole as the joke protagonist, as he is only one of a number of joke types that could fill the slot.) But as a puzzle, the solution—the appropriateness—is complete given the theoretical question of how a house with a square floor plan could be built with only southern exposures.

The artificiality is contained solely within the puzzle question but not in the puzzle answer. In the joke, the "solution"—the appropriateness—is spurious.

It is important not to confuse a fantastic scenario in a joke with either the efficient incongruity or its appropriateness. Many jokes have fantastic or unlikely scenarios. "A horse walks into a bar . . ." (Keillor 2005, 131); "A five-dollar bill walks into a bar . . ." (129); "What do you get when you drop a piano down a mine shaft?" (209). In the elephant joke "How do you hide an elephant in a cherry tree? You paint his toenails red," there is clearly a fantastic scenario of hiding an elephant in a tree. That is not the operating incongruity in the joke, however. The incongruity resides in the notion that painting the elephant's toenails might serve to hide the animal. Painting the elephant's toenails red is, nevertheless, appropriate since red toenails could—in theory—blend in with the cherries in the tree. The appropriateness is clearly spurious because painting the elephant's toenails could hardly achieve the desired result. The remaining seven tons of the otherwise gray animal would undoubtedly stand out. Note, however, that painting the elephant's toenails orange, yellow, or blue would leave one without a joke altogether. Such answers would simply create non sequiturs as they provide no appropriateness whatsoever. Painting the elephant's toenails red at least serves as an appropriate, if spurious, contribution to its camouflage.

The fact that jokes, in most cases, are easily and intuitively grasped does not mean that the analysis of jokes is a simple or straightforward affair. Explicitly identifying the incongruity, the appropriateness, and the spuriousness of that appropriateness may often prove difficult. Furthermore, what is incongruous, appropriate, and spurious is not necessarily mapped onto distinct parts of the joke or lodged in discrete mechanisms. What follows is the analysis of a series of jokes from the relatively easy to those I consider to be far more difficult.

A relatively easy joke:

Wife: My two specialties are meatballs and peach pie.
Husband: I see, and which one is this? (Keillor 2005, 232).

The incongruity is that the husband cannot differentiate between two foods that are about as different as can be. One is a savory meat dish, the other a sweet fruit pastry. His inability is appropriate, however, if one presupposes that the wife's cooking is so bad that the two cannot readily be distinguished. This appropriateness is spurious, because no matter how poor the wife's cooking, the two dishes would remain in terms of form, color, odor, consistency, and taste at some level distinguishable.

Veni, Vidi, Velcro—I came, I saw, I stuck around. (Keillor 2005, 12)

This joke depends, first of all, on recognizing the saying *Veni, vidi, vici*—"I came, I saw, I conquered"—as Julius Caesar's description of his speedy victory over Pharnaces II at the Battle of Zela in 47 BCE (Obviously, it is only the attribution to Caesar and a knowledge of the meaning of the phrase that are necessary for understanding the joke.) Given this knowledge, the word *Velcro* creates an incongruity. Although the word has something of a Latin quality (it is actually a portmanteau word constructed from the French *velour* [velvet] + *crochet* [hook]), it refers to a type of fabric fastener in common use. The fastener can take some effort to pull apart, and thus Velcro becomes appropriate when translated as "I stuck around." Of course, *Velcro* does not mean "I stuck around" in Latin or any other language, nor would Julius Caesar have said it as a boast of his military accomplishments in Pontus. It is an appropriate, though spurious, usage of the word.

> As long as there are tests, there will be prayer in public schools. (Keillor 2005, 11)

The incongruity centers on the question of what the issue of school prayer has to do with test taking. Prayer in school is a matter of law. The First Amendment of the US Constitution, which states that Congress should make "no law respecting an establishment of religion," serves as the basis for courts prohibiting public prayer in schools and at other sites paid for with taxpayer money. Tests, of course, will cause many students to silently pray—both strictly and loosely defined—that the questions they are asked are easy, that they are not examined on materials they have not studied, or that they will somehow succeed despite their inadequate preparation. Consequently, prayer is relevant to the matter of tests in school. But the issue that goes under the term *school prayer* only concerns organized, public, religious expression. *School prayer* and *prayer in school* are not quite the same thing. What one hopes or says to oneself is not within the purview of the law (nor could it be monitored if it were), so the appropriateness of *school prayer* as the term is generally understood and test taking is spurious. The silent appeals of students before or during their tests bears little relation to the political issue evoked by the term *school prayer*.

> One day, Sven and Ole were hunting and suddenly a man came running out of the bushes yelling, "Don't shoot! Don't shoot! I'm not a deer." Ole raised his gun and shot him.
>
> Sven said, "Ole, why did you shoot that man? He said he wasn't a deer!"
> Ole answered, "Oh! I thought he said he was a deer" (Keillor 2005, 235).

Ole is a character in a series of jokes from the Upper Midwest of the United States, and he is Norwegian and typically stupid. His friend Sven is Swedish, but he is as, or even more, clueless than Ole (Leary 2001). The above joke could easily be told about any stereotypically stupid joke characters (e.g., Polish Americans, Newfoundlanders, Irish, et al.).[17] It even might be told about the former vice president of the United States, Dick Cheney, not because he was perceived as stupid, but because he shot a companion while quail hunting on a ranch in Texas back in 2006. (This suggests that there can be more than one way to link a joke with a real-world protagonist.)

The incongruity in this joke is clear: Ole shoots a man who is yelling, "Don't shoot, I'm not a deer." The incongruity is appropriate because Ole claims to have misheard what the man said as "I am a deer." Mishearing may often serve as a legitimate excuse for a host of otherwise unacceptable actions (Hempelmann and Attardo 2011, 134; Oring 2011b, 153). The appropriateness in the joke is transparently spurious because the man was not a deer, did not look like a deer, and, furthermore, deer do not speak. Ole claiming to mishear what the *deer said* completely undermines the appropriateness of his justification for shooting him.

The following joke is considerably harder to dissect:

My name's Pavlov; ring a bell? (Keillor 2005, 1)

The incongruity arises when the hearer of the joke is confronted with two distinct meanings for "ring a bell." One is an idiom meaning, "Does it sound familiar?" There is also the literal meaning of the phrase—the ringing of a bell—which normally would not be called to mind except that Pavlov evokes the name of the psychologist Ivan Pavlov who conditioned dogs to salivate in response to the ringing of a bell (actually a buzzer, but it seems the Russian was mistranslated ["Ivan Pavlov" 2019]). The simultaneous evocation of the idiomatic and literal meanings of the phrase "ring a bell" creates an incongruity that is made appropriate by the name Pavlov. It is only the name Pavlov (Quasimodo might also work) that directs the listener's or reader's attention to the literal meaning of the phrase. "My name is Williams, ring a bell?" has no such capacity.[18] The name Pavlov alerts one to the existence of an incongruity between the idiomatic and literal meaning of the phrase and at the same time makes that incongruity appropriate, for the two senses of the phrase have meaning: one with respect to Pavlov purely as a person's name, the other with respect to the psychologist Ivan Pavlov, who experimented with dogs' purported responses to ringing bells. The appropriateness, however, is spurious because ringing or responding to the ringing of actual bells is a concept totally irrelevant to the activity of introducing oneself to another person.[19]

The Pavlov joke is somewhat unusual in that a double meaning is the source of the incongruity. More often, a double meaning in a joke serves to establish the appropriateness of an incongruity. For example, "Save the whales for the valuable prizes." The incongruity turns on the dissonance between preserving a form of marine life and winning prizes. The appropriateness lies in the double meaning of the word *save* which can mean "rescue" or "protect" as well as "accumulate" as in saving coupons or stamps to redeem for a kitchen appliance or an item of home decor. Again, the spuriousness of the appropriateness lies in the fact that only one sense of *save* can be employed at a time. A word cannot legitimately operate with two distinct meanings in the context of a single utterance.

Numerous jokes may depend upon the literalization of conventional metaphors or idioms as in the Pavlov example. The literalization creates something like a pun, a word or phrase with two possible referents. In an article concerning artificial intelligence and personal assistants (like Siri, Alexa, and Cortana), the author reported asking his personal assistant, "How old are you?" The assistant replied, "Well, my birthday is April 2, 2014, so I'm really a spring chicken only I am not a chicken" (Vlahos 2019, 60). Here we have an incongruity—a chicken that is not a chicken—that comes about through the literalization of a metaphor. Originally *spring chicken* referred to a young chicken that was born in the spring and had not lived through the winter (and whose meat was consequently more tender). Eventually the term came to refer to any young or inexperienced individual. "He's just a spring chicken" or "She's no spring chicken" are not untypical constructions. It is appropriate for the assistant to claim that she is not a chicken if the term is taken literally rather than figuratively. But it is spuriously appropriate in that a literal meaning is substituted for a figurative one in the same utterance. It is spurious in the same way as the pun—it operates with two different meanings for the same term in a single communication. There are a host of such idiomatic expressions whose literal meanings are usually ignored unless something serves to point them out and make them humorous: "Lend me your ears" ("I'll return them later"); "I'll keep an eye out for you" ("just remind me to put it back in"); "Keep your shirt on" ("even though your shirt is off"); "I'm eating my heart out" ("might you pass the salt?").

The next joke is, perhaps, even more difficult:

"If we aren't supposed to eat animals, why are they made out of meat?" (Keillor 2005, 18)[20]

To grasp the incongruity in this joke, we need to rephrase the question amplifying some of its presuppositions: why prohibit the eating of animals when their flesh—meat—is tasty and nutritious and which humans have consumed for tens of thousands of years? Note that in this formulation the humor has almost entirely disappeared. The way the question is formulated in the joke creates an incongruity because it is oblivious to the notion that the prohibition against eating animals has nothing to do with whether animals are tasty, nutritious, or have proven a long-standing foodstuff. The reverse is, in fact, true. The prohibition arises precisely because animals have long served humans as food. If animals were not a foodstuff there would be no necessity to prohibit eating them. It is the killing of animals for food that is the impetus for the prohibition.[21]

The appropriateness of the incongruity depends on registering a difference between animals and meat. Animals are living beings. *Meat* is a term for the body of an animal apprehended as edible product. By creating the impression that there is a distinction between *animal* and *meat*, the appropriateness of the incongruity emerges. Why prohibit the eating of animals when they are made of something so obviously and traditionally edible? There are grounds for this distinction. We go to the supermarket and never see a living animal and only rarely a dead one. We shop for steak or hamburger, not cow; for pork or bacon, not pig; for veal, not calf. The appropriateness of the incongruity is spurious, however, because the prohibition is specifically about killing animals for human consumption. The prohibition against eating animals is straightforwardly a moral prohibition against eating meat.

> An old lady who never married specified in her will that her tombstone say, "Born a virgin, died a virgin." That was too many words to put on the stone, so they just wrote, "Returned unopened" (Keillor 2005, 149).

The humor of this joke does not trade on the incongruity of sex and death although those categories might be retrieved from the joke. It depends on the analogy of the body to a package. The analogy in itself does not create humor. In fact, the conception is a traditional one. "The body is only a package that encloses the soul" elicits no amusement.[22] Nor is the idea of "opening" necessarily amusing. "The body is a package which God opens and in which He encloses the soul" also lacks any hint of humor. It is the extension of the metaphor to a package processed by the United States Postal Service that creates the incongruity. We do not usually think of the human body in terms of postal service categories or procedures. But since the woman proposed an epitaph that reduced her life to the maintenance of her virginity, she could be thought of as not having been "opened" by means of sexual intercourse and consequently she can be appropriately compared to an unopened package that is being returned to its sender—God.

But though the inscription is at some level appropriate, it is nevertheless spurious. She had lived a life. She was figuratively "unopened" in one aspect only (granted, one that she herself emphasized). Her life was not necessarily without significance. Nor is US Postal Service phraseology the appropriately dignified language for a funerary inscription.

It is important to note that with the jokes in this chapter, I am not concerned with any meanings or messages that the jokes might bear; for instance, whether, in the absence of sex, the woman's life might be considered a wasted effort, akin to the sending of a package to a recipient who never receives it or returns it without ever learning what is inside. Such concerns relate to what I call the *evaluation* of the joke (Oring 2003, 35–37). Whether a joke reader or hearer evaluates the epitaph joke in this way is another matter. While the evaluation of a joke usually depends on the mechanics of the joke, the evaluation should not be confused with those mechanics. Here I am focused only on what causes a text to be regarded as a joke, and this is determined by the perception of a spuriously appropriate incongruity.

The spuriousness of the appropriateness of jokes need not merely be a function of language.

> The *Schadchen* [Jewish marriage broker] was defending the girl he had proposed against the young man's protests. "I don't care for the mother-in-law," said the latter. "She's a disagreeable and stupid person."
>
> "But after all, you're not marrying the mother-in-law. What you want is her daughter."
>
> "Yes, but she's not young any longer, and she's not precisely a beauty."
>
> "No matter. If she's neither young nor beautiful she'll be all the more faithful to you."
>
> "And she hasn't much money."
>
> "Who's talking about money? Are you marrying for money then? After all, it's a wife that you want."
>
> "But she's got a hunchback too."
>
> "Well, what *do* you want? Isn't she to have a single fault?" (Freud 1960, 8:61)

This joke does not depend on its language. The joke is a conceptual one. The incongruity lies in the claim of the marriage broker that the prospective bride has only a *single* fault after the young man has raised concerns about the woman's mother, her age, her attractiveness, and the money that she can bring to the marriage. The broker's indignation is appropriate, however, because he has dismissed each of the young man's objections in turn. Indeed, he has turned each fault into a virtue. The woman's hunched back he cannot redeem so he declares it to be the woman's sole fault, and no one can expect to find a woman or any human being with absolutely no faults. The spuriousness of the appropriateness is that it is the broker alone who is persuaded by his own sophistry. No reader or listener to the joke would have registered anything but a catalogue of faults that would characterize the woman in question as unmarriageable.

Graeme Ritchie seems to have a bit of trouble fitting the following joke into an incongruity-resolution model:

A reporter saw a crowd gathered around a road accident. Anxious to get a scoop,
he told the bystanders: "Let me through, let me through, I'm the son of the victim."
The crowd made way for him. Lying in front of the car was a donkey.

Ritchie rightly claims that no real incongruity is resolved in the punchline since
a donkey could very well be the victim of a road accident (Ritchie 2009, 7–8).
This is one of a class of jokes in which something seemingly appropriate is suddenly reconceived as incongruous rather than a previously registered incongruity
being made appropriate in the punchline (Oring 2003, 1–3). Reporters often do
misrepresent themselves in order to get a story. That is appropriate, if somewhat
morally questionable, but it is not incongruous per se. When it is discovered that
the victim of the accident is a donkey, the reporter's claim becomes incongruous.
In claiming that he is the victim's son, the reporter, it turns out, has announced
himself to be the son of a donkey—an ass. That is appropriate given his subter-
fuge. But the reporter is an ass only metaphorically. He is not actually the son of a
donkey. The appropriateness is spurious.

A cop pulls a woman over and says, "Let me see your driver's license lady."
The woman replies, "I wish you people would get it together. One day you take
away my license and the next day you ask me to show it." (Keillor 2005, 199)

The analysis of this joke is somewhat difficult. Specifying the incongruity and
its appropriateness is not immediately obvious. It is easy enough to "get" the joke
but harder to explicate. "I wish you people would get it together" in and of itself
does not create an incongruity, although it signals some sort of impending criticism or challenge. The driver is suggesting that the police are somehow at fault.
People, however, often argue with the police during a traffic stop.

The revelation that the woman was driving without a license—as in "I can't
show you my license since it was suspended"—is not sufficient to create a joke.[23]
The joke can only reside in the woman's formulation of her predicament: "One
day you take away my license and the next day you ask me to show it." One
might be inclined to see the joke's incongruity in the "opposition" embedded in
this complaint, but I believe that would be a mistake. Yet the revelation that the
woman is driving knowing that her license had been suspended does condition an
incongruity. Even though she is not in possession of a valid license—actually, for
having had her license suspended, which signals that she is a singularly poor or
irresponsible driver—she tries to shift the onus onto the police. This is the source
of the incongruity. Nevertheless, her complaint is in some measure appropriate
since those same authorities responsible for taking away her license are, in fact,
now asking to see it. This complaint is spurious, however, since the revocation of

her license was a revocation of the right to operate a motor vehicle and not merely the removal of a piece of identification from her wallet. Had she complied with the suspension, no situation could have arisen in which a cop would have asked to see her license.

It is not difficult to find a host of examples in which the appropriateness of the incongruities in jokes is spurious. Consider the long list of "light bulb" jokes that depend upon a question of "How many X's does it take to change a light bulb" (the X to be filled in by a variety of ethnic, occupational, regional, political, or other social statuses). The answer almost invariably is a number greater than the single individual that would be presumed to be sufficient for the task along with an explanation of why more were needed based upon some stereotypical trait of the X's in question. For example, "How many Californians does it take to screw in a light bulb?—Ten. One to screw it in and nine others to share the experience." "How many law students does it take to change a light bulb?—Six. One to change and five to file an environmental impact report" (Dundes 1987, 145). In each case the incongruous number of personnel required to change the bulb is made appropriate by a justification of the additional number in terms of the activities, beliefs, or psychological dispositions attributed to the group in question. Of course, these justifications are spurious because it does not really require an additional nine Californians to share in the experience of bulb replacement or five additional law students to file an environmental impact report. American Polish (Polack) jokes work in a similar way, except that they focus on only two character traits—stupidity and dirtiness (Dundes 1987, 115–138; Davies 1990, 84–101). In fact, the archetypical light bulb joke would seem to have started as a Polish joke: "How many Poles does it take to change a light bulb?—Five. One to change the bulb and four to turn the table he is standing on." Even though the method of turning a table rather than twisting a wrist might prove a possible, therefore appropriate, way to screw in a light bulb, it would hardly be a method ever employed even by purportedly stupid people and is therefore spurious.

A maître d' goes over to a middle-aged Jewish couple eating in his restaurant. He asks them, "Is anything all right?" (Keillor 2005, 114). The incongruity is that the formulaic phrase of a maître d'hôtel is, "Is everything all right?" with the implication that if something is amiss, he would immediately remedy the problem. The stereotype operating in the joke is that older (American) Jews tend to be critical of the service they receive in a restaurant—the air conditioning is set too high, the table is too close to the kitchen, the soup is too cold, the portions are too small—and are likely to be vocal about it (see Mason 1988). But this behavior, as with all stereotypes, characterizes only a small minority of Jews, and no one is critical of absolutely everything. So, the assumption of the maître d' is appropriate for the stereotype at the same time greatly exaggerates the reality and is consequently spurious.

> A woman walked into a bar and asked for a double entendre. So the barman gave
> her one. (Keillor 2005, 144)

The technique of this joke is subtle. A *double entendre* refers to a word or phrase that has two meanings, one of which is innocent and the other risqué. The term is also applied to a joke that simultaneously trades on both an innocent and sexual meaning. The woman asks a bartender for a double entendre, which would initially be interpreted as a request for a drink since that is what a customer normally requests from a bartender in a bar. As there are any number of drinks with fanciful names—grasshopper, scotch mist, Manhattan, old-fashioned, Cuba libre, cosmopolitan, Harvey Wallbanger, sidecar, corpse reviver, and even sex on the beach—a double entendre would not be out of keeping as a name for a mixed alcoholic drink. Furthermore, the word *double* is a meaningful term in the language of a bar as it signifies that there is twice the alcohol that would make up a single drink of the same type. "Make it a double" is an instruction to a bartender to double the amount of alcohol in the drink that was ordered. (Perhaps a better joke would result had the woman said, "I'm feeling frisky tonight; give me an entendre and make it a double," but the grounds for this joke would be different.) In any event, the most economical analysis of the joke is that when a customer orders a double in a bar, as in "give me a double whiskey," the bartender can give her "one," that is, one double whiskey. But when she asks for a double entendre, there are a number of possible interpretations. She has asked for a drink with the name double entendre and the bartender gave her one. Or she asked for a drink with the name entendre but wanted it doubled, that is, with two shots of alcohol. Or she might have requested a risqué joke. But if the request is interpreted as a request for a joke, it is possible that the bartender either gave her one double entendre or gave her only one entendre, that is, a single entendre. There is no such thing as a single entendre, however. Therein resides the joke's incongruity. The appropriateness of the incongruity depends on the word *one*, which can be interpreted in two senses: as one double entendre or as half of a double, or a single. The spuriousness of this appropriateness is the same as the spuriousness of a pun; two distinct meanings for a word are not legitimate within a single utterance.[24]

There are two types of jokes that I initially thought escaped the restriction that the appropriateness of incongruities proves spurious. The first type is jokes that I have previously called *tautological jokes* (Oring 2016, 41); jokes in which a response to a question offers the same or less information than is already implied in the question:

"I see there is a funeral in town today."

"Yeah."

"Who died?"

"I'm not sure, but I think it's the one in the coffin." (Keillor 2005, 94)[25]

Outside the Jewish Quarter in the Old City of Jerusalem a tourist asks a local boy: "Where is the Wailing Wall?"

The boy answers, "In Israel." (Giora 1991, 470n4)

Not quite a tautological joke, but related is:

Exam question: Identify six Arctic animals.

Student answer: Four seals and two polar bears.

The second set of jokes are what have been called by folklorists *pretended obscene riddles* (Brunvand 1998, 119–121).

What is it that a cow has four of and a woman only has two of?—Legs.

What is a four-letter word ending in "k" that means the same as intercourse?—Talk.

What is it a man can do standing, a woman sitting down, and a dog on three legs?—Shake hands.

What is it on a man that is round, hard, and sticks so far out of his pajamas you can hang a hat on it?—His head. (Bauman 1970, 22)

Looking first at the tautological jokes, it is obviously incongruous in the context of a funeral to identify the dead person as "the one in the coffin." The answer produces no information beyond what is already in the possession of the one who is asking the question. After all, the inquirer sees the coffin, presumes there is a body in it, and knows, consequently, that he is observing a funeral. Likewise, it is incongruous to tell a tourist standing just outside the Jewish Quarter in the Old City of Jerusalem that the Wailing Wall is in Israel, when the wall is in the Jewish Quarter, outside which the inquirer is standing. It is also incongruous to identify four seals and two polar bears as six Arctic animals when there are only two kinds of animals being identified. Nevertheless, the answers in each case would seem to be completely appropriate. After all, the dead person *is* the one in the coffin, the Wailing Wall *is* in Israel, four seals and two polar bears *do* comprise a group of six Arctic animals. The answers would, on first inspection, seem fundamentally sound and completely appropriate to the question being asked. They do not seem spurious at all.

But the appropriateness becomes spurious when one reckons what is intended by the questions. There is a disjunction between the questions as they are uttered in context and the questions when considered as abstract linguistic formulations. In the first joke, the questioner is really asking for the *identity* of the dead person. In the second joke, the tourist is asking for *directions* to the Wailing Wall, which he already knew to be in the city. The exam, in the third joke, intends the student to identify six distinct *species* of Arctic animal. What the questioners intended to ask is not addressed by the answers since the answers are appropriate only to the literal language of the questions and not to their intention. In other words, the answers are completely appropriate to the questions semantically but not pragmatically. Consequently, the incongruities in these jokes are appropriate, but only spuriously so, since they ignore the information that is obviously being requested. Contrary to my initial assumption, this group of jokes would not contravene a postulate that a joke depends upon the appropriateness of an incongruity that is in some way faulty or spurious.

The pretended obscene riddles are different from ordinary riddles—*true riddles* (Taylor 1943, 129–130)—in the sense that an incongruity is not generated in the riddle question. They are simply questions that call for specific answers that conform to the question's requirements. The riddle questions, however, are framed to direct a hearer's thoughts to sexual parts or behaviors. The incongruity lies between these imagined obscene answers and the completely innocent ones. Yet these innocent answers seem to be completely appropriate to the questions. As in the tautological jokes, they meet the requirements of the questions completely.

The appropriateness of the innocent answers, however, is spurious given the loading of the riddle questions for sexual solutions. As in the previous set of tautological jokes, the answers are appropriate but spurious given the intent of the questions. The answers that should come to the hearers' mind when asked these questions—teats, fuck, piss, and penis—are the completely appropriate answers given the questions' construction. In fact, were these responses given to the questions, there would be no joke.[26] The innocent answers—legs, talk, shake hands, and head—are literally appropriate to the questions but not to their intent. The answers are spurious when the implicatures of the questions are taken into account. Again, it is not the semantics of the questions that queer the appropriateness of the answers but their pragmatics.

The next and last joke example is difficult to analyze, for it is easy to misidentify what constitutes the incongruity and the appropriateness.

"Why do they report power outages on TV?" (Keillor 2005, 18).

To grasp the structure of this question as a joke, it is necessary, once again, to register the implicature in the question. The question presumes that there is something odd about reporting such outages, although, at first, they would seem to be as newsworthy as anything else likely to be reported by a local television news station: house fires, firefighters rescuing cats from trees, water main breaks, soldiers returning home from combat zones and surprising their wives and children. The joke could be more straightforwardly reformulated: Don't you think it is odd that they report power outages on television news? This is the basic incongruity. Such reports should, after all, seem unremarkable; indeed, they are broadcast all the time without arousing undue notice. Once it is registered, however, that the audience that might benefit most from such news are those who suffer the outage, the incongruity becomes appropriate. Those who suffer the outage (1) already know their power is out and (2) they could not, in any event, see the television report since they have no electricity. Consequently, the incongruity is appropriate. The appropriateness, however, is spurious. Reports of fires, traffic accidents, robberies, shootings, and such are rarely news to their victims. Nor do the victims generally have access to the television reports of these events in real time. Victims make the news; they do not generally consume it except, perhaps, after the fact. The mistake I made in trying to analyze this joke was to overlook the incongruity resident in the implicature of the question and immediately jump to the idea that the locus of the incongruity was that the power outages are known to their victims before the news report is broadcast. But that is not the basic incongruity of the joke. The incongruity is resident in the unstated "why," or strangeness question, and the appropriateness of the incongruity is that such reports communicate news to people who already know it and are unlikely to benefit from it. Spuriousness resides in the recognition that the news is usually not directed toward those suffering calamities both large and small. News is largely a spectators' sport.

While I was pleased to discover the basis on which the responses to the above jokes could be considered incongruous, appropriate, and spurious, we should remain cautious as to whether *all* appropriate incongruities in jokes are necessarily spurious. This will require further research, not only on my part, but on the part of others who are attuned to the question of joke construction and understand the claim that is being made. As for my analyses of the above joke texts, I welcome alternate analyses and critical responses. But I would expect that alternate analyses would consistently identify what it is that specifically makes these texts jokes.

Folklorists who have written about jokes have often cited the term *appropriate incongruity* (e.g., Eliason 2007, 42; Blank 2013, 78–79; Gabbert 2020, 23n4; Kelley 2020, 165). The term, however, is primarily employed as a catchphrase. In other words, there is an acknowledgement that jokes depend upon some sort of incongruity, but jokes are never *dissected* to see what that incongruity is, how it is made appropriate, or whether that appropriateness is spurious. For the most part, folklorists (and others) do not fully grasp that the phrase is meant to describe what makes an organization of language and the ideas that language evokes into a joke. To the extent that folklorists have been involved in studying jokes, they have almost exclusively focused on their contents, not their construction. While they note subject matters of class, ethnicity, religion, race, gender, death, disaster, and whatnot in the contents of jokes, there is almost no attention to how that content is actually structured. Consequently, folklorists are left to make sense of jokes strictly in terms of their content, often employing some functional theory—such as release and relief—to explain the emotional benefits that are presumed to result for both tellers and their audiences (e.g., Dundes 1987, 11, 37, 52; Eliason 2007, 35; Gabbert 2020, 21). Few scholars in any discipline spend their time analyzing a sizeable number of jokes (and this is partly why so many jokes are analyzed in this chapter). Folklorists, who are more oriented than most toward the close analysis of oral texts, might do just that, and could then be in a position to gauge the extent to which jokes are what I am claiming them to be.

Of course, folklorists are not computational linguists. They have not been tasked with creating algorithms for either the identification or generation of humor. Amazon and Apple will not be contacting them anytime soon for their input as to how Alexa or Siri might be able to recognize when their customers are joking and when they are speaking seriously. Folklorists, however, are called to explain and interpret humor that is exchanged within and between social groups. In investigating how jokes work; how cultural and linguistic content is structured in the creation of jokes, in actually identifying and analyzing appropriate incongruities, folklorists may be in a position to grasp something of their possible meanings and their significance in the social worlds of those who hear and tell them (e.g., Oring 1973, 1981).

Oppositions, Overlaps, and Ontologies

The General Theory of Verbal Humor Revisited

It was without a compeer among swindles. It was perfect, it was rounded, symmetrical, complete, colossal.

—Mark Twain, *Life on the Mississippi*

The General Theory of Verbal Humor (GTVH) was first proposed by Salvatore Attardo and Victor Raskin in 1991. It was an elaboration of the Semantic Script Theory of Humor (SSTH) published six years before by Raskin (1985a) with additional thoughts by Attardo on the different levels of abstraction that might be identified in a joke (Hofstadter, Gabor, and Attardo 1989, 438–439). Some questions were raised about the theory when it was first proposed as to whether, without transformational rules, it could generate jokes and only jokes, and whether it could really handle funny rhymes, excessive alliterations, or spoonerisms, (e.g., Morreall in Attardo and Raskin 1991, 333–334, 339–340), but these for the most part did not upset the promulgation and the widespread adoption of the theory both within and outside of linguistics. In any event, GTVH was claimed to be a theory of humor competence, not humor production. It was meant to be a description that could differentiate between what a native speaker would regard as a joke-carrying text and a non-joke-carrying text in the same way that a grammar might predict what a native speaker would regard as a grammatical and ungrammatical utterance (Raskin 1985a, 49–59).

More serious and sustained criticisms of GTVH were raised by Graeme Ritchie in 2004 (69–80). In 2011, I questioned the hierarchy of Knowledge Resources (KRs) posited by GTVH, the reported experimental confirmation of this hierarchy, as well as the degree of faithfulness of GTVH's model of jokes to the close

 https://doi.org/10.7330/9781646425198.c005

analysis of specific texts (Oring 2011b). Here I would reprise and extend some of the basic concerns about GTVH and its predecessor SSTH and the implications for subsequent theorizing.

The main hypothesis of SSTH on which GTVH is based is that a text can be characterized as a joke-carrying text if:

1. The text is compatible, fully or in part, with two different scripts;

2. The two scripts with which the text is compatible are opposite in a special sense defined;

3.* The two scripts with which the text is compatible are said to overlap fully or in part. (Raskin 1985a, 99)[1]

In other words, the key terms in the theory are *script, compatibility, oppositeness,* and *overlap.*

A script is a chunk of semantic information that surrounds a term and the concept it designates (and which is internalized by a native speaker). Technically a script is represented by a graph with lexical nodes and semantic links between the nodes (Raskin 1985a, 81), what in plain speak might be called a term and its web of associations.

SCRIPT OPPOSITION

A joke-carrying text would be one that contained two opposite scripts. Opposite scripts can be those that negate the other or are antonyms of the other. But semantic script theory adds that two scripts can be opposite in a local sense within a particular discourse (Raskin 1985a, 108). Thus, SSTH characterizes the oppositeness in the joke "He is a man of letters; he works for the Post Office" as "He is *a writer* vs. he is *not a writer*" (Raskin 1985a, 29, 109).

In SSTH, it would seem that any script might be designated as opposite to every other one simply by putting the word *not* in front of it (Ogden 1967, 55; Ritchie 2004, 73–74). Except for a writer script, all other scripts are necessarily *not writer* scripts. *Opposition* is put forward by SSTH as a technical and operationalizable term, but it is no such thing. Semantic oppositions do exist. There may be gradable, directional, orthogonal, and antipodal opposites; contradictories; and contraries (Lyons 1977, 270–289). They are only a subset, however, of the kinds of differences that appear in jokes.[2] Difference is not the same as opposition (Ogden 1967, 37).

To make a joke dependent on a "man of letters" script, one must invoke a script that does not involve writing but that does involve letters in some other literal or figurative way. Actually, there are a number of scripts that might serve besides that of postman. He is a man of letters: he paints advertising billboards; he operates a linotype machine; he alphabetizes the card catalog in the library; perhaps even, he splices genes. Can a sign painter, a linotype operator, a librarian, a postman, and a microbiologist equally be considered *oppositions* to the concept of writer? To suggest that they are "local" oppositions (Raskin 1985a, 108)—that is, oppositions that can only be recognized in a particular stretch of discourse—does not, I believe, address the problem in what is put forward as a global theory of verbal humor. In fact, that is one of the problems with my own *appropriate incongruity* perspective as incongruity and appropriateness can only be specified post hoc in particular local contexts.

If a joke could then be created using two scripts that in no sense could be categorized as opposite, would they then automatically become opposite? If so, it would seem that oppositeness has little theoretical value. It would be jokes that create oppositions rather than oppositions that create jokes. Actually, such a test has been performed. In *Alice's Adventures in Wonderland* by Lewis Carroll, the Mad Hatter asks a riddle in the course of the Mad Tea Party: "Why is a raven like a writing desk?" When Alice gives up and asks for the answer, the Mad Hatter says that he hasn't the slightest idea. Carroll did not intend this riddle to have a solution, but that did not stop Carroll enthusiasts—and later Carroll himself, under pressure from such enthusiasts—from proposing solutions. The best and most succinct, perhaps, is: "A raven is like a writing desk because Poe wrote on both" (Carroll 1960, 95n3). So, are we to say that in formulating this riddle answer that ravens and writing desks are brought into "opposition"?

One might also ask what SSTH would make of the formulation: "He is a man of letters but produces nothing of literary value." Here it might be argued that there is script oppositeness, in SSTH's sense of the term, in that a man is declared to be a man of letters—a writer—but is not a genuine writer when reckoned in terms of the quality of his literary output. Indeed, SSTH might have difficulty distinguishing this sentence from a joke, as it could be said to contain both script oppositeness and script overlap. The appropriate incongruity perspective, however, would point out that the appropriateness of the "man of letters" who produces nothing of literary value is not spurious; consequently, no humor is produced. A postal worker, sign painter, or a linotype operator are only "men of letters" in a spurious sense, for none are belletrists although they deal with *letters* (see chapter 4). The writer who produces inferior pieces of writing is a "man of letters," if only of an inferior sort. One could have a serious discussion as to what constitutes the level of literary merit that would qualify a writer as a "man of letters." One could not have a similar discussion about a postal worker, sign painter, or linotype operator (Oring 1992, 2–3; 1995; 2003, 5–9, 14–15; 2016, 48).

The concept of oppositeness is not and has never been well defined (Ritchie 2014, 73–74). Different scripts are necessarily opposed to one another when the opposition of A is simply reckoned as anything that is ~A. Under this conceptualization a daffodil is the opposite of a carburetor; a raven is the opposite of a writing desk; a linguist is, perhaps, the opposite of a snake oil salesman. Although linguistics has successfully harnessed plus/minus notation in discriminating phonemes and lexemes in componential descriptions, it does not seem useful in characterizing the scripts in a broad range of jokes. Consequently, oppositeness in SSTH should be characterized, as some computational linguists have characterized it, merely as *incongruence* (Lubatov and Lipson 2012, 151).

SCRIPT OVERLAP

For a text to be a humor-carrying one according to SSTH, the opposed scripts need to be in some sense fully or partially *compatible* (Raskin 1985a, 99). The only type of compatibility proposed by SSTH is script overlap; that is, different scripts share similar components. Overlap is never precisely defined in SSTH. Rather, it is illustrated:

> "Is the doctor at home," the patient asked in his bronchial whisper. "No," the doctor's young and pretty wife whispered in reply. "Come right in." (Raskin 1985a, 100)

SSTH identifies an initial medical script that is characterized by an individual with symptoms of illness—a bronchial whisper—seeking entrance to the home-office of a physician. Surprisingly, the doctor's wife declares that the doctor is *not* at home yet invites the patient in. Equally curious is that the invitation, like the inquiry of the patient, is delivered in a whisper. These odd states of affair (an *incongruity* according to the appropriate incongruity perspective) initiate a search for a second script, which is compatible with the first in which the wife's whispering and invitation make some kind of sense. The characterization of the doctor's wife as "young and pretty," which would seem irrelevant to the medical script, eases the recognition of a "lover script," which is compatible with the wife's whispered invitation to the patient to enter the house while the doctor is away. In other words, the overlap between the patient and lover scripts according to SSTH generates the joke-carrying text (Raskin 1985a, 117–127).

Given the description I have just offered, I would argue that the main hypothesis of SSTH fails to identify the necessary and sufficient conditions for a joke-carrying text. What is absent from the main hypothesis is the notion that the reader or hearer of a verbal joke encounters some kind of incongruity that precipitates the search for an alternative script that "makes sense" of that incongruity;

FIGURE 5.1. Doctor-Lover joke.

in my terms, that makes the incongruity appropriate. SSTH recognizes the existence of such incongruity-creating devices but characterizes them as *contradiction* or *ambiguity* found in "many" but not "all" jokes (Raskin 1985a, 114). Because it has not included this notion of contradiction, or rather incongruity, in the main hypothesis, the main hypothesis is deficient in defining a joke-carrying text.

Semantic theorists claim that SSTH/GTVH could be falsified if there were a joke that was "*not based on overlapping and opposed scripts*" (Raskin, Hempelmann, and Taylor 2009, 289). It will be left to the reader to decide whether some of the jokes that are analyzed below can be adequately conceptualized in terms of overlapping and opposed scripts. But the falsification of SSTH/GTVH can also be accomplished by showing that in the presence of opposed but overlapping scripts, no joke is created. This occurs regularly as most texts—and certainly most literary texts—can be described in terms of oppositions. Consider a short text that contains oppositions and overlap but does not seem to rise to the level of a joke-conveying text: "A man and his dog went for a walk together." There is the opposition of human versus animal. There is the further opposition in the interests of both the human and the animal. The dog is going to urinate and defecate. The man is not going to urinate or defecate but to ensure that the dog does. Yet these "opposed" personnel and interests overlap in the script of "going for a walk together." Why is there no humor in this text and others like it?

Raskin offers the following as a "botched" version of the patient/lover joke:

A funny thing happened to a friend of mine. He had bronchitis and went to see his doctor. The doctor's wife who was young and pretty opened the door. He asked whether the doctor was in, and naturally, he had to whisper because he had lost his voice. The woman misunderstood him entirely and decided that he was whispering because he did not want to be overheard. She thought therefore that he had amorous designs on her and happily . . . [whispered an invitation] to come in because, of course, her spouse was conveniently away and the two of them were alone. (Raskin 1985a, 145)

This text is not botched, nor does it suffer from a surfeit of detail as Raskin suggests. The text contains both patient and lover scripts as well as an overlap between the two scripts in the whispering of the characters. This text takes the form of a comic tale (*Schwank*)—though it is reported rather than dramatized. What it lacks is a punchline that triggers a sudden reconceptualization of the relevant scripts (Oring 1992, 81–93). But if there is no punchline in the above text, the concept of the punchline is absent from the main hypothesis of SSTH as well. There is no mention of punchlines: only script opposition and script overlap. Had the main hypothesis included the notion of a punchline, it would necessarily have been brought to an encounter with incongruity as a necessary condition of joke-carrying texts (Oring 1992, 83). A covert compatible script suddenly discovered in a text is what makes an incongruity in a joke appropriate and qualifies the text for joke status. It is not that comic tales are devoid of humor; they are simply not jokes. The comic tale invariably reveals too much and hides too little (90). There is no forced reconceptualization (Oring 1992, 83; Ritchie 2002) of the text.

The matter of script opposition and overlap becomes more complicated in some jokes than might be supposed by the analysis of the patient/lover joke, which all too many researchers have regarded as the standard model. For example,

A man who had taken to drink supported himself by tutoring in a small town. His vice eventually became known, however, and as a result he lost most of his pupils. A friend was commissioned to urge him to mend his ways. "Look, you could get the best tutoring in the town if only you would give up drinking. So do give it up!" "Who do you think you are?" was the indignant reply. "I do tutoring so that I can drink. Am I to give up drinking so that I get tutoring?" (Freud 1960, 8:52)

First, let us identify the possible scripts in this joke. There is *tutoring*, a type of work. There is the *drinking of alcohol*. There is the *friend* who is instructed to perform what today in the United States would be called an intervention to persuade the man to curtail his drinking. These are the scripts that are easily retrievable from the surface of the joke text.[3] But nothing in this joke depends on a simple overlap of any of these scripts. No elements of a tutoring script are shared with a drinking script. A friendship script might overlap with a drinking script—friends often drink together—and a friendship script might overlap with a tutoring script were a friend to tutor a friend, but it is clear that these kinds of overlaps cannot be reckoned as the source of this joke.

The joke, however, produces an incongruity at the point the friend attempts to intervene to alter the drinker's behavior. The drinker is indignant. This in itself is not incongruous as many alcoholics resent the attempts of friends and relations to alter their behaviors. It is the drinker's justification of his indignation that generates the text's humor. Those listening to or reading the joke recognize, along with the character of the friend, that drinking is a serious problem; one that is impairing the drinker's ability to secure a livelihood. The incongruity in the joke is that drinking is not viewed by the drinker as a problem even though it results in the loss of work. The punchline reveals this incongruity to be appropriate since, from the drinker's perspective, the tutoring work is valued solely as the means by which to secure money for drink. In other words, the joke hinges on a reversal of the direction of a presumed cause and effect. One presumes that drink is a problem because it hampers the ability to secure work. The other presumes that work is solely an activity that enables the worker to secure drink.

In order to cast this joke into SSTH's categories of opposition and overlap, one would have to describe a script *opposition* between drinking and tutoring or between drinking and working more generally (as in, "Work is the curse of the drinking classes" [a quote often attributed to Oscar Wilde]). But these scripts do not overlap on any of their components as in the patient/lover joke. If overlap is merely meant to include *any kind of relation* between scripts or categories, then it would simply reproduce my own notion of *appropriateness*.

Another example:

"Is this the place where the Duke of Wellington spoke those words?"
    "Yes, it is the place; but he never spoke the words." (Freud 1960, 8:61n1)[4]

Based on how it analyzed other jokes (Raskin 1985a, 108–110), SSTH would probably argue that the opposition in the joke is: Wellington spoke some specific words in this place versus Wellington did not speak those words in this place. It should be noted—and this is important—that while this is an opposition, it does not necessarily constitute a script opposition. There are two *propositions*, but not necessarily two distinct *scripts*, that are in opposition.

Even were we to stipulate to SSTH's construal of the opposition, the reckoning of how these two formulations are made compatible is another story. The respondent's answer does bring these into conjunction through a partial concession to each proposition, but only by means of a paradox: the identification of the place is correct, but the words were never spoken. This is the source of the incongruity, however, and not the means of making appropriate or resolving that incongruity. Further work is needed. One way the incongruity might be made appropriate is by recourse to ellipsis: the script of what Wellington said in that place is, in fact, only a script of what he is *believed* to have said in that place. A belief script, however, is not explicitly invoked, but it would make sense if the respondent were replying to a question of popular belief rather than historical fact. Note, however, that explicitly mentioning a belief script in the text would destroy the joke. "Yes, this is the place where Wellington is believed to have spoken those words, but he, in fact, never spoke them" is a perfectly legitimate response lacking any joke-conveying qualities whatsoever. Nor does "No, this is not the place, for he never spoke the words" generate a joke. It is only in replying "yes" to the place but denying that he spoke the words that a joke is created. (The opposite is not true: acknowledging that he indeed spoke the words but denying that this is the place he spoke them would not result in a joke.)

There is a second way to conceptualize the appropriateness of the incongruity in this joke. The place and the words that Wellington, or anyone, might speak are impartible. If words are spoken, there must be some place where, and time at which, they were spoken. If Wellington never spoke the words, there is no place that he might have not spoken them (or one might argue that he had not spoken them everywhere). A non-event does not take place in either space or time. The respondent who says "yes" and then denies that Wellington spoke the words may be proposing that a non-action be treated the same as an action—an absence is treated as a presence, as something that also occurs in space and time. For example, we often speak of darkness as though it were a substance coequal with light and this presumption can create an appropriate incongruity as in the joking question "What is the speed of dark?" (Oring 2016, 89).

One last example:

The Great Barzini's career was failing. After 30 years as a magician, escape artist, and strong man his audiences had dwindled to almost nothing. In an attempt to revive his career, he announces that he will sit on the stage and allow a member of the audience to come up and strike him on the forehead with a twenty-pound sledgehammer and will sustain the blow unharmed.

On the day of the performance, the house is full with more people lined up outside trying to get in. Confidently, the Great Barzini in an elegant costume assumes his position in a chair on the stage, and a member of the audience is found to administer the blow. Barzini thrusts his head forward, and the man swings. Barzini and the chair go tumbling backwards. Barzini is completely unconscious. He is taken to the hospital where he remains in a deep coma. He is totally unresponsive; he makes no movements, utters no sounds. And so he remains for ten years. One day a nurse is attending to his IV drip when she thinks she notices some slight movement in his facial muscles. She calls over one of the doctors, and as they lean over Barzini, his eyes suddenly pop open, his arms shoot out, and he exclaims, "Ta-dah."

There are two obvious scripts in this joke: a performance script and a hospital script. There is no obvious overlap between these scripts. The final "ta-dah" is certainly an element of a performance script that is inserted into the hospital *scene*, but the performance script has no intersection with the hospital script. There is no overlap as there is in the patient/lover joke.

The point of the analysis of these joke examples is to indicate that a notion of script overlap as presented by SSTH does not obtain for all jokes. The notion that two scripts can be related by means of an intersection in a subset of their components, as in the patient/lover joke, will not bear up under scrutiny. Many jokes establish the appropriateness of their incongruities by other means.[5] On the other hand, if what is meant by script overlap in SSTH is that there is *some way* of relating two scripts, then SSTH in no way can be distinguished from any other form of incongruity theory. Overlap becomes just another word for appropriateness or resolution.

THE GENERAL THEORY OF VERBAL HUMOR

The General Theory of Verbal Humor was an outgrowth of the Semantic Script Theory of Humor. This theory included a number of what it called knowledge resources, which were components of the joke not mentioned in semantic script theory. These components included language (LA), narrative strategy (NS), situation (SI), target (TA), logical mechanism, (LM), and script opposition (SO). As no clear change occurred in the conceptualization of script opposition between SSTH and GTVH, only logical mechanism need concern us here.

It should be noted that in the move from SSTH to GTVH the matter of script overlap was quietly dropped. There was no further discussion of it. The original formulation of GTVH notes the importance of the punchline and acknowledges that "all the other parameters of the joke work towards it" (Attardo and Raskin 1991, 299), although no formal definition of *it*—the punchline—is provided. The punchline is simply subsumed within the knowledge resource of language (LA), which suggests it is a merely linguistic formulation, a matter of joke style. If the punchline is critical to the joke—as most scholars and even laymen would acknowledge—it needs to be defined in terms of *joke structure*, not style.

The logical mechanism, which is a novel element in GTVH replacing script overlap in SSTH (although the overlap terminology was not entirely abandoned), is not defined at all; it is only illustrated. Thus, the logical mechanism in the Polish joke "How many Poles does it take to screw in a lightbulb? Five. One to hold the bulb and four to turn the table he's standing on" is characterized as figure-ground reversal (Attardo and Raskin 1991, 303). The logical mechanism is purported to be the means by which opposed scripts within a joke are made compatible (Raskin

1985b, 39; Attardo and Raskin 1991, 331; Attardo 2001, 25). Questions have been raised even about the characterization of the logical mechanism of this Polish joke (Oring 2011b, 208), but even were we to stipulate to its accuracy, the question of logical mechanism remains. Salvatore Attardo acknowledged that logical mechanism was the most problematic component of the joke and noted that Raskin even questioned its significance because it did not behave in accordance with the predictions made by GTVH with regard to a hierarchy of knowledge resources.[6] Elsewhere it has been shown that this hierarchy is fanciful as it was construed, and the experiment that claimed to confirm it was flawed (Oring 2011b, 211–212). Ultimately, Attardo regarded the logical mechanism as the means by which an incongruity in an incongruity model of a joke was resolved (Attardo 2001, 25). So, the General Theory of Verbal Humor turned into a theory of appropriate incongruity or incongruity resolution.[7] What is important about the introduction of logical mechanism into the scholarly discourse on jokes is that it had the potential to focus attention on the *means* by which the incongruities in jokes are made appropriate, or, again, if only to seem ecumenical, how incongruities in jokes are "resolved." A list of mechanisms has been proposed.

role reversals	exaggeration
vacuous reversal	meta-humor
garden-path	role exchanges
almost situations	juxtaposition
inferring consequences	figure-ground reversal
coincidence	analogy
proportion	false premise
parallelism	ignoring the obvious
field restriction	chiasmus
vicious circle	faulty reasoning
potency mapping	self-undermining
missing link	cratylism
implicit parallelism	referential ambiguity
false analogy	

(Attardo, Hempelmann, and Di Maio 2002, 18)[8]

The meaning of some of these terms will not be immediately clear; one would need to look at the original sources, definitions, and examples offered (Paolillo 1998; Attardo, Hempelmann, and Di Maio 2002). Others will seem recognizable if not precisely specifiable. It should also be noted that script overlap does not appear as one of the mechanisms for resolving incongruity. This seems odd since it was the sole means described by SSTH in making script oppositions compatible. Nor is it clear that script overlap is subsumed wholly in any of the other mechanisms. For example, I would have trouble ascribing the mechanism of the patient/lover joke to any of those listed above.[9]

The term *logical mechanism* is in some respects unfortunate since the means by which an incongruity in a joke is made appropriate is never truly logical, nor is it, for that matter, usually a discrete mechanism (Oring 2011c, 151). The formulators of GTVH know that the means by which incongruities are made appropriate are not logical, but paralogical, pseudological (Attardo and Raskin 1991, 307; Attardo 2001, 25), or, in my own terms, *spurious* (Oring 1992, 3; Oring 2003, 5–9, 14–15; see chapter 4). Several questions arise. To what extent are these mechanisms well defined? Are these mechanisms clearly distinguishable from one another? How comprehensive is the list? Are there some obvious mechanisms that have been overlooked? More generally, why would such mechanisms create a perception of humor? Aren't many or even most of these mechanisms also characteristic of all kinds of verbal texts and behaviors that are not humorous?

Some mechanisms of jokes are relatively clear and distinct. The pun, for example, which appears (unfortunately) in the list under the term *cratylism*, has been a means of establishing appropriateness in any number of jokes. "Knock, knock." "Who's there?" "Needle." "Needle who?" "Needle little money for the movies." Certainly the pun in this example evidences overlap as it is relevant to two different scripts—the object of a *needle* and the claim of a *need*.[10]

Reversibility—the chiasmus—is also a tried-and-true joke technique, although specifying what exactly is reversed may prove trickier to pin down. The reversal "Put not your trust in money but your money in trust" depends upon a syntactical reversal that is explicit in the text. A chiasmus does not automatically produce humor. Much of biblical poetry is based upon chiasmata, and there is not much in the way of humor to be found there. What creates the humor in the case of the joking aphorism about money and trust is not simply the syntactic reversal but the change wrought in the meaning of the object of the altered sentence. The meaning of *trust* as "faith" is transformed into that of a legal entity for the administration of property (which may have beneficial tax consequences). A sound philosophical truth has been converted into an economic truth with something of a morally discrepant implication.

> "What's the difference between capitalism and communism?"
>   "Capitalism is the exploitation of man by his fellow man."
>   "What is communism?"
>   "Just the opposite."

In this joke: (1) no reversal is actually displayed in the joke text and (2) a hearer of this joke must entertain two types of reversal, one semantic and one syntactic.

The semantic reversal depends upon understanding nurturance or sustenance as the antithesis of exploitation. This, I would argue, is the sense first registered in the online processing of the joke when it is suggested that communism is the opposite of capitalism. The syntactic reversal, which I would argue only registers subsequently, simply transposes the subject and object so that there is no net change in the meaning of the whole: man exploits his fellow man in both formulations and, consequently, in both economic systems. In this joke, there are two kinds of reversal operating conceptually, neither of which is explicitly represented in the surface of the text.

The following joke might be described in terms of faulty reasoning:

> A gentleman entered a pastry-cook's shop and ordered a cake; but he soon brought it back and asked for a glass of liqueur instead. He drank it and began to leave without having paid. The proprietor detained him. "What do you want?" asked the customer.—"You've not paid for the liqueur."—"But I gave you the cake in exchange for it?"—"You didn't pay for that either."—"But I hadn't eaten it." (Freud 1960, 8:60)

The faulty logic of the customer is clear. A man is given a cake, which he had not as yet paid for, and then claims that cake as his own asset in an exchange for a glass of liqueur. When the shop owner challenges the man to pay for the liqueur, the man claims that he gave the cake in exchange for the drink. Stated in this fashion, the joke tends to disappear. I would argue that in the joke there is an intuitive sense of the customer's fraud, which is somewhat disguised in the customer's statement that he hadn't eaten the cake. The faulty reasoning is detectable without being immediately specifiable. If the exact nature of the fraud could be instantly specified, the joke would tend to disappear as it did in my reformulation of it.

Faulty reasoning alone will not create a joke, however:

> A guy goes into a flower shop and orders a bouquet of roses which he plans to send to a woman who had recently broken up with him because she had become attracted to another man. He tells the shop owner that he wants roses some of which will quickly fade to suggest to her the impermanence of her new attachment. The shop owner tells him, "Roses are flowers and some flowers quickly fade. So, don't worry. Some of these roses will quickly fade." (see Kahneman 2011, 45)

If you are troubled by the fact that this text doesn't seem to rise to joke-carrying status despite its obvious reliance on a mechanism of faulty logic, then you and I are together in wondering what the exact relationship of the faulty-logic mechanism is to the creation of jokes.

Many of the mechanisms listed above are also characteristic of non-humorous texts and discourse. Certainly, they are not all paralogical or spurious by definition. Inference of consequences, coincidence, proportion, parallelism, analogy, and chiasmus do not inevitably, or even usually, produce humor. Even the use of faulty reasoning, which is by definition paralogical, does not—as we have seen in the above text—automatically create a humorous scenario. People propose illogical arguments all the time and are roundly criticized for them.

It is not difficult to identify some otherwise obvious mechanisms that seem to escape the above list. An incongruity can be made appropriate when an object, situation, or person is viewed from a different perspective.

"Son, I think it's time we talked about sex."
"Sure, Dad. What do you want to know." (Keillor 2005, 155)

At first, this joke might look like simple *role exchange* (a mechanism included in the list). The son seems to be taking on the role of the father in that he will instruct the father in sexual matters. But that is not really what is happening. The son has not approached his father in order to instruct him about sex—which might suggest role exchange. The joke rather depends on the change in perspective as to which of the two joke characters likely possesses more information about or experience with sex. The initial assumption is that the parent would. The punchline suggests to the listener that it is the son who might. Such changes in perspective have been called the "Rashomon effect" after Akira Kurosawa's film in which conflicting stories of a crime are told from the perspectives of its various characters (Heider 1988).

It is worth returning to the example of the joke about the Great Barzini and his act involving being hit in the head with a sledgehammer. Recall that there is no overlap between the performance and hospital scripts. Rather, an element from the performance script—the exclamation "ta-dah!"—is attached to the very end of the hospital scenario. If we peruse the list of logical mechanisms, we might discover the term *juxtaposition* and be satisfied that we had identified the logical operator in this joke. I believe, however, that we would be wrong. Juxtaposition is more likely to create incongruities than resolve them (Ritchie 2004, 75). In the Barzini joke, juxtaposition creates the anomaly. Why would Barzini employ an expression of triumph when his hospitalization demonstrates that his performance has proved an utter failure?

When the joke is considered in terms of the Rashomon effect, we can see the appropriateness of Barzini's gesture. From the perspective of the medical staff and of the joke listener, Barzini has been unconscious for ten years. There is no basis for his belated expression of triumph. From Barzini's perspective, however, those ten years of hospitalization do not exist. His consciousness extends directly from the instant before the hammer hit him in the head to the moment his eyes popped open in the hospital. For him, there is no interruption. His performance is of a piece and, consequently, his triumphant flourish is completely appropriate (though spurious from an objective point of view). The Rashomon effect is what is operating in this joke.

ONTOLOGIES

Humor studies has been living with SSTH and GTVH for almost forty years. For nearly twenty years, humor scholars have been tantalized with the promise of a computer-based implementation of these theories (Raskin 1996; 2008, 7–12; Raskin, Hempelmann, and Taylor 2009), and the Ontological Semantics Theory of Humor (OSTH) has been put forward as the fulfillment of these promises (Taylor 2010, 221–222). A computer-based program of humor generation and comprehension depends upon *ontologies*, semantically structured encyclopedias of linguistic and cultural knowledge. Ontologies are essential for natural language processing and are not in themselves peculiar to the processing of humor. But humor processing requires some additional knowledge in terms of the recognition of what have been regarded as semantic incongruities, ambiguities, oppositions, overlaps, appropriateness, resolutions, or compatibilities. At present, I am skeptical about the prospects for OSTH for several reasons:

1. OSTH is based on SSTH and GTVH and continues to employ the terminology of script opposition and script overlap; notions which are problematic and which, at best, are applicable only to a subset of jokes.

2. If OSTH depends upon notions of logical mechanism from GTVH, it is likely to be flawed because of incompleteness in the identification of logical mechanisms and the absence of precise definitions of those mechanisms that have purportedly been identified. Often, the means by which incongruities are made appropriate in jokes escape these mechanical specifications altogether (e.g., the Wellington joke).

3. Despite the explicit, although belated, recognition by proponents of SSTH and GTVH that they are at root incongruity theories, SSTH and GTVH have failed to operationalize and incorporate notions of appropriate incongruity or incongruity resolution. Script opposition as it has been described is not the same as incongruity. Numerous texts might revolve around oppositions that are in no way humorous, and there are many jokes that do not seem to easily lend

themselves to analysis in terms of script oppositions. I believe a computer might be easily programmed to recognize semantic oppositions in literary texts. I also believe that the oppositions identified will only occasionally be those that engender jokes.

My approach to the study of jokes has been from the point of view of appropriate incongruity. I am, fortunately, a folklorist and my concerns have been to understand how contents are structured within the text of a joke and in joke corpuses in an effort to see what a joke might mean in a social-situational or broader cultural context (e.g., Oring 1973). Appropriate incongruity seems sufficient for this task. An appropriate incongruity perspective has also been extremely useful in assessing whether the analyses of jokes proposed by others seem accurate and persuasive. To date, I have found a number of joke analyses by humor scholars that would appear to be off the mark (Oring 2011b, 212–219; 2016, 39–41). Consequently, an appropriate incongruity perspective has both analytical and critical force. I admit that appropriate incongruity is a post hoc conceptualization with little or no generative power. I cannot at this time operationalize either the notion of incongruity or appropriateness.[11] This is not to say that they might not be operationalizable, only that I currently have no idea how to do it. Graeme Ritchie, after attempting formal descriptions of "forced interpretation" jokes in symbolic language, also concedes that his descriptions can lead to no algorithms or software implementations in the absence of precise definitions of "inappropriateness" and "contrast" (Ritchie 2002). My sense of both SSTH and GTVH is that they are post hoc conceptualizations as well. Only after something is regarded as humorous do underlying oppositions, overlaps, and mechanisms become visible.[12]

Ultimately, the point is not to assert or argue about whether my concerns and criticisms have substance. OSTH has now reset the terms of the debate. Consequently, the adequacy of the formulation should be demonstrated with the following test. Identify a joke domain—for example, doctor/patient jokes, teacher/student jokes, human/Martian jokes, whatever (so long as they are not formula jokes or jokes with obvious stylistic markers). This will restrict the breadth of whatever ontology might be necessary for the identification of such jokes. At this stage of the process, one cannot expect that an ontology would be adequate to identify each and every joke that might be thrown at it. I would leave it to the proponents of OSTH to identify a joke domain, even if it were a fairly restricted one. Then a body of verbal texts of a specifiable and significant number should be submitted for identification by the computer program. These texts will be submitted by humor researchers *not* engaged in the ontological semantics project. These texts should include those that are identified as joke texts by human subjects as well as texts constructed for the purposes of the experiment that are identified as *not* being joke texts by those same subjects. The corpus of texts should then be submitted to the computer program with the expectation that discriminations between joke and non-joke texts reasonably match those made by human subjects. The only restrictions on the ontological semantics theorists are: (1) the texts submitted for analysis should be published; (2) the jokes submitted for computer analysis and identification should not be changed in any way after receipt; (3) no changes can be made to the ontology or the computer program once those same texts have been received;[13] and (4) there should be a specification of a time limit for the ontological semantics theorists to get their ontology and programs prepared for the experiment. Even the ontological semantics theorists admit that the implementation of a theory needs to be completed in a finite amount of time (Raskin, Hempelmann, and Taylor 2009, 287). Indeed, I would like to be alive to witness the results of the test. If the experiment proves successful, then I will happily concede (maybe not happily) that SSTH and GTVH live up to their claims about how joke texts work and that my concerns to date would seem to be unfounded. Until that time, my deep suspicions remain.

My concerns about the Ontological Semantics Theory of Humor do not represent the worries of a humanist fearing that the computer recognition or even production of humor—again, production is the far easier task—would constitute a final assault on claims for the nobility and irreducibility of the human spirit (whatever that may mean). I am actually sanguine about the possibility of the computerization of humor. I believe that a computer with a sufficiently large, complex, and sophisticated ontology and rules for how to recognize incongruous categories and the spurious means by which those categories can be brought into some psychologically valid alignment might be possible. I cannot at present think of a reason that the knowledge and rules that I employ to produce and recognize jokes could not be successfully modeled and deployed by a machine. I am only suspicious that the Semantic Script Theory of Humor and the General Theory of Verbal Humor are the platforms upon which such a computer model can be successfully built.

Memetics and Folkloristics

The Theory

Like a good poet, nature avoids precipitous transitions.
—Heinrich Heine, *Travel Pictures*

Richard Dawkins first defined the meme in his 1976 book *The Selfish Gene. Meme* designated a "unit of cultural transmission, or a unit of cultural *imitation*. . . . Tunes, ideas, catch-phrases, clothes fashions, ways of making pots or of building arches" are all examples of memes (Dawkins 2006, 192).[1] The word *meme* itself was immediately seized upon by scholars and laymen alike. Within ten years of its coinage, it was included in the *Oxford English Dictionary*. The adjectives *memic* and *memetic* are listed as well, but strangely there is no entry in the great dictionary for *memetics*—the science of memes—despite a significant literature devoted to the subject. What I am interested in exploring here is what the idea of memes and the science of memetics might contribute to the field of folkloristics.

Because the concept of a meme was created by Dawkins as an analogy to a gene, it is important to understand something of the biological perspective from which memes and memetics derive. Richard Dawkins argued that even before the emergence of life on this planet, there must have been a primeval soup made of water, carbon dioxide, methane, and ammonia, which, in the presence of lightning, sunlight, or some other energy source, produced molecules of a more complex nature. Indeed, such organic molecules—purines, pyrimidines, amino acids—have been produced under laboratory conditions. Today such organic molecules would have been broken down by bacteria, but then bacteria had not yet been created. Eventually, a molecule came about that had an unusual property; it was capable of

 https://doi.org/10.7330/9781646425198.c006

copying itself. This possibility of self-copying is not as bizarre as it might seem. It is only necessary to imagine a chain of molecules A, each section of which attracts some other particular molecule. Should that complementary chain of molecules split from A, the new chain of molecules B could in turn attract its complementary molecules, thereby reproducing the original chain A.[2] The number of self-reproducing molecules would likely grow in relation to all other molecules in the primeval soup because the formation of other complex molecules is only a hit-and-miss affair. Self-copying molecules, once they get started, take over. The formation of these complex molecules is no longer a matter of chance chemical encounters.

Dawkins terms such self-copying molecules *replicators*. But in any type of copying, errors inevitably occur. Some of these miscopies would reproduce, and eventually there would be several varieties of replicators in the primeval soup. And some of these varieties would be more stable—less prone to break apart—than others and thus become more numerous in the soup. Such replicators of high *longevity* would become dominant because they would have more time to make copies of themselves. Molecules that reproduced themselves with greater frequency—that had greater *fecundity*—would also come to be more numerous than those with lesser rates of reproduction. In the course of time, molecules with even higher longevity and fecundity would emerge and thus there would be an evolutionary trend toward higher longevity and fecundity. In Darwinian terms, nature would select molecules for their greater longevity and fecundity. Another trait nature would have selected for is *copying fidelity* or *heritability*. A molecule that makes a copying mistake every thousandth generation would become more numerous than a molecule that makes a copying mistake every tenth generation even if they are equally long-lived and fecund (Dawkins 2006, 14–18). Copying errors, however, are essential to evolution. Without copying errors, no new forms would emerge. Evolution—Darwinian evolution—depends on both faithful and unfaithful replication (Allen 1983, 88).

The primeval soup was not capable of supporting all the replicator molecules. There would have been competition for resources and some replicators would have succeeded at the expense of others. Some replicators would have "figured out" how to chemically break down other replicators and use their component molecules for their own replication. Others may have developed chemical walls around themselves to prevent such attacks. They built *vehicles* or *survival machines* (i.e., bodies) to protect themselves, and in time these machines would have become more elaborate (Dawkins 2006, 19). Natural selection favors good survival machines as it does the longevity, fecundity, and fidelity of replicators. DNA is a good replicator and single- and multicellular organisms are good survival machines because they are the basis for all life on earth today.

DNA makes up the chromosomes in cellular nuclei and the chromosomes are made up of genes. The definition of gene is not fixed. Often a gene is considered to be a section of DNA on a chromosome responsible for the production of a protein (sometimes called a *cistron*).[3] In Dawkins's view, a gene is a portion of a chromosome that "lasts for enough generations to serve as a unit of natural selection" (2006, 28). It has incredible longevity. It is a unit that is small enough that it is unlikely to be split in the process of crossing over in the production of gamete cells. (Chromosomes in humans last only a single generation. Children have entirely different chromosomes than their parents, although their genes are derived from both their parents.)[4] In some cases a gene may be composed of several closely linked cistrons. Thus, a gene, in Dawkins's view, is a portion of DNA that is likely to survive through hundreds, thousands, or even millions of generations. It is "nearly" immortal.

Dawkins's definition of a gene is framed within an evolutionary perspective. While it is variation that creates those slight advantages that over time result in the emergence of new biological forms, there must be stability as well. If everything changed in every generation, there would be no time for the slight advantages that are concomitant with some variations to be selected and become dominant. Selection operates slowly. It takes time to determine whether that organism and its descendants reproduce more successfully over the long haul than organisms without that change. An organism with a slight genetic alteration might be successful in reproducing in the short term only because of good luck (2006, 38–39). The fitness of a particular variation in an organism is something that is only conceivable in statistical terms. Despite the essential part of variation in evolution, a stable unit is required for natural selection to operate. For Dawkins, that unit is the gene (36).

This brings us to the final point in Dawkins's evolutionary biology: *gene selfishness*. Genes are ruthlessly selfish. They are single-mindedly devoted to their own survival and their own reproduction. Being selfish, genes usually create individual survival machines that are ruthlessly selfish as well; that is, they produce organisms that are likely to ensure the survival and reproduction of the genes they carry.[5]

To say that genes are selfish is not to say that genes have motives or foresight. Genes do not and cannot want or anticipate anything. "Selfish genes" is meant to be a shorthand to describe genes as units that survive by virtue of the fact that they produce survival machines that promote the genes' successful reproduction. If they did not create machines that successfully furthered their reproduction, these genes would eventually disappear. "Evolution is the process by which some genes become more numerous and others less numerous in the gene pool" (2006,

45). What Dawkins means by "selfish gene" is that it is the gene—not the individual organism, not the group, not the species—that is the unit selected by nature for survival or extinction (Dawkins 2006, viii).

Dawkins's "selfish gene" shorthand may be dangerous and misleading, and his book might have attracted less attention had his exposition been more prosaic and less tendentious. There seems to be some predisposition in evolutionary biology, however, toward teleological expressions. Charles Darwin's terms "favoured races" (2008 [1859], iii), "natural selection" (17), "competition" (55), "struggle for existence" (55), "adaptation" (63), "striving" (65), "race for life" (177), and "fitness" (461) also suggest goals, purposes, or intentions even though the terms can be formally defined without reference to any of these. To recapitulate, the "selfish gene" means that nature selects for genes that manufacture survival machines—organisms—that are most successful in ensuring the continuance of the genes of their manufactory.

Dawkins's notion of the gene seems, to me at least, tautological. The gene is defined as those parts of DNA that survive long enough to be the unit of natural selection (Dawkins 2006, 28–29). But since the gene is defined as the unit that survives through the generations, it is the unit that has already been selected for. If it had not been selected for, it could not have survived over the long run. If one sets out to argue that the gene is the unit of natural selection, it would probably be best not to define it as that unit that has been previously selected for.[6]

Biological evolution is tough terrain for scientific explanation. The history of life on the planet is long. Descent by modification is slow. Fossil evidence is discontinuous. No one has actually witnessed the emergence of a new species from an old one. Given Darwin's principle of natural selection, biologists are necessarily led to imagine how and why species take the shapes that they do. Dawkins claims to be interested in the morphological, physiological, and behavioral aspects of organisms that are "undisputedly adaptive solutions" to environmental conditions, yet his book is filled with speculations, guesses, hypothetical scenarios, and what he himself calls "subjective soliloquies" (1983, 405; 2006, 69). Suppositions of what might *logically* constitute fitness, however, may not constitute fitness in actuality.[7] Evolution by means of natural selection—no matter how brilliant Darwin's insight or how long it has served biology—is a theory, not a fact (contra Dawkins 2008, 339). It is important to employ facts in a continual testing of theory. If facts are massaged to demonstrate the presumed rightness of a revered theory, science loses its perspective and its value. After all, Claudius Ptolemy's equally brilliant model of the universe held sway for some fourteen hundred years. There may be other forces at work in evolution besides natural selection. Darwin thought so. Even Dawkins thinks there might be (2008, 185).

Yet Dawkins's book is not a fabrication from whole cloth either. There is reasoned argument, mathematical modeling, computer simulation, hypothesis testing, and even prediction. There are certain biological realities that lend themselves to selfish gene theory. One is animal altruism. An organism that typically behaves altruistically—sacrificing its well-being for the sake of another—raises serious questions about the individual as the unit of selection. Shouldn't an altruistic organism go extinct and any genes for altruism go along with it? Dawkins sees altruism as a matter of gene selection. When an animal behaves altruistically, it is not haphazardly altruistic. Altruism is directed most frequently toward animals that share more of the same genes. Consequently, altruistic behavior is more likely to be directed toward offspring, parents, and siblings who, on average, share half an organism's genes; toward grandchildren and grandparents, aunts and uncles, and nieces and nephews, who on average share one-fourth an organism's genes; toward first cousins and great-grandparents and great-grandchildren, who share on average one-eighth an organism's genes; and toward second cousins, who share one twenty-eighth of that organism's genes (Dawkins 2006, 92–93). A child, consequently, in this genetic accounting, is worth two nephews or two aunts, and a first cousin is worth a grandchild. Dawkins goes on to show how selfish gene theory can account for clutch size (115–116)—that is, the optimum number of eggs laid—parental investment in offspring (124, 171–173), sex ratios (143–144, 176–179), mate choice (157–163), herding and flocking (167–169), alarm calls (169–170), and mutual grooming (183–184) better, or at least no worse (120), than group selection. Not being a biologist, I am in no position to seriously evaluate Dawkins's theory of gene selection. It seems to have received positive responses from a number of evolutionary biologists, and it has been described as an original contribution to evolutionary biology (Hamilton 1977; Medawar 1977; Smith 1982). I also gather, however, that the issue of the unit of natural selection remains very much alive (Sober 1984; Mayr 1986; Wilson 2001).[8]

In the brief final chapter of *The Selfish Gene* (that is, the final chapter in the first edition of the work [1976]), Dawkins introduced his concept of the meme. He hoped to extend his insights from the realm of biological to cultural evolution. Memes are entities that can be imitated, copied, and thus constitute a new kind of replicator launching a new kind of evolution. However, they are selected for on the same basis as those first replicators in the primeval soup—longevity, fecundity, and copying fidelity. Thus memes, like genes, are selfish and seek (again, using Dawkins's shorthand) to occupy as many brains as possible. The success of memes, however, has nothing to do with the preservation of genes or the success of organisms (2006, 193–194).[9] Memes constitute a new kind of evolution and are entirely independent of the biological machines they inhabit. Memes seek only to promote themselves—not the organisms or the genes on which those organisms depend.[10] This is part and parcel of what Dawkins termed "universal Darwinism," the idea that *any* phenomenon or system—so long as there is replication, variation, and hereditability—is shaped by the same selective forces that Darwin described for the evolution of species (Dawkins 1983, 422–423; Blackmore 1999, 10–23).

Dawkins's suggestion of a new unit in the cultural realm upon which selection might operate inspired a host of writers in a bevy of books to flesh out, organize, rationalize, and criticize the new science of memetics: Richard Brodie, *Virus of the Mind* (1996); Susan Blackmore *The Meme Machine* (1999); Robert Aunger, *The Electric Meme* (2002); Kate Distin, *The Selfish Meme* (2005). An online *Journal of Memetics: Evolutionary Models of Information Transmission* began publication in 1997. There is even *The Complete Idiot's Guide to Memes* by John Gunders and Damon Brown (2010). Memes were a meme by any definition of the term.

What eventually emerged from all this elaboration was a memetic philosophy (I am reluctant to call it a science). Memes were memes because they were imitated. In the early stages of human evolution, there were relatively few memes. The first memes must have given some survival advantage to their human hosts. Someone who could imitate the process for making a tool, for example, was probably more likely to survive than someone who couldn't. Those who could acquire memes probably proved to be attractive mates, and consequently, genes for imitative ability would be selected for and predominate in the gene pool. In these early stages of human development, memes were selected for on the basis of the biological advantages they conferred on their human hosts and thus were more closely articulated with biological evolution. Memes, in fact, could have been responsible for the enlargement and the development of the human brain (Blackmore 1999, 74–81). As humans emerged as proficient and prodigious imitators, memes could proceed on their own. They no longer were tied to biological survival. They could replicate and spread even if their hosts had no biological issue so long as there were new hosts for the memes to infect. Thus, a meme for celibacy was not necessarily a deterrent to that meme's fecundity or longevity even though a great number of its human hosts never reproduced. In fact, a clergy committed to celibacy would have enormous amounts of time free from the tasks of raising and maintaining families to spread, through word and deed, the meme of celibacy. This clergy would have been disadvantaged in passing on a gene for celibacy—were such a gene to exist—but a Roman Catholic clergy has been tremendously successful in transmitting the meme over the last two thousand years (Dawkins 2006, 198–199). Similarly, women practicing birth control who are out in the workplace are better vehicles for their birth-control memes than mothers isolated in their homes are for their reproductive ones (Blackmore 1999, 138). Altruists are more likely to spread memes than non-altruists because they have more contacts, are better liked, and consequently have greater influence (154).

Memes are selfish as genes are selfish. Their only goal is to proliferate. Memes are in competition not with genes but with other memes. Good memes are successful memes; memes that manage to inhabit the greatest number of human brains. They are not good because they are important, useful, or moral (Blackmore 1999, 56). They do not necessarily contribute any benefit to the individuals whose brains they inhabit or to the species as a whole. If they can spread, they will. Their success has nothing to do with their benefits to humans but how they benefit themselves. Memes command the resources of the brain to make copies of themselves (14, 27).

One problem with memes is that a meme is not precisely specified. Are the first four notes of Beethoven's Fifth Symphony a meme or is the whole symphony (Blackmore 1999, 53)? Technically, as both can be and are imitated, both are memes, although clearly the former is reproduced far more frequently than the latter. Blackmore claims that a gene is not a well-defined entity either. A gene may be a cistron (a chain of nucleotides that control the building of a single protein) or hereditary information that lasts long enough to be subject to selection.[11] According to Blackmore, the fact that a gene is not well-defined does not impede progress in genetics. Consequently, the difficulty in specifying a meme should not prove a barrier to progress in memetics (1999, 53–56).

"If a friend tells you a story and you remember the gist of the story and pass it on to someone else . . . you have not precisely imitated your friend's every action and word, but something (the gist of the story) has been copied" (Blackmore 1999, 7). So, what is the meme? It is the gist of the story. But what is that gist? The motifs that comprise the story; the plot, the theme, some combination of these that might resemble what folklorists call a *type*? Again, it is important to be able to answer these questions in order to ascertain what is being selected for in any purported Darwinian process. And why would the meme for a story be the gist of the story rather than the story itself? Would the meme of Beethoven's Fifth Symphony be the "gist of the symphony" rather than his musical score instrument by instrument, note for note?[12]

Cultural transmission is often not a matter of imitation at all. It is not obvious that an element of culture inherits all of its properties from some other element of culture that it is presumed to replicate. Cultural transmission frequently depends upon the ability to infer and to recognize goals and intentions and depends upon not only what is seen and heard but upon prior information and knowledge (Sperber 2000, 163–173). The transmission of a folktale, for example, does not depend—as Blackmore recognizes—upon copying the story word for word. Rather, a schema of the story is remembered along with some elements of its content and those are employed to *re-create* another story (Lord 1960; Bloch 2000, 199). The story is not copied as a chain of nucleotides would be copied in the process of mitosis.

The difference between a story and its copy might be considerable. In retelling a story, narrators may combine—accidentally or deliberately—motifs and plot elements from one story with motifs and plot elements from some previously heard stories. They may switch settings and replace characters and emphasize different themes. The transformations can be startling. This raises the question of cultural creativity. What does memetics make of new cultural products? Even granting that "there is nothing new under the sun" (Eccles. 1:19), if Beethoven's Fifth Symphony in C minor is a meme, exactly what is that meme a copy of?

Darwinian evolution depends upon copying fidelity—accurate imitation with only very small and very intermittent errors in the copying process. Dawkins himself admitted to being on somewhat "shaky ground" when it came to insisting on the copying fidelity of memes. It is not clear that there is not constant mutation and blending in meme transmission (2006, 194–195). And blending is fatal for any theory of natural selection (Livio 2013, 37–59). A meme must be sufficiently stable for natural selection to operate. And if natural selection is indeed operating, it seems important to specify both *what* is being selected and *why* it is being selected in any particular environment. It is unlikely that memetics can make much progress without a precise notion of what a meme is, what is being replicated, and why.

If memes are in competition with other memes, the question naturally arises: what makes for a successful competitor? Memes are more likely to succeed if they are attention grabbers, easy to imitate, and keep their hosts mentally engaged (Blackmore 1999, 41, 57).[13] Novelty is an attention grabber, although novel memes must fit into already acquired meme complexes (Distin 2005, 59–60).[14] Memes, it has been argued, may be more successful if they are keyed to human biological dispositions; for example, sex, food, or danger (Brodie 1996, 86–97).[15] They also do better if they are traditional, make sense, seem familiar, involve faith, and are evangelized (1996, 94). They particularly stick when they are simple, unexpected, concrete, credible, emotionally charged, and presented in story form (Heath and Heath 2007, 14–18). Some memes—such as chain letters—contain instructions that urge their readers to copy them. They may also warn of the misfortunes likely to befall those who fail to faithfully follow the directives (Blackmore 1999, 18–19). Successful memes often inhabit the brains of artists, celebrities, and the politically powerful because such people are frequently imitated (130–31). In general, some individuals are *meme fountains* because their sociability, loquacity, and likeability make them the source of memes for numerous others. Other people, however, are *meme sinks* because they are poor conduits for meme transmission.[16] They are exposed to fewer memes and pass on even fewer of those they do possess. While the means and channels by which a meme spreads affect their success, many memes that are in competition often have access to the very same mechanisms and avenues of dissemination. What makes one meme flourish while another fails?[17]

A question arises as to whether the *truth* of a meme is a criterion for its success. Distin believes that memes that are accepted as true are more likely to be selected than those that are held to be untrue (2005, 59). For a scientific theory to thrive, for example, it must enjoy some degree of explanatory success, fit within established theoretical frameworks, and account for the available evidence (58). Blackmore argues that natural selection has equipped humans with perceptual and cognitive systems that accurately model the world. Consequently, humans are disposed to choose memes that are true over those that are false (1999, 180). Brodie, however, does not find truth to be a strong selector for memes (1996, 168, 216). Both Distin and Blackmore recognize that many memes are false. Sometimes false memes can attach themselves to complexes of otherwise true memes and thus be adopted and spread as part of a package (Brodie 1996, 153; Blackmore 1999, 180). Other memes simply *claim* to be true and are accepted and spread on the basis of the claim alone (Blackmore 1999, 180–181). Blind faith itself can be a meme (Dawkins 2006, 198).

The question of truth points to one of the problems underlying memetics. If memes are pretty much all that inhabit the human mind, what could be the basis for discerning whether a meme were true or not? All the relevant programs of truth assessment—science, philosophy, religion, commonsense—are themselves nothing more than complexes of memes that have been created, modified, selected, and transmitted. The evaluation of meme truth would be no more than a memetic commentary on memes. There would be no place to stand from which to move the world.

The problem of "good" and "bad" memes is analogous, although not identical, to the problem of truth. Dawkins already intimates in *The Selfish Gene* that some memes are negative—the God meme, for example, and its associated meme-complexes that are often designated as "religion." The threat of hellfire is "a particularly nasty technique of persuasion" according to Dawkins, and it has been the source of a great deal of human anguish both in the past and the present (2006, 197). Dawkins believes that sometime in the course of human evolution, consciousness emerged, and consequently humans need not be the powerless subjects of blind replicators—whether genes or memes (200). Both Dawkins and Brodie designate some memes as *viruses* that *infect* the mind (Dawkins 1993; Brodie 1996, 63–64). They believe, however, that humans can be free to choose the memes they acquire and spread (Dawkins 2006, 200; Brodie 1996, 213). With difficulty, humans can learn to think for themselves, pursue what they truly want, and live in freedom and happiness (Brodie 1996, 218, 220, 229).

The difference between a meme and a virus, however, is simply the sense of whether Dawkins, Brodie, or any other memeticist regards it as positive—that is, beneficial to humans (Blackmore 1999, 22). This is hardly a theoretical distinction. In the cultural realm, viruses and memes are one and the same, and an analogy based on the distinction between a gene and a virus from biology does not apply (Distin 2005, 74–77; Jeffreys 2000, 230–231; Ellis 2003a, 82–83). In a Darwinian universe, there should be no entity or organism that can serve as a standard of measurement for the "goodness" of anything. An underlying principle of Darwinism is that nature doesn't care, and whether something is good or bad for humans, other life forms, or even life itself is utterly irrelevant. Consequently, whether a meme is beneficial or detrimental to individuals or human societies should be utterly irrelevant to memetics, even if it is not irrelevant to us (see Schrempp 2009).

The question of whether humans are slaves to memes or are their masters turns on whether there is a distinction between the human mind and the information that mind processes; that is, upon the status of human consciousness (Distin 2005, 170). Are memes simply programs that run through a brain that is little more than a very sophisticated computer? Or is the human mind a computer that is aware of the programs it is running and able to evaluate them, discriminate between them, favor some, and abort others? It is hard to know exactly what the properties of the mind are and what its resources could be in a process of evaluation, selection, promotion, and impedance. On the basis of what values, standards, or measures could consciousness discriminate? Wouldn't those values, standards, and measures likewise prove to be no more than memes? And if consciousness stands above memetic thought and can monitor and control its processes—to what extent can universal Darwinism claim that human thought is subject to *natural* selection? Human consciousness would seem to be independent and engaged in *artificial* selection just as Darwin envisioned it. Darwin proposed natural selection as an alternative to the idea of artificial selection—that is, the kind of conscious selection that pigeon fanciers use to create their various breeds. Natural selection was Darwin's hypothesized mechanism for design in nature in the absence of an intentioned, intelligent selector.

The archetype for the intelligent designer is not God but Man. Because of consciousness—which Dawkins fully accepts (1989, 200)—a human can reflect on the past, imagine a future, and set out in the present to shape ideas and materials from the past for future use. Humans visualize goals and work toward them.

This offers another possible account of cultural evolution, one that does not depend upon natural selection. Cultural evolution might prove to be Lamarckian, not Darwinian. That is to say, cultural evolution might depend on the striving toward goals and the acquisition of characteristics that can be passed on. Culture develops as the result of conscious choice and building on assimilated experience rather than accidental variation and natural selection.[18] Robert Aunger, in creating his physicalistic theory of memetics, does everything imaginable to avoid what he terms "Lamarck's folly" (Aunger 2002, 238–239, 242). Of course, there was nothing foolish about Lamarck's theory. It was simply wrong in accounting for species change at gross levels. Cutting off the tails of mice, as August Weismann did, to see whether their offspring would be born without tails was a gross test of Lamarck's theory (Weismann 1893, 397).[19] Recent discoveries, however, indicate that a gene's expression might depend on environmental factors and can be inherited by subsequent generations (Hurley 2013).[20] A priori commitments to Darwinian formulations of cultural evolution represent prejudice, not science. If it is determined that the Lamarckian shoe fits for cultural evolution, one should be obligated to wear it. In fact, if even a small portion of culture can be accounted for in Lamarckian terms, the whole Darwinian thesis goes right out the window.[21]

Susan Blackmore attempts to deny that cultural evolution is essentially Lamarckian. She insists on the difference between copying the product and copying the instructions with Lamarckian inheritance applying only to the former. For example, if someone watches someone make soup, they may watch the cook but then add more salt than the cook does or leave out the garlic when they prepare the soup. Someone who watches them prepare the soup will inherit the acquired characteristics of increased saltiness and decreased spiciness. But if the original cook passes on the *recipe*—the instructions—the second cook will follow those instructions, and even if they deviate in some way in producing the soup according to that recipe, the variation will not be inherited by a person to whom they pass on the recipe. That person will have the original recipe for the soup as prepared by the first cook and can make the soup in an identical way (1999, 59–62). For some reason, Blackmore does not imagine people deliberately altering recipes (instructions) and passing them on. Thus, an acquired change in the recipe—the addition of oregano, for example—is passed to future generations that receive the recipe. The addition of oregano is not a random variation that is blindly selected for. It is deliberate, introduced to achieve a particular goal, and it is heritable.[22]

Actually, as far as folkloristics is concerned, the Lamarckian copying the product that Blackmore describes is actually much closer to the character of folklore transmission than copying the recipe. Folk musicians, unlike classical musicians, may have no written instructions (no score) for the music they play. Undoubtedly, there are ways of conceptualizing a tune when one hears it without memorizing it note for note or writing it down. Figuring out how folk musicians extract instructions from a performance would be a very worthwhile area for investigation. But what musicians—or other folklore performers—are exposed to is often a product and not a set of instructions. That is why a song, tune, or story can vary so spectacularly in the course of its dissemination.

It might be argued that conscious choice is also subject to natural selection. People may have goals and strive toward them, but their choices and the effects of these choices are selected for by nature. If so, why not, in the interests of economy—if nothing else—simply consider consciousness part and parcel of all memetic programs subject to natural selection? That would, of course, deny the possibility of real conscious choice and independent selection. There could be no special status for consciousness. There could only be a memetic programming of the human brain of which consciousness is merely a part. Dawkins, however, argues for genuine consciousness and genuine choice for human beings. Consequently, it would seem that he would have to be open to the idea that cultural evolution might escape the Darwinian algorithm.

So, what does memetics have to do with folklore? What contribution can it make to its study? It seems to me that any folklorist who wants to make use of memetics has to wrestle with several issues. Memes, in essence, are nothing more than *ideas* (Lynch 1996, 2; Pimple 1996, 239n5; Aunger 2002, 176). When the word *idea* is substituted for *meme*, memetics immediately loses a great deal of its glamor. Darwin's achievement in biology was to show how species could come into existence in the absence of special acts of creation and how design in nature could exist in the absence of a designer. Natural selection was the key to showing how what we perceive as order could emerge from a never-ending stream of accidents.[23]

It is hardly revolutionary, however, to suggest that ideas are descended from other ideas and that human brains play some part in creating, modifying, and organizing them. This notion is both ancient and commonplace. We have not been as perplexed about the origin and natural order of ideas as we have about the natural order of things. Cultural evolution has not been a mystery. If, for example, Dawkins would like to explore the evolution of the God meme, he could not do better than to look at Edward Burnett Tylor's account of the development of monotheism from polytheism, polytheism from the belief in nature spirits, the belief in nature spirits from primitive animism, and primitive animism from inferences about the phenomena of sleep, dreams, and death (Tylor 1871, 1:387–453). Admittedly, Tylor's evolutionary framework was not Darwinian but progressive, and the notion of natural selection played no part (Oring 2012b, 174).

Whether Tylor was correct in his reconstruction of the evolution of religion is another matter entirely. The point is that science has long regarded ideas—such as monotheism—as the outgrowth of other ideas. Memetics claims to be the solution to something that has not hitherto been a problem.[24] Consequently, memetics must do more than *claim* that Darwinian evolution is applicable to the stuff of the human mind.

Memeticists are aware that memetics must at some point interface with psychology. The human mind seems an important factor in determining a meme's success or failure. Why do certain memes appeal to human brains while others do not? Why do certain ideas resonate for one individual but not for another (Blackmore 1999, 16, 55; Dawkins 2006, 62, 198; Plotkin 2000, 70; Distin 2005, 62, 64)? Wherein lies the catchiness of a catchy tune?[25] This is precisely the opening through which folklorists, anthropologists, sociologists, and psychologists enter the picture. They investigate the ideas, register their variations, study their environments, trace their movements, and proffer some explanations for their distribution, power, and effects. To date, memetics has only identified some very obvious mechanisms that facilitate the spread of ideas. It has failed, however, to identify the qualities that make certain ideas spreadable. Until memetics can do that, it will remain of dubious value.[26]

What memetics must also show is how the natural selection of ideas actually works. It needs to show that certain ideas survive and others fade away because these ideas are fit or unfit in particular environments.[27] Meme *fitness* is the key. The demonstration of fitness or unfitness in the cultural realm for memes seems harder than in the biological realm for genes. In biology, one must be able to argue that a particular variation is fit or unfit for survival within a particular natural environment, and therefore the genes that produced the variation either proliferated or were extinguished. There are objective environmental conditions—the availability of food, water, shelter, mates, and a myriad of others—that might logically and actually impinge on the maintenance and reproduction of an organism under the guidance of its genes.[28] But it would be easy to point to many memes that should seem unfit because of their failure to accurately model events in the world, because of the danger to which they expose their hosts, or because of their incompatibility with other ideas that, nevertheless, thrive. *The success of a meme has not been measured in terms of its contribution to the survival of its host or to anything else other than its own proliferation.* In other words, a successful meme can only be reckoned in terms of its own success.[29] Any tautological tendencies that might reside in selfish-gene theory are flagrant in selfish-meme theory (Aunger 2000, 8). In her introduction to *The Selfish Meme*, Distin worried that the meme hypothesis might risk "collapsing into the trivial assertion that some ideas survive whilst others disappear" (2005, 3). By the time a reader has finished this otherwise intelligent and accessible volume, it would seem that her worst fears have been realized.[30]

Memes and memetics are themselves memes that spread with considerable alacrity in both academic and popular culture. The online *Journal of Memetics*, however, which began publishing in 1997, published its ninth and final volume in 2005. In that final volume, there appears an article that graphs the number of papers mentioning the word *memetic*. It shows a rise from close to zero in 1987 to a high of seventy in 2002 but dropping precipitously to about twenty-five two years later.[31] The author argues that memetics was in fact a "short-lived fad" that had emphasized abstraction over substantive explanation.[32] Memetics did not provide new understandings of phenomena or offer explanations and predictions beyond what were available without the gene-meme analogy (Edmonds 2005; Kuper 2000, 188). Those folklorists who idly employ the word *meme* should be aware of the theoretical baggage that follows in its train. They must determine what constitutes a meme, reckon with the appropriateness of the gene-meme analogy, decide whether a meme is in fact the basic unit of culture, and assess whether memes are copied with only the barest minimum of distortion. Finally, they must show that the history of ideas can be understood in terms of natural selection and that the fitness of particular ideas can be demonstrated rather than merely asserted or presumed. Those who would seriously look to apply memetics to folkloristics should be alert to the issues that are central to the endeavor and all the difficulties that effort might entail.

CHAPTER SEVEN

Memetics and Folkloristics

The Applications

You are my creator, but I am your master—Obey!
—Mary Shelley, *Frankenstein*

In the previous chapter, the claims of memetics were outlined and questions concerning their logic and utility were raised. The discussion was rather abstract since memeticists were less concerned with applying memetics than showing how memetic theory *might be true*. Beyond the occasional example, there were no attempts to apply memetics to the explanation of corpuses of cultural materials. In this chapter, the focus is on the introduction of memetic theory into folkloristic discourse and its application in understanding folklore and folklore-related materials. It examines four applications of memetic theory in some detail.

The first discussion of memes in the folklore literature occurs in Kenneth D. Pimple's "The Meme-ing of Folklore," published in *Journal of Folklore Research* in 1996.[1] Pimple briefly introduces Richard Dawkins's concept of the meme and the concept of gene and meme selfishness. Pimple holds that memes are in the business of promoting human survival. Memes tell us how "to be able to court potential mates and raise offspring" (Pimple 1996, 237). This idea is contrary to Dawkins's own formulation (2006, 193–194, 198–199) and to the views of most memeticists except in the earliest stages of meme/brain development (Blackmore 1999, 67–81). It is a view that is closer to sociobiology than to memetics (Wilson 2000).

In any event, what is curious about Pimple's essay is his rationale for introducing memes into the folkloristic conversation. He does not use memes to explain folklore. He discusses them to help in thinking about the *definition* of folklore.

    https://doi.org/10.7330/9781646425198.c007

Pimple claims that there is a continuum between the natural and the artificial. In biology, genes fall close to the natural end of this continuum. With respect to culture, *folk* refers to those memes that likewise cluster at the natural end of the continuum. Folk—face-to-face—communication is less mediated than other forms. The more complex the infrastructure, the less natural and more artificial the practice and product will be. "It takes only one voice to make a folk singer, but it takes dozens of technicians for a singer to perform on television" (Pimple 1996, 238). The definition of what is *folk* thus depends upon a distinction between natural and artificial. Whatever the merits of this distinction might be, it does not seem to be one dependent on a notion of memes. Pimple prefers the term *memes* to *ideas* because of its tie to evolutionary theory. However, other than to state that evolution is not unilinear and that it is not coincident with progress, Pimple makes no use of evolutionary theory at all (1996, 239n5). He does not attempt to show that some memes are adaptive while others are not, or even to suggest that natural modes of communication might be more or less adaptive than artificial ones. Consequently, the entrance of memes into folklore discourse was rather slant; the term was introduced while the theory was left behind. Memes were not used for either analysis, explanation, or prediction.

Since Pimple's "The Meme-ing of Folklore," several folklorists have mentioned *memes* (Sherman 2004, 292; Noyes 2009, 238). Another has noted that folklore is a subset of the set of memes (Foote 2007). A few more have cited Dawkins's definition and noted its analogy with a gene, but they too have not actually employed the concept for analysis or explanation (McNeil 2009; Blank 2012, 8). Others have made use of the concept but only slightly. Thus, a legend may be a meme struggling to survive in a competitive environment (Fine and O'Neill 2010, 159) or currency chains—messages written on paper money and passed on—prove to be such an irrational and wasteful use of time that they stand in opposition to practitioners of "profit memetics" (Olbrys 2005, 306). Charles Duffin, in thinking about the role of the audience in the dynamics of ballad production, mentions Cecil Sharp's comments about the community role in the process of selection of a singer's innovations and the accusation of Darwinism made against Milman Parry's understanding of epic formulas. Duffin notes the relation of Parry's formulas to memes but makes no use of memetics (2004, 135–137). All in all, folklorists have been aware of memes, have mentioned them in passing, but, for the most part, memes have not had to do much in the way of heavy or even moderate lifting.

Monica Foote goes a little further when she describes the variation generated in *userpicks* (user pictures)—little icons that the members of a blogging community create and employ to represent themselves in their posted messages. Foote spends some time exploring the concept of meme and believes that memetic theory might offer a model for how folklore is transmitted and evolves (Foote 2007).[2] However, she never returns to her userpicks to explain which ones survive and propagate. All the variations in the userpicks that she describes seem to coexist. It is not clear that there is competition among them or, if there is, how that competition plays out.

The most sustained user of memes has been Jack Zipes. In *Why Fairy Tales Stick* (2006), as well as in a number of articles, book chapters, and chapter sections, Zipes tries to apply memetic theory to fairy tales (2008; 2009, 87–119; 2011; 2013).[3] Zipes regards individual fairy tales in their various forms of expression (oral, literary, cinematic, computer gaming) as good examples of memes. He argues that fairy tales must have been stable and relevant for them to "stick." Tales that remained relevant were passed on; tales that became irrelevant were forgotten. The basis of their relevance is their ability to carry vital information for adaptation to the environment (2006, 7–13). The tales indicate something about both genetically determined and cultural behaviors. They enable tellers and audiences to "discuss the rational bounds of social constructs of their own making and to voice their desires and social and political concerns" (15).

According to Zipes, only to the extent that tales are relevant and fulfill basic needs can they be considered memes (2008, 111).[4] The tales then seeks to perpetuate themselves, and in doing so, they adapt to changes in the environment (15). Thus, fairy tales adapt to the environment *and* provide information that enables humans to adapt to the environment as well. It would seem that the tales serve as some sort of index of environmental changes and then allows humans to adapt to those changes (2006, 26). More specifically, as fairy tales usually deal with crises, they raise questions about how one is to survive in a cruel and exploitative world. They communicate the need to be selfish to survive, yet they raise questions of whether there are ways of living and reproducing that "do not involve the transgression of other bodies."[5] Fairy tales are, according to Zipes, "survival stories with hope" (27).

Zipes's approach is not entirely congruent with orthodox memetic theory. He believes that fairy tales—memes—must contribute something to human survival or they would disappear. Zipes believes that what is true for genes should be true for memes as well. Genes that repeatedly fail in contributing to the survival of their hosts will eventually be eliminated from the pool. Dawkins, however, regards memes as replicators that are independent of the survival of their biological hosts. They perpetuate themselves because they *can*; not because of any benefits that they confer (Dawkins 2006, 193–194). Memes can spread even if their hosts do not survive or reproduce. The only requirement is that they do not kill their hosts before they are passed on.

There is an upside to Zipes's view, however. Because Dawkins's memetic theory argues that memes are only advantageous to themselves (2006, 199–200), Dawkins feels no need to demonstrate meme fitness—a meme's success *is* the demonstration of its fitness.[6] But if it is maintained that fairy tales must fulfill basic human needs and thus contribute to the survival of their hosts, the evidentiary basis is different. One must be able to show how a meme—a fairy tale—contributes to the survival and reproductive success of those who relate, hear, or read it.

Although what is required in the way of demonstration is clearer, that does not necessarily make demonstration a straightforward affair. Zipes discusses a number of fairy tales, but there is only space to present and discuss one of them here. Zipes claims that the lead tale in all the editions published by the Grimms, "The Frog Prince," is about sexual selection, reproduction, and the evolution of culture (2008, 111). It is certainly about mating—in the Grimm version the princess at first refuses to fulfill her promise to sit with the frog at the table or admit him to her bed. Her father the king, however, insists that she honor her pledge. She admits him to her room but throws him against the wall. The frog then turns into a handsome prince with whom she sleeps until morning. The prince then carries her back to his kingdom.

According to Zipes, this tale "advocated for the restoration of the patriarchal word and world order to which young women were to subscribe" (2008, 112). If marriage in the upper classes in this period, however, was not based on love, and the father in fact determined who his daughter was to marry, what exactly had to be "restored" (115)? What principle did the tale teach that was not already recognized by everyone? If Zipes is going to tie the stability and relevance of fairy tales to evolutionary theory, basic questions need to be addressed. Are arrangements by the father for the marriage of a daughter the best mating strategy from a biological point of view? Does patriarchal authority promote survival and reproduction (117–118)? Might patriarchal authority unwisely trump a biologically based disposition that has been selected for over millions of years—the disposition of pure physical attraction?

It is not entirely clear that Zipes is truly concerned with reproductive success. He feels that the tale gets widely disseminated because it allows people "to reflect upon the possibilities and hazards of mating and to draw their own conclusions" (2008, 122). What might not lead to reflections on mating, however? Novels, songs, television shows, plays, proverbs, jokes, engagements, marriages, and everyday behavior and gossip might also lead people to reflect on mating. What is special about the reflections that fairy tales promote? Furthermore, what evidence is there that such reflections take place? Zipes cites no fieldwork on the social situations of fairy tale telling, reading, or viewing. Does "The Frog Prince" actually engender such reflection? Do we have records of conversations on mate selection in which the tale has been told? If such reflection does take place, does it not matter where such reflection leads? If it does not lead to sound conclusions about reproductive success and the preservation of children to the age of reproduction, of what good is it (129)? Zipes seems to think that the basic question to be answered throughout the world is how to "mate most effectively, to enjoy sex, and get the most of the union" (118). I am not sure what he imagines the criteria for "effective" mating are, but why presume that reflecting on a fairy tale—or anything else—is likely to foster it? From an evolutionary point of view, what good is enjoyable sex if it does not lead to successful reproduction? Reflections on fairy tales, in fact, might cause people to delay marriage and procreation, make them unhappy with their spouses, destroy the integrity of the family unit, and put children in jeopardy. If the whole of Zipes's argument is that fairy tales touch on topics of importance in human society—love, marriage, economic hardship, parental neglect, sibling rivalry, sexual predation, violence, social injustice, and death—why is memetics or evolutionary theory needed to make this claim? What does memetics add to the understanding or explanation of the tales?[7]

Contemporary feminist literature, as Zipes points out, makes extensive use of "The Frog Prince" tale. Zipes suggests that this literature demonstrates that the tale continues to play a central role in thinking about mating strategies. Yet he also shows that some of this literature turns away from issues of marriage and mating. Feminist versions may reject the "happily ever after" conclusion of the traditional tale. Males may be absent or superfluous and their sexual instincts domesticated. The emphasis may be less about marriage or mating than the establishment of an individual identity (2008, 133–135). Establishing identity may be an important contemporary concern, but it may not contribute to the effective reproduction of genes, the individual, or the species. In fact, it might be argued that those societies in which the establishment of individual identity is a central concern are the ones with the lowest birthrates. Zipes feels that this tale will endure as long as it speaks to the ability of men and women to "develop mating strategies that stem from their natural dispositions and mental capacities and to make sexual choices influenced by changing social orders" (137). If Zipes merely means to say that people will continue to represent matters of sex and mating in their language and literature, there is little to dispute. A tale about a frog that beds or marries a human will necessarily be about mating to some extent. To claim that the endurance of the tale is a consequence of its dealing with mating is another matter entirely.[8] What Zipes would need to show is that the tale endures because it conveys something *particular* that contributes to reproductive success. He would also need to show that other tales and discourses about mating that do not contribute to reproductive success fail to be transmitted and disappear. Without formulating such an argument buttressed by evidence, the "stickiness" of "The Frog Prince" or other fairy-tale memes becomes an extremely dubious affair. Zipes knows that some tales found in the early fairy-tale collections have thrived while others have not. "The Frog Prince," "Cinderella," and "Little Red Riding Hood" became enormously popular; "Ricky of the Tuft," "Princess Rosette," "The Friendly Frog," and "Jorinda and Joringel," not so much (Johnson 1961; Hunt 1884). The enormous *differences* in the popularity, distribution, and endurance of particular fairy tales should be the starting point for memetic and evolutionary explanations.[9] Explanation should not reduce itself to assertions that fairy tales survive because the topics they deal with are important ones and fulfill basic biological needs. While fairy tales *are* "conventionalized speech acts" (Zipes 2006, 14), "often engender crises" (26), voice "utopian wishes" (15), and "stories with hope" (27) as Zipes maintains, everything that he claims about fairy-tale survival, adaptation, and evolution is disputable, contradictory, and often tautologous.

Bill Ellis's memetic perspective is directed at contemporary legends rather than fairy tales (2003a, 75–92). Ellis argues that contemporary legends may have no determinable meanings and that folklorists are wrong to identify meanings as factors in folklore transmission. At best, legends force their listeners to construct meanings, and those meanings are provisional, idiosyncratic, and constructed at the moment of legend communication. They can best be glimpsed, if at all, in the meta-commentaries generated in legend-telling events (89). Most of the legend meanings that have been proposed are likely meanings created by folklorists in *their* acts of interpretation rather than the meanings of participants in legend transmissions. Legend scholarship, Ellis alleges, has been impeded by the interpretative approach. He claims that no interpretation is any better than any other. Legend narratives may "behave more like organisms in an ecosystem which develop through natural selection to exploit the conditions in which they are passed on" (76).

Because contemporary legends have no meanings, Ellis is drawn to analogies between contemporary legends and biological viruses. Viruses contain information, but only information necessary to their own replication. There are no "hidden meanings" to be discerned (91). Consequently, Ellis sees Dawkins's thesis about selfish memes and his characterization of "mind viruses" (Dawkins 1993) as potentially relevant to legend study. For Ellis, memes are folklore and mind viruses are contemporary legends (Ellis 2003a, 83). A meme is a unit of replicable information; a "mind virus" is a packet of information that manipulates its host to reproduce and distribute it.[10] A mind virus is a meme that parasitizes the mind. It is held to be inherently right, true, or virtuous so that it compels the mind to convince others of its truth and virtue. As a virus is only interested in its own multiplication, it can be dangerous to those to whom it spreads. As viruses are not scrutinized critically or evaluated in terms of available evidence, they prove to be self-sustaining. They are an indication of human gullibility (Dawkins 1993, 20; Ellis 2003a, 78–79).

At first, Ellis regarded Dawkins's notion of mind viruses as anecdotal, unquantifiable, and untestable. Ellis also implied that the distinction that Dawkins maintains between mind viruses and other memes and complexes of memes—such as science—might be questionable (2003a, 79, 82–83). Not all mind viruses have negative effects.[11] Some false contemporary legends actually bring about good results. There are "redemption rumors" (Fine 1991), which urge people to send get-well or business cards to an ailing child and actually result in medical treatment for the child or increased attention to and funding for a medical problem (Ellis 2003a, 81–82). Thus, the response of people to rumors and legends—Dawkins's mind viruses—are not measures of gullibility but result in concrete and positive outcomes. In fact, much that goes under the name of "science," Ellis argues, involves little in the way of critical assessment and hypothesis testing. There is much mindless duplication both in science practice and in science education.[12]

The question, however, should not devolve to whether an unfounded or untrue legend can have positive or ill effects any more than to whether science can have positive or ill effects. Both are distinct possibilities. Indeed, the negative effects of science are probably much greater than the negative effect of rumors and legends because scientific practice and the knowledge it produces coalesce in powerful institutions. Science has done considerable damage.[13] Legend has yet to acquire a coherent institutional basis. When grading the negative impacts of science versus religion, however, the question seems somewhat of a toss-up since both are situated in powerful institutions. The answer probably depends on which side of the divide one stands and what criteria are employed in the calculation. Millions of deaths might be tolerated, even welcomed, by someone holding ideas about the Apocalypse and the Second Coming. Similar scales of annihilation might also seem acceptable to those who design chemical, biological, and thermonuclear weapons as a means to ensure freedom, national survival, the preservation of cultural values, or perhaps just their own salaries.

If Ellis was at first critical of the imprecise, anecdotal, and untestable nature of mind viruses, he felt that Dawkins's analogy was somewhat redeemed by Dawkins's publication, with coauthor Oliver Goodenough, of a chain letter termed the "St. Jude mind virus" (Goodenough and Dawkins 1994). It was a typical chain letter, but the letter, like RNA or DNA, contained instructions for its own replication. Recipients of the letter were instructed to make and distribute twenty copies of the letter with asseverations that those who had already fulfilled these directives had received tremendous rewards while those who had not met with unmitigated disasters. Here was proof that mind viruses actually existed with codes for their own replication. Furthermore, Goodenough and Dawkins noted that the letter spread with the rapidity and range of biological viruses and caused distress at least as real as the physical distress caused by the common cold. (Goodenough and Dawkins even confess to their own "mild, irrational anxiety" when deciding not to pass it on.) Furthermore, many people had to be "immune" to the virus for, if everyone was receptive, within eight successive generations, every person on earth would have received the letter 4.5 times. As this was not the case, many people would seem not to have passed it on.[14] The authors muse that the instruction to make twenty copies was probably too onerous and that the letter might have spread more widely if recipients were instructed to pass on only two copies (2004).[15]

The fact that chain letters include instructions for their own replication is startling only in terms of the biological analogy that Dawkins is proposing between memetic and genetic worlds. In fact, most items of folklore do not contain such explicit instructions. In most cases, legends do not include them. Dawkins seems to designate as mind viruses only those packets of information that are believed to be true because belief *compels* their dissemination. Jokes, however, are almost never believed but seem to spread almost as widely and as quickly as legends and chain letters. There would also seem to be a difference between instructions for replication and the existence of a mechanism for replication. Instructions may be present, but no mechanism for following them is present or enabled. Biological viruses contain instructions for their replication, but they have no mechanism for replication until they penetrate a living cell. When an analogy is made between biology and culture, the problem is exponentially harder. Even if a piece of folklore contains instructions for its own duplication, who, after all, follows instructions? Ask any parent, teacher, physician, or assemble-it-yourself furniture manufacturer about the propensity of children, students, patients, or consumers to follow instructions. To say that some people are resistant is to beg the question, Why are some people resistant while others are not (Dawkins 1993, 19)?

Goodenough and Dawkins claim that they were immune to the St. Jude virus and that their publication on the virus constituted a kind of "meme therapy" because they attached their own packet of scientific information to a highly contagious virus. Although they did not make twenty copies of the chain letter and send it on, they published the chain letter in a journal that has thousands of potential readers. Whether the information packet neutralized the "virus" is an open but empirically decidable question. It is possible that they spread it further than an ordinary chain-letter recipient. Jokes, folktales, and games demonstrate that folklore dissemination does not depend upon belief, and even legends are as likely to be passed on by those who do not believe them as by those who do (Kapferer 1993; Ellis 2003a, 75).

In choosing to distinguish between folklore and contemporary legends, Ellis advances a distinction of which he himself is rightly skeptical. It is not clear what the differences between the two might be other than Dawkins's belief that science is critical, useful, and liberating while viruses are insidious, exploitative, and mind numbing. Is contemporary legend not a form of folklore, and how does it differ from other forms that proliferate and spread? And if contemporary legends spread more quickly and widely than a folksong, for example, is there a fundamental difference in the means of their dissemination? Do outbreaks, epidemics, and pandemics differ in anything other than their reach?

These questions aside, Ellis has some interesting ideas about how to think of contemporary legend from an epidemiological, rather than an evolutionary, point of view (Aunger 2002, 49). He suggests that contemporary legend can be viewed not only as a virus invading an individual or community; a legend could also be regarded as a reaction to an invasion—an immune response. The debate that legends often provoke and the humorous anti-legends that are generated may be a response to the presence of a foreign packet entering an individual's or group's informational system. Legends are "best resisted by prior inoculation of similar ideas, or else by a strategy of inverting and ridiculing the infectious legend shell" (Ellis 2003a, 86).[16]

Legends, like viruses, are often self-limiting. New legends tend to spread quickly but usually settle down in some stable but low-level mode in what resembles an evolutionarily stable strategy (Ellis 2003a, 86). Of course, one would have to show that this is, in fact, an evolutionarily stable strategy (ESS), which is to say that alternative strategies can be identified, their outcomes can be quantified, and it can be shown mathematically that they cannot better the outcomes of the strategy in question (Dawkins 2006, 69–72). Ellis suggests that the "Stolen Kidney" legend first circulated as an alleged incident, but it then jumped to the fictitious environments of the comic strip *Dick Tracy* and the TV series *Law and Order*, which demanded less energy from and less risk to its host to survive. I am not quite certain what Ellis is suggesting here. Perhaps he means that when a legend runs its original course, it settles in fictional forms where its truth is not an issue, but which provides a location from where it can stimulate new legend outbreaks sometime in the future. Followers of *Law and Order*, however, know that the series often bases its shows on incidents drawn from news events, so incorporation of the legend in an episode might increase rather than decrease the sense that the kidney theft legend represents a common practice and thus stimulates the legend's transmission.[17]

The distinction between the *texture* and *text* of folklore was first introduced into folkloristics by Alan Dundes in 1964. According to Dundes, the texture of a piece of folklore is its linguistic formulation: its particular phonemes, morphemes, phraseology, rhymes, rhythms, and style. The text is the sense of the item of folklore itself which, while not actually separate from the texture, can nevertheless be distinguished. The sense of the rhyming proverb "Red sky at morning, sailor take warning" could be translated into another language, although none of its rhyming features might survive the translation. Ellis sees this distinction as analogous to Dawkins's distinction between the gene and the survival machine: the texture of the legend being the machine (the body) and the text being the encoded information. He urges that attention be paid to those aspects of legend texture that make the story a good one and make it most likely to be replicated. It is questionable, however, whether what makes a story a good one and replicable can be attributed to its textural feature alone. First, many legends cross language and cultural boundaries and lose many of their textural features. Second, it is often the *sense* of a story that is arresting, rather than any particular element of texture. That people are drugged and wake up in a bathtub full of ice to discover that one of their kidneys has been removed may be a sufficiently arresting idea to transmit irrespective of how that idea is encoded in one or another narrative report. While textural—aesthetic—features do matter, what makes the story memorable and replicable may not be a matter of texture at all.

Ellis suggests that the *concealed function* (Barnes 1986, 70) that characterizes a number of contemporary legends may be such a textural feature that makes a story memorable; for example, the trucker who pursues a woman driver at night, repeatedly flashing his headlights and scaring her out of her wits, turns out to be trying to save her from a murderer in the back seat of her car that he can see but she can't. Until the very end of the story, the hero would seem to be the villain (Ellis 2003a, 88–89). Why, however, is this concealed function a textural feature at all? It seems more a textual one. It relates to the structure of plot rather than to the qualities of language. If the legend text were translated into some other language, that structural element would likely be retained. It also may be that concealed functions come to signal that a legend is untrue rather than true. As the members of society become acclimated to the existence of contemporary legends though books, television shows, and films, the concealed function might be just that literary effect that conditions its own incredibility (Oring 2012b, 100, 147).

The texture of a piece of folklore is highly variable. The phonemes, words, phrases, tones, and rhythms of a legend are likely to change dramatically from one telling to another and from one teller to another, certainly more than the text's basic message is likely to change. Consequently, there is nothing stable enough in legend texture for selection to work upon. If texture can vary wildly from telling to telling, it suggests a rupture between the code (the text) and the survival machine (the texture). How would the same code generate bodies of such extraordinary diversity? The code would not generate reasonable facsimiles as it does in biology. In Dawkins's selfish gene theory, it is genes that are ultimately selected for, but they can only be selected for if they produce survival machines that are *fit* to survive and replicate. The genes must encode for a relatively stable body that survives and reproduces. If those bodies survive and reproduce, the genes that govern them will survive as well. If, however, the body changes dramatically with each replication, there is nothing stable on which selection can operate. Survival would be a hit-and-miss affair and so would the survival of the genes that generate such somatic diversity. If legends prove to be "constantly mutating entities" (Ellis 2003a, 90), how can they serve as the object of Darwinian selection?

Ellis finally suggests that contemporary legends might be part of a community's *immune response* to potentially harmful media information. But unlike antibodies in biology, which can only be transmitted from mother to newborn, anti-legends can be transmitted horizontally and spread widely. Successful advertising campaigns, for example, seem to provoke corresponding "contamination legends" (2003a, 85, 89). But have contamination legends been plotted against successful advertising campaigns and successful advertising campaigns plotted against contamination legends across the board? It would seem that there is much successful advertising that does not generate a corresponding contamination legend. So which campaigns provoke an "immune response," which do not, and why? This is, first and foremost, a matter for empirical investigation.

Legends may indeed react to powerful media messages. There may be many forms of folklore that function in this particular way. Joke cycles may be a response to the discourse and images created and purveyed by the news media (Oring 1987; 1992, 29–40). Children's rhymes often respond to the ubiquity and allure of advertising (Mechling 1986, 97–103; Bronner 1988, 109–110). *Resistance* is a term that is regularly employed in epidemiology as well as the study of culture (although the latter is likely the prototype for the former). Resistance has long been a major theme in folklore study (Greenway 1953; Dorson 1958, 108–128). The interesting question is not whether certain forms of folklore may be characterized as forms of resistance but why resistance may be present in one case but not in another and why some forms of resistance are overt and deliberate while others seem covert and unwitting.[18]

Ellis is right that legend interpretations may be more in the minds of folklorists than in the minds of those who transmit and receive legends. His claim that no interpretation is better than any other is more problematic. Some interpretations unequivocally misread data. Some interpretations are more economical and depend upon fewer distinct assumptions. Some interpretations corral more data and data at distinct levels—for example, texts, commentaries, interview responses, and behaviors. And some interpretations parallel interpretations of data from other domains and are in accord with other bodies of theory. Some interpretations are potentially falsifiable (even though folklorists have not spent a great deal of time trying to falsify them [Oring 2003, 41–57; 2004; 2011b, 206–212; 2019c, 145–147]). If there can be worse interpretations, there certainly can be better ones.

I do not think that in most, or even many, cases a folklorist need determine the "personalities" of tellers to interpret a legend narrative (Ellis 2003a, 75).[19] Folklorists do need to explore the range of messages that a text can bear and examine the relations between those messages and the narrators who tell them and the people who respond to them. They do need to attend to the commentary that surrounds legend narration and to elicit such commentary in interviews (Dundes 1966). A narrative, however, cannot mean *anything*. If it could, narrators could dispense with all but a single text that could be made to carry whatever meaning they hoped ever to convey. The "kidney heist" might bear a number of meanings, but that it addresses concerns about whether humans can safely travel to Mars and establish a successful colony is probably not among them. At present it is hard to imagine how the study of contemporary legend can make do without some form of interpretive approach, even if Ellis is right about folklorists failing to ask themselves some hard questions about the interpretations they have proposed.

Ellis endeavors to explore the analogy between the spread of disease and the spread of contemporary legends. He sees some interesting analogies, analogies worthy of closer study. Folklore transmission was once at the center of folklore studies. The historic-geographic method was something akin to an epidemiological inquiry with the reconstruction of the *Urform* of a tale somewhat equivalent to identifying Patient Zero in a biological epidemic. Yet positing that legends are viruses with "autonomous ability to spread from brain to brain" (Ellis 2003a, 76) leaves a great deal to be desired. If there is no indication of why certain memes spread while others do not, or why certain memes spread widely while others remain local, less in the way of explanation may be offered than one rooted in straightforward textual interpretation.

The transmission of a legend or anti-legend should have to provide some benefit to the individual, according to Ellis, and therefore tellers would tell legends to those from whom they might expect some reward in return. They should spread, in other words, according to patterns of strong social obligation rather than be haphazardly broadcast (Ellis 2003a, 90). This seems a reinterpretation or misreading of memetic theory. While genes must confer some benefit to the individual—otherwise that individual will not survive to reproduce—according to Dawkins and other memeticists, memes do not have to confer any advantages to their hosts at all. All the memes need do is survive and proliferate. Consequently, there should be no necessity that legends or anti-legends spread only to those with whom one has close social obligations, although it perhaps would not be surprising if legends were first transmitted to close friends and relatives just as colds often are.[20]

Ellis is more interested in epidemiology than evolution.[21] Consequently, what needs to be done is to compare patterns of legend spread and virus spread. Do they distribute themselves in a similar manner or is that similarity simply assumed? What are the reasons for infection and non-infection in both cases? One can imagine that a person previously exposed to a particular legend or type of legend might be impervious to the legend or the type the next time it is encountered. But one could also imagine that the legend or legend type would have had to be shown to be untrue for such "resistance" to develop. When someone hears an odd bit of news from a friend and is told the same news in a slightly different form by another friend, they tend—in the absence of contrary information—to believe it. If they hear the same bit of news but with significant variations—in one case the odd event occurred in New York, in the other in Shanghai—the case is more dubious. The news may be doubted because the odd event is unlikely to have transpired at the same time in such different and distant places. So, it becomes important to identify the kinds of factors that make individuals "resistant" to belief in certain legends. As in biology, identifying the mechanisms is everything.[22]

Bill Ellis was not the only one to approach legends from a memetic point of view. In a series of creative experiments, Chip Heath, Chris Bell, and Emily Sternberg attempted to determine whether urban legends that aroused emotion were more likely to be transmitted than those that focused on plausible and useful information (2001). They focused on the emotion of disgust because the ideas that aroused disgust could be easily identified and manipulated in stories.[23] Their first experiment showed that stories that were rated higher in levels of disgust by experimental subjects were the same stories that subjects said they were more likely to pass along, more likely than stories that contained true and useful information or a moral lesson. The second experiment showed that when stories were manipulated to increase their levels of disgust, the more disgusting versions were the ones that subjects said they were more likely to transmit. The third experiment involved rating urban legends in terms of the number of disgust motifs they contained and then seeing whether these legends were more likely to appear in the ten most popular urban legend websites. They sought, in other words, to determine whether disgusting versions were *actually* passed on (as opposed to subjects simply saying that they would pass them on). The researchers found that the number of disgust motifs in a story was a good predictor of website popularity. For every additional disgust motif that a story included, the chance of the story being found on an additional website went up by 20 percent (2001, 1038). Overall, the authors concluded that *emotional selection* operates in the transmission of urban legends. Those stories that contain more elements of disgust and generate stronger disgust responses are more likely to be passed on.

No folklorist would be surprised at the suggestion that stories that arouse emotion would prove more compelling and popular than those that do not. Almost twenty-five hundred years ago, Aristotle argued that audiences are persuaded "when they are made to feel emotion" (1991, 38–39).[24] It is true that disgust has not largely been an emotion of concern to folklorists (but see Jones 2000). As Heath, Bell, and Sternberg suggest, students of legend have tended to resort to arguments about diffuse, preexisting anxieties (e.g., Oring 2012b, 149). But Heath, Bell, and Sternberg not only suggest the salience and attractiveness of emotionally arousing legendary materials, they also invoke Richard Dawkins's terminology and evolutionary paradigm: urban legends are memes, and "memes should evolve to fit an environment determined by shared psychological and social characteristics" (Heath, Bell, and Sternberg 2001, 1040).

Given this evolutionary paradigm there are certain questions that need to be addressed. First, Darwinian evolution presupposes that organisms or memes are in competition. With what is an urban legend competing? Are more or less disgusting variants of the same legend competing with one another (as in the second experiment)? Are disgusting legends in competition with disgusting legends with different content and plots? Are disgusting legends in competition with legends that plumb different emotions than disgust? Are emotional legends competing with legends that focus primarily on plausible, practical information and moral principles (as in the first experiment)? Are legends competing with other kinds of narrative or with other verbal genres like folksongs or jokes? If the emotional selection identified in the experimental environment were operating in the natural world, why did the researchers find that only 25 percent of a random selection of legends from the three largest urban legend websites elicit disgust? And why did only 50 percent of the twelve disgust-legends the researchers chose for their second experiment prove to be in the high disgust condition while the other 50 percent were not? Given that these legends had been around for some time and would have gone through a large number of retellings (i.e., replications), why would the less disgusting variants have survived?[25] Why wouldn't they have been replaced by their more disgusting competitors?[26]

Second, selective factors for traits are only relevant in a defined environment. The reduction in the population of the light moth (*Biston betularia betularia morpha typica*) and the increase of the dark moth (*carbonaria*) were a result of the pollution produced by the Industrial Revolution in England in the mid-nineteenth century (Livio 2013, 32). What are the environmental conditions that favor the spread of one legend over another? Like the black moth, disgust—or any other emotion—must succeed or fail in some environment. That is why certain rumors and legends spread rapidly and widely in situations of "crisis, conflict, and catastrophe" when information from institutional sources is often absent or deemed untrustworthy (Koenig 1985, 3).[27]

Third, if there is selection for disgust, it is not simply that more disgusting legends survive and proliferate. Humans are not mere copyists. They recreate the stories they hear and make their retellings more disgusting. They anticipate—consciously or not—the interest and response that a more disgusting legend might arouse and work to fulfill that expectation. This kind of change is not the *random* variation that Darwin imagined. It is *motivated*; it is directed toward a goal. It is Lamarckian rather than Darwinian.[28]

While I have no problem with Heath, Bell, and Sternberg's experiments confirming that people favor and say they will pass on stories that arouse emotion (actually I do),[29] it is the leap to a Darwinian paradigm for story proliferation that I am uncomfortable with. Once again, it is the demonstration that folklore forms proliferate or go extinct under particular environmental conditions that is missing. The leap to Darwinian evolution from this series of experiment seems premature.

Michael D. C. Drout's *How Tradition Works: A Meme-Based Cultural Poetics of the Anglo-Saxon Tenth Century* (2006a) is another study in memetics that deserves some attention even though it is not a folklore book. It deals with written texts—not oral materials—but Drout is concerned with establishing a meme-based theory of tradition. In addition, Drout received his MA in English from the University of Missouri in 1993, where he studied with John Miles Foley. In other words, he is informed by and addresses matters related to the concerns of folklorists.

In his consideration of tradition, Drout does two useful things. First, he does something that folklorists often fail to do, he defines *tradition*: "A tradition is an unbroken train of identical, non-instinctual behaviors that have been invariably repeated after the same recurring antecedent conditions" (2006a, 9). He recognizes that for humans, exact repetition is not really possible, but he suggests that people can recognize the "same" actions even when they are not strictly speaking the same (11–12). While I certainly can appreciate this viewpoint, I wonder whether it is sufficient for a memetic theory in which *replication* rather than *re-creation* or *similarity* is fundamental.

Drout roots tradition in behavior—something specific must be *done* in response to specific conditions. There may be traditions, however, that never materialize in a specific behavior. For example, the *idea* of ghosts—the returning dead—is rather widespread in ancient and contemporary societies. This idea takes a variety of forms, is instantiated in a variety of media, is an idea that exists for both believers and non-believers and is both seriously and humorously entertained. This idea is acquired from the past but may stimulate no behavior or, alternately, provokes a wide spectrum of behaviors in a variety of circumstances. So, is the belief or non-belief in ghosts traditional? Given his definition, Drout might rule it out. But if the idea of ghosts is not traditional, what is it?

Drout's definition of tradition would seem a purely etic one; it is formulated without reference to human conceptualizations of their own behaviors.[30] Something that people label a *tradition* might not be a tradition according to the definition, and something that people do not consider a tradition may very well be one. It is further worth noting that a tradition would not seem to depend upon repetition within any particular group. If some Americans should replicate the behavior of some people in India, that behavior would constitute a tradition. "Whose tradition is it?" is a question that seems less meaningful for memeticists than for many folklorists.[31]

The second useful thing Drout does is characterize tradition in terms of certain invariant memetic components; what he calls *recognitio, actio,* and *justificatio.* That is, for every tradition there must be *recognition* of those conditions for which a traditional action is appropriate; there is an *action* that is performed; and there is a *justification* given for why the action is performed. Regardless of whether one operates with a memetic theory, these aspects of a tradition are useful to distinguish because they may vary in different degrees and at different rates. An action may remain the same while the antecedent conditions triggering that action change, or the justification may change while the antecedent conditions and action remain substantially the same. Drout considers that if the action changes too much, the whole tradition may be transformed beyond recognition. Yet this suggests that if the action remains substantially the same but is triggered by different conditions, or is justified with a different rationale, it might nevertheless be considered the same tradition. This raises the question of how much *recognitio* and *justificatio* are really intrinsic to this notion of tradition. After all, if a tradition is defined as a specific action performed *in response to* the same antecedent conditions, how much can those conditions change without breaking the chain? Drout imagines how changes to *recognitio* and *justificatio* might increase or decrease the fitness of the entire complex of memes—that is, affect the ability of a tradition to reproduce and spread. He regards changes to the *actio* as more likely to decrease fitness (Drout 2006a, 16). Of course, if the *recognitio* and *justificatio* are part of the memeplex (the complex of memes), some major elements of the tradition are being lost by definition when they change. So exactly what parts of a memeplex are the ones that are of concern and *really* constitute the tradition?

Drout employs hypothetical examples to illustrate the increasing or decreasing fitness of a tradition with changes in the *recognitio* and *justificatio*. For example, a *justificatio* for a tradition that is "because if you don't [do it], we will all die" is supposedly stronger than "because it makes the crops thrive" (2006a, 15). This might sound good in theory, but in real time and space it might prove terrible for maintaining a tradition intact. It is an all-or-nothing proposition. Should someone deviate—accidentally or deliberately—from the *actio* without everybody dying, there might be good grounds for abandoning the tradition altogether. One is reminded of the situation in Hawaii in the early nineteenth century when King Kamehameha II sat down to eat a meal with his mother and wife, thus violating a major taboo. When nothing happened as a result of this sacrilege, Kamehameha disbanded the priesthood and destroyed the temples (Howells 1962, 36; "Kamehameha II" n.d.).

Change in *justificatio* can preserve the fitness of a tradition through what Drout calls "word-to-world fit." Since traditions interact with the environment, a justification should not run up against conditions in the real world (Drout 2006a, 16–19). Certain *justificatios*, however, are impossible to test—such as the one of receiving rewards in the afterlife—and therefore are unchallengeable. But even when memes run up against the world, as when prayers go unanswered, or bad things happen to good people and vice versa, religions may go on, oblivious to a lack of word-to-world fit. Faith often demands surrender to God's will regardless of what takes place in the real world. There is no objective standard that can challenge faith (Dawkins 2008, 346).

For Drout, *justificatios* that are sufficiently vague will fit the world better than specific ones. Specific ones have the liability of sometimes failing to fit conditions. Consequently, there would be selection pressure in favor of vague justifications. The vaguest, perhaps, is what Drout calls the "Universal Tradition Meme"—the justification that "we have always done so," which can support any tradition with which it is associated (2006a, 17). The universal tradition meme "parasitizes" any traditional memeplex by substituting itself for its *justificatio* and can preserve vast complexes of human behavior. Memes that join together have a greater chance of being preserved than if they exist on their own. Even a meme with some negative attributes may survive if it is wedded to a memeplex that has some beneficial attributes (2006a, 19–20).[32] All this leads to something that looks like a basic memetic law: "A [harmonized] cluster of memes . . . all using the Universal Tradition Meme as their *justificatio* components, makes up a tradition. This tradition should continue to replicate itself" (22).

Since all this theorizing takes place in the absence of the consideration of real traditions, it is hard to know exactly how to evaluate it. The Universal Tradition Meme is vague because it is not about a cause and an effect. Specific *justifcatios* are likely to be characterized as cause-effect propositions: If we don't do A, B will happen; or if we do C, D will happen. For example, "If ye shall harken diligently unto My commandments . . . I will give the rain of the land in its season" (Deut. 11:13–14). Also questionable is whether the Universal Tradition Meme is as universal as it is made out to be. People generally do not need to rationalize continuities in the ways they do things. The Universal Tradition Meme seems to be proffered when *alternatives* to behavior are recognized. "This is the way we have always done it," is intended to exclude the possibility of doing it some other imaginable way. Thus, the Universal Tradition Meme makes tradition a matter of cultural identity—the way *we* have always done it (Drout 2006a, 22). This seems the source of power of the Universal Tradition Meme, not its vagueness. The tradition becomes a part of the sense of self and community. This is why such traditions are likely to persist. Identity lies behind what Drout calls "the self-consciousness of traditionality" (22). It is not because such self-referential traditions encode their information more than once—in the tradition itself and in the references to that tradition, as he claims (23). The tradition is rather a statement of who one is and where one stands in the world.[33] Nevertheless, the Universal Tradition Meme may have its own problems. It invariably invites the question that perhaps what we have been doing all along is wrong. Within the Universal Tradition Meme, in other words, lie the seeds of its own destruction.

What is problematic about Drout's memetics is what is problematic about memetics generally: (1) it proposes a new vocabulary to describe exchanges of ideas and information that hitherto had been described without that vocabulary and (2) it asserts but does not demonstrate that natural selection is operative in the evolution of culture. The evolution of culture by natural selection is an assertion predicated solely on Darwinian logic. It has not been demonstrated by Drout, Dawkins, or other memeticists. The matter of establishing fitness remains crucial. Drout at least recognizes the tautology inherent in the notion that what has survived is what is fit (2006a, 7). He suggests that fitness might be reckoned in terms of the superior design of a meme: "It should be possible to apply design or engineering principles to memes to determine why some of them spread and why others die out" (8). Although promising, this statement is rapidly superseded by the statement that "whether . . . an individual is fit or not is *whether or not it is able to replicate*" (50, emphasis in original), which belies any real concern to define fitness in objective, engineering terms.

Drout does suggest, however, that memes that are easier to remember and that are aesthetic are more likely to be replicated and spread. Both propositions seem reasonable, but here reason may be the catch. Why did the Anglo-Saxons or Scandinavians not employ rhyme to enhance the memorability of their poetry? They relied almost exclusively on meter and alliteration, although rhyming poetry was known to them.[34] It would not be enough to say that it was contrary to their aesthetic because if memorability enhances the replication and spread of memes, as Drout claims, rhyming should have been reconciled with alliteration in a yet more powerful form of mnemonic verse.

Of course, cultural information does not always have to be remembered. It can be recalled from permanent storage—a scroll, tablet, painting, codex, book, photo, sheet music, CD, DVD, or the World Wide Web—and is read or performed and then dismissed and re-forgotten. What is remembered is usually an idea about what is stored: a plot, theme, major character, or perhaps a musical or linguistic phrase. Rarely is a memeplex remembered in its entirety. Often what is remembered is where to go to retrieve the information. Of course, memorability is critical in an oral society where external information-storage devices are both limited and few. But remembering the sense of a meme and recalling where it is stored is not a matter of remembering the same things.

Drout does recognize that memeplexes encoded in texts can be revived at a later time and suggests they are somewhat insulated from the word-to-world fit standard. Thus, writing or any external storage medium gives a de facto survival advantage to memes and memeplexes regardless of their memorability, aesthetics, or any relation to the external environment. Drout proposes an analogy between books and the seeds of plants that preserve their information through barren periods only to sprout when conditions grow more favorable (2006a, 37). Indeed! But I am not sure what is to be gained by over-biologizing the analogy. That writing can serve as a basis for the preservation and revival of culture is hardly a discovery of memetics.

Aesthetics would indeed seem relevant to the replication of a meme, but how is this to be assessed? If we look to past societies, as Drout does, the only sense of what the aesthetic might have been is what was "most copied and adapted." Thus, the only way to assess an aesthetic is through what has been repeatedly used. In other words, an aesthetic is hypothesized on the basis of what has been previously replicated, what is most replicable is not hypothesized in terms of a known aesthetic. Once again, we are left with tautologies (2006a, 41–43).

Drout is not bothered, as Dawkins is, by the possibility of high mutation and recombination rates for memes. Dawkins felt that in the course of replication, mutations must be minimal and occur only rarely for selection to operate (Dawkins 2006, 12, 16–18, 33, 194). Drout feels that high mutation and combination rates for memes gives natural selection much more to work with (2006a, 54). Drout also feels that differences in memes that occur after transmission may be superficial features that are invisible to selection (55). That may be true, but the question remains: What is being selected for if there is high variability in cultural products? With such variability, could selection have time to work at all?

Minute changes in a memeplex over time can lead to dramatic differences between ancestors and descendants. For Drout, this is not a problem. "No matter how much a tradition changes, as long as the chain remains unbroken . . . we continue to have a tradition" (27). But descendants do not result only from the mutation of information within the original memeplex. Memes also change and combine with other memes in the human brain. They emerge as hybrids. Meme A may be combined with B and C; in the next generation, D is added and A is dropped; then E is added and B is dropped; finally, F is added and C is dropped. All that remains is D, E, and F. Nothing remains of the original memeplex. There is clearly an identifiable chain, but there is no surviving tradition (either emically or etically). "Is this the tomahawk that killed General Custer?" "Yes, but the handle has been replaced and the blade is new."[35]

Changes in tradition can be revolutionary rather than evolutionary. Drout invokes the following example only to illustrate how interpretation can lead to the mutation of a written text, but I would suggest that Saint Paul's transformation of circumcision of the flesh to a circumcision of the spirit was just such a revolutionary change, not a slight metaphorical emendation of the Jewish commandment (2006a, 33). Circumcision of the spirit meant that physical circumcision—as well as all the other commandments of the Torah—no longer needed to be fulfilled. Combined with the idea that Jesus was the son of God and Mary—from a Jewish perspective, a thoroughly pagan notion—the relation between Judaism and Christianity was severed. While there are ideas that are common to both, and although Christianity began as a sect of a small group of Jews in Judea, would it be correct to characterize Christianity as an evolutionary outgrowth rooted in some "mutations" of Jewish doctrine and practice? After Paul, Christianity was a Greco-Roman religion, not a Jewish one. It is not even clear that the Judaism that developed after the destruction of the Temple in Jerusalem in 70 CE was a continuation of what had come before (Wex 2006, 6). Certainly, if one defines tradition in terms of *behavior*, as Drout does, it would seem more appropriate to describe Christianity and rabbinic Judaism as leaps, rather than modifications, of Second Temple Judaism. It is as though birds emerged from dinosaurs over the weekend.[36]

Drout's turn to memetics is based on his desire for a "materialist option" in understanding the workings of culture. Memetics reduces culture to units akin to the atoms and molecules of chemistry. Memes enter the brain, are copied, and combined. There is no need to posit a human soul (2006a, 54). As Darwin eliminated the designer from the understanding of nature, memetics would exclude the designer from culture. There is no need to posit conspiracies contrived by powerful people to maintain their wealth and influence (56, 58–59). There are, of course, many explanations of culture change that have been offered that do not depend upon conspiracy theories. But Drout's memetics goes beyond what most people think of as conspiracy theories. He is skeptical of consciousness entirely. The skull is a petri dish and a human brain the medium into which memes are introduced, copied, combined, and from where they spread to other petri dishes. Intention and choice are beside the point.[37]

The bulk of Drout's book is devoted to the analysis of cultural materials from a memetic perspective. One of his areas of research is the history and literature of the Anglo-Saxon tenth century, and it is to these materials that he applies his memetic perspective.[38] His focus is the Benedictine Reform, its development and influence. The monastic order under the *Rule of St. Benedict*, introduced by Dunstan, Æthelwold, and Oswald in England, came to replace the groups of priests who ran the great cathedrals. These priests were accused of profligacy, thrown out, and replaced with monks and monastic rule. The success of the *Rule of St. Benedict*, according to Drout, was that it was written, and everyone was subject to the rule, including the abbot. Along with a second written rule, the *Regularis Concordia*, the daily life of the monk was so prescribed that it left little room for competing memes to enter. The monastery was embedded in a never-changing cycle of liturgical time, which ended only with the death of a monk or by Christ's return. Acceptance into the monastery was difficult and leaving the monastery was nearly impossible. The rule was read to all the monks three times over the course of a year. In their scriptoria, monks copied the rule, and with multiple copies available, it was more likely to spread. A monasticism defined by written and invariant rules was more likely to replicate itself than non-text-based monasticisms.[39] This centrality of the rule served as a kind of memetic hygiene because it was likely to prevent the introduction into monastic life of any memes that did not accord with it. Breaches of the rule were punished according to their seriousness: exclusion from the common table, exclusion from psalm singing, whipping, excommunication, or expulsion from the monastery (Drout 2006a, 75–105).

Certainly, reference to an invariant written text is likely to promote stability. Folklore scholars know that a song or tale is likely to remain more stable in oral tradition when singers or tellers have recourse to written or printed texts. But it is important to keep in mind that Drout is analyzing written rules. There are no ethnographic accounts of tenth-century monastic life. As the monasteries were completely independent of one another, it is difficult to know if interpretations of the rule by one abbot differed significantly from those by another or how much day-to-day practices might have varied between monasteries. If differences did arise, were any of these selected for? Other questions also arise. Why did the monasteries remain independent units rather than form confederations—as they seem to have done on the Continent—that could serve to check deviations that might have arisen in individual houses? Had a corrupt clergy led to the downfall of the priests and the rise of the Benedictines? Did the success of the Benedictines owe much to a general rejection of the non-monastic priests they replaced? Why did Anglo-Saxon kings—Edmond, Eadred, Edgar—support the Benedictine Reform? Would such a reform have succeeded without royal backing (2006a, 106)?[40] What was the nature of the evolution of Benedictine monasticism in England and how did it differ from Benedictine monasticism on the Continent? As Benedictine monasticism had been introduced into England before the tenth century, why didn't it succeed in that earlier time (82)? Is understanding the Benedictine Reform really improved by regarding the whole as a question of the stability and reproduction of information rather than matters of economics, power politics, social organization, and ideology? Is understanding enhanced or impoverished by trying to get rid of human consciousness and intention? What is it about a rule, no matter how fixed, that makes people—but only some people—want to follow it?

Drout is concerned that the *Rule of St. Benedict*, even with its translation into Anglo-Saxon, would never have been known to more than a very small percentage of the population. Consequently, he is at pains to establish that the Benedictine Reform held sway beyond the walls of the monastery. Why this is necessary is not entirely clear. Even from a memetic point of view, a successful meme need not inhabit every mind any more than a successful bacterium need inhabit every gut. Nevertheless, Drout concerns himself with Anglo-Saxon wills that had been deposited with the monasteries at the time of the Benedictine Reform (2006a, 125–166) as well as with the influence of what has been called "hermeneutic Latin" on the Anglo-Saxon translation of the *Rule of Chrodegang*, a rule for canons compiled by the bishop of Metz in the eighth century (179–217). There is no space to consider these here, but I can't see that reference to memes adds value to either analysis. While Drout seems right that the perduring qualities of monastic institutions would make them good organizations for supervising wills, it seems important to register that the *Rule of St. Benedict* makes no provision for such activity. It does refer to donations to the monastery by the families of oblates, the income of which is reserved for that family (chapter LIX). There is no mention, however, of executing wills. In fact, it would seem that this monastic function would constitute a new meme that has entered what has been described as an otherwise highly resistant memeplex. It suggests that depositing wills with monasteries is better explained by reference to social structural considerations than by memetics.[41]

In the final section of his book, Drout examines four poems from the Exeter Book that have been labeled *wisdom poems*: "The Gifts of Men," "Precepts," "The Fortunes of Men," and "Maxims I." He argues that monastic memes insinuated themselves into these poems in an effort to have an impact on the wider secular culture. The poems are didactic and communicate what is valuable in life. I am neither a scholar of the Anglo-Saxon tenth century nor a medievalist, but the analysis did not seem convincing. The poems are heavy on worldly Anglo-Saxon virtues and rather subdued with respect to Christian ones. The analysis at a number of points is equivocal (2006a, 261, 270, 284), and Drout *guesses* that the authors of the poems were monks with ties to the nobility who were trying to influence that nobility to think well of the monastery (247–249). Or in memetic terms, "The wisdom genre possessed . . . cultural authority, accessing the form allowed Benedictine Reform memes to be more easily spread throughout the culture" (250). I am not sure why the expression of a Christian virtue is necessarily a monastic one, nor am I certain what kind of influence the Exeter Book and these poems had in tenth-century society. Are there many references to the poems in the Anglo-Saxon literature? Is inclusion in the Exeter Book necessarily a sign of memetic success? I don't know the answers to these questions, but with or without the mention of memes, the interpretation of the "wisdom poems" seems an uncertain effort to extract history from literature.

While Drout admits that he does not possess a complete memetic theory of culture, he feels that the theory is sufficiently robust so that new discoveries in psychology will not destroy it (2006a, 293–294). I am not sure that his theory is that robust, and I worry that a theory that claims to be impervious to challenge from new discoveries may either be too vague to be challenged or be held true a priori. I am also leery of a theory that is crafted primarily to be materialistic rather than to best explain the data. Nevertheless, I appreciate Drout's attempt—all serious attempts—to apply memetic theory (in its various forms) to a body of cultural materials. The proof of the pudding, after all, is in the eating. I am not hostile to the possibility of memetic explanation; I am only skeptical.

My criticisms of memetics are essentially questions. If answers are forthcoming, I might change my mind. At present, however, I think the theory as it is currently formulated is flawed: the definitions and delineations of basic concepts are vague; the applications leave much to be desired; tautologies lurk everywhere; and, most importantly, the principle of selection is never convincingly demonstrated. I do not see that the materials explained could not be accounted for as well or better without the invocation of memes. I fully understand the wish for a unified theory of cultural dissemination and development, but a theory should not be advanced on the basis of wishes alone. It must prove a better explanation; it should not be predicated on tautologous arguments; and it should not do violence to the data. Nevertheless, as a "mutation" of culture theory—memetics may have some unanticipated benefits in folkloristics. For if memetics can push folklorists to stop talking solely about the particular traditions they love and start focusing on the macro- and microprocesses of tradition itself, it will not have been without significant folkloristic value (Oring 2012b, 220–239).

CHAPTER EIGHT

Four Laws of Folklore

By denying scientific principles, one may maintain any paradox.

—Galileo Galilei, *Dialogue Concerning the Two Chief World Systems*

In "Back to the Future: Questions for Theory in the Twenty-First Century," published in *Journal of American Folklore*, I discussed the interpretive enterprise in which folklorists have been engaged over the past fifty years (Oring 2019c). I suggested that folklorists might return to formulating testable hypotheses about folklore, and in one of the endnotes, I cited Edward B. Tylor's famous dictum in his 1871 work *Primitive Culture*: "If law is anywhere, it is everywhere" (1871, 22). In her response to my essay, Dorothy Noyes stated: "[I do not] think [we should] . . . strip down to laboratory conditions and try to isolate independent variables, if only because if laws do exist it will take a long time to find them while the world passes by in the meantime. But many thinkers better equipped than I have demonstrated to the satisfaction of many of us that the social world does not operate by the same principles as classical physics" (Noyes 2019, 181).

I would agree that the social world—and the world of folklore in particular—probably does not operate by the same principles as classical physics. But should we presume that it works according to no discernible principles at all? Why should laws govern only a narrow range of events in the universe? Would we be wasting our time to see whether we can identify principles to which those objects of our attention conform? And might not the search itself, whether ultimately successful or not, produce new knowledge and lead us to new insights about our common enterprise?

https://doi.org/10.7330/9781646425198.c008

What do I mean by a law? Basically, a law is a statement of a relatively invariable relationship between some X and some Y (Brown 1963, 134). For example, the force of attraction between two objects is directly related to their masses and inversely to the distance between them. Or ritualized joking relationships occur between relatives that are potential sexual partners. Or the rate of suicide in a society increases with an increase in the degree of anomie. Or the price of goods and services in a market society increases as demand for those goods and services increases. Thus, a law has a certain underlying form even though it may be variously formulated in ordinary language.

A law usually begins as a hypothesis rooted in an empirical generalization (Kaplan 1964, 84, 91–92): the discernment of a relationship that seems to characterize an array of observations. But the generalization must move beyond the stage of a hypothesis. It cannot stand on the dataset upon which it was initially established. For example, between 1920 and 1960, it was the big party candidate with the longest last name who won the US presidential election (Kaplan 1964, 92). In 1916, however, Woodrow Wilson defeated Charles Hughes (last names of equal length), and in 1964, Lyndon Johnson defeated Barry Goldwater (the longest last name lost). There is also a generalization that every animal has roughly the same number of heartbeats in a lifetime. An elephant outlives a mouse by a wide margin, but its heart rate is so much slower that they both live about the same length of time in heartbeats. This generalization, however, is vitiated by bats and birds, which have phenomenal heart rates but live, on average, long lives (Ridley 2000, 200–201). A final example is Bode's law ("Titius-Bode Law" n.d.), first published in the eighteenth century, which formulates the distance of the planets from the sun. Except for the gap between Mars and Saturn (where it was assumed a planet remained to be discovered), it approximately described the orbits of Mercury through Saturn. The discovery of Uranus in 1781 seemed to confirm the law, but the law was upended by the discovery of Neptune in 1846, and Pluto and the Kuiper Belt in the following century. So, in addition to extending beyond the range of data that gave rise to it, a law must, at least initially, appear to be true (Kaplan 1964, 92).[1]

There are probably no laws—not even in physics—that do not have exceptions (Kaplan 1964, 96). Even Newton's laws do not always hold.[2] Laws are also constrained by the conditions under which they operate and should be accompanied by statements of those conditions. Thus, Galileo's law of uniform acceleration for free-falling bodies predicts that a feather will fall at the same rate as a hammer. On earth, however, air resistance interferes with the expected outcome. The law should hold true for the feather and the hammer, however, were they dropped in a vacuum. (A demonstration was conducted on the moon by Commander David

Scott of the Apollo 15 mission, where the hammer and the feather appeared to fall at the same rate [Zane 2006]). The prices of goods and services will not go up as demand for them increases if there is a simultaneous and comparable increase in the supply of those goods and services. Economic laws are often formulated on the assumption that rational actors are buying and selling, but actors have been shown to be anything but rational in their economic activities (Kahneman 2011).

The idea of laws for folklore is not at all new. There was a time that folklorists were interested in proposing laws. Folkloristics was not originally conceived as a search for the *meaning* of texts and the *significance* of behaviors but as a search for an *explanation* of them. Folklorists later lost interest in this endeavor. What I propose is to resurrect several laws proposed by folklorists. A few caveats are in order, however. First, there are no laws for folklore in general because folklore is not a unitary phenomenon. Folklore is sometimes defined as art, sometimes as tradition, sometimes as texts or behaviors orally communicated, sometimes as informal culture, and sometimes as an expression or property of a particular kind of social group. Consequently, whatever laws may exist will not be laws of folklore but laws that characterize those groups, behaviors, texts, and events that have been of central interest to folklorists. Second, folklorists and others did not always designate the laws they proposed as *laws* per se. They may have employed other terms or not labeled them at all. Nevertheless, they have proposed principles of relationship between variables that would largely conform to the characterization of law discussed above. Third, these proposed laws may not ultimately prove to be true, but that is a matter for investigation. The point here is to show that folklorists have traditionally been interested in proposing law-like principles and to raise the question as to why these interests evaporated. I also submit that the pursuit of general principles for folklore might prove a worthwhile addition to the discipline's concentration on the meaning of individual texts and events. My contribution to this discussion is limited only to the way these laws are articulated, to the proposal of corollaries, and to suggestions as to how the formulation of laws might lead to a reimagining of folkloristics. Basically, I am reminding folklorists of their past and thinking about a possible disciplinary future.

A first law of folklore that I would identify is that folklore—in whatever form—changes over time. This, however, is hardly a law of folklore but rather a cosmic law. Stars explode and collapse, galaxies crash into one another, new stars are born from intergalactic dust, molecules break apart and recombine, living things die, and new organisms come into being. Change is a law of everything, and a law of everything is likely to prove sterile. The notion that folklore changes over time is a law that leads nowhere. It conditions no particular understandings and provokes no further research. A law of change must concern some subset of the phenomena that is of interest and specify something about how, when, or under what conditions certain kinds of change occur.

Folksong variation has been an interest of folklorists almost since the field got its name. The comparative study of folksong texts has resulted in the characterization of various kinds of change: localization, universalization, personification, conventionalization, literalization, dramatization, lyricization, fragmentation, division, merger, cross-over, expurgation, contraction, bowdlerization, sentimentalization, moralization, rationalization, oicotypification, recomposition, parodization, and degeneration (Burns 1970, 250–253; Abrahams and Foss 1968, 18–19, 34). Some of these kinds of changes are the result of forgetting, mishearing, misunderstanding, or some combination of the three (Abrahams and Foss 1968, 17). Others are changes that are consciously or unconsciously implemented such as expurgation, moralization, or parodization (34). Of course, these terms largely serve to *describe* change rather than characterize principles of change. No general principle has been put forward to explain, for example, why elements of a song are localized in one instance and universalized in another. Both the degenerative and creative changes seem, for the most part, irregular and identifiable only after the fact.

One exception is a proposal by Tristram P. Coffin that characterizes a general course of ballad change and might justifiably be called a law. In Coffin's view, a poem created by an individual enters oral tradition. It has three components: "frills" of poetic style, details of action, and an emotional core. Oral tradition first wears away its subliterary frills, and some of the details of the action are lost as well. Then the ballad takes one of two routes: either (1) *essential* narrative details disappear until only a hodgepodge of verses centered around a dramatic core remains or (2) *unessential* details drop away until only a lyric remains centered around its emotional core. In other words, a ballad moves over time either toward a nonsense song or toward a lyric (Coffin 1957, 210).

It is this second formulation that might be reckoned as Coffin's law of ballad change: in a chain of oral transmission, a ballad will contract into a lyric centered on its emotional core. This certainly was a principle emphasized by Roger Abrahams and George Foss in their book *Anglo-American Folksong Style*, although they never employed the term *law* (1968, 19–29, 37–60). Coffin not only proposed this law but theorized it as well. In Coffin's view, memory depends and interest is focused on those aspects of a song that arouse emotion. The details of action may be forgotten, but not the emotional core.[3]

Coffin illustrated this law with the Child ballad "Mary Hamilton" ([Child #173]; Child 1965 [1882–1906] 3:384–385; Coffin 1957). However, the law has not been scrutinized in terms of the available evidence. Although Coffin claims that other ballads also reflect a reduction to an emotional core,[4] his law has not been put to the test for the full array of 305 ballad types found in Francis James Child's collection, nor for the 546 ballad types listed in George Malcom Laws's indices of American balladry (Laws 1957, 1963). Nor has it been subjected to empirical test. It would not seem impossible, for example, to craft an experiment to see what happens to narrative and lyrical elements in chains of repeated and serial repro-duction of a ballad (as in Bartlett 1920).

A second law of folklore is derived from some of the laws proposed by the Danish folklorist Axel Olrik (1965 [1909]). Olrik was a philologist, and his laws were rooted in his work on myths, heroic epics, ballads, and folktales that appeared in manuscript. He was concerned with identifying which parts of old manuscripts were likely based on oral traditions, and his laws were meant to serve as a means of diagnosis. Consequently, some of his laws might not at first sight seem apposite to the personal-experience stories, urban legends, and jokes that folklorists often grapple with today. For example, his law of opening (*das Gesetz des Einganges*) and law of closing (*das Gesetz des Abschulsses*) state that a folk narrative begins with calm and moves to excitement but moves from excitement to calm at its end. Although these laws would appear applicable to many folktales and ballads, they would not seem to characterize a number of legends or jokes collected today.[5] Nevertheless, several of his laws impress as being relevant even to these genres: notably, the law of two to a scene (*das Gesetz der scenischen Zweiheit*), the law of contrast (*das Gesetz des Gegensatzes*), and the law of repetition (*das Gesetz der Wiederholung*), with its corollary law of three (*das Gesetz der Dreizahl*). In brief, what these laws state is that there will be at most two characters with distinct identities in any narrative scene; these two characters will contrast markedly in their attributes (e.g., rich/poor, wise/foolish, good/evil); and if there is a repeti-tion of a scene in a Euro-American narrative, that repetition would be threefold (generally fourfold in Native American and in South Asian narratives [Olrik 1965, 132–133, 134–136], but fivefold in Nez Percé myth [Stross 1971, 111], and seven- or ninefold among the Land Dyaks of Borneo [Geddes 1957]).[6] These laws pertain to the structure of folk narrative; they do not merely identify aspects of narrative style. The laws of two to a scene and contrast describe the structural properties of a narrative scene in terms of an opposition of the dramatis personae. The law of repetition (threefold or otherwise) is a statement about tale syntax.[7]

What is amazing is that since Olrik first proposed these laws, there has been no systematic effort to see to what extent they hold. His work, of course, has been repeatedly cited as particular laws have been applied to describe individual cases (e.g., Stross 1971; Porter 1976; Danielson 1979; Goldberg 1986; Schmidt 2005; Henderson 2010). But how far do Olrik's laws extend: to what range of genres and in what range of cultures? Under what conditions do they fail and why (Ben-Amos 1992, ix)? What corollaries might they engender? To what extent do these laws also describe literary texts that do not derive from or deliberately imitate oral sources?[8] These questions have not, to my knowledge, been answered or even asked, although Olrik himself suggested that these were matters to be pursued (1965, 141).

It might not be difficult to test some of Olrik's laws by creating texts that deliberately violate them. Narratives could be created with three to a scene, with dramatis personae minimally contrasted, or with two rather than three repetitions in order to see how these texts change when they are launched into chains of oral transmission. Would the texts be reformulated in compliance with Olrik's laws? No one knows because no one seems to have suggested, let alone attempted, the experiment.

Just as surprising is the absence of any attempts to theorize Olrik's laws. Why should these laws—if valid laws they prove to be—obtain for oral narratives? What is the connection between orality and these rules of narrative production? Have they something to do with memory, aesthetics, or sheer cultural inertia? How, in the course of a century, has a theory to account for these laws not been proposed?

A third law of folklore was put forward by Arnold van Gennep in his book *Rites de Passage* (*Rites of Passage*), first published in 1909.[9] Van Gennep's law also identified a structural principle and, in that sense, resembles the laws proposed by Olrik.[10] Van Gennep recognized that rituals that attended the crossing of a geographical frontier had a tripartite structure: rites of separation, rites of liminality, and rites of incorporation (van Gennep 1960, 11). He further recognized that these stages of territorial passage served as a template for rituals of social passage more generally—the passage from one socioreligious state to another (15–25). Van Gennep discussed these stages as preliminal rites that served to separate individuals from their previous statuses, the liminal or threshold rites of the transitional stage, and postliminal rites that served to incorporate individuals into their new social positions.

Van Gennep focused his attention on rites associated with pregnancy and childbirth, initiation, betrothal and marriage, and funerals. Although these did not exhaust the range of social transitions, they were the most important ones to be found cross-culturally. The duration and complexity of the rites might vary in different cultures or under different conditions. (For example, the birth of twins among the Basoko in the Congo required more elaborate rituals and lengthier ritual phases than were normally associated with single births [1960, 47]). Certain occasions emphasized one phase over another; for example, rites of separation were prominent at funerals (146), rites of incorporation at marriages (117). Sometimes, the liminal or transitional stage could become almost autonomous in pregnancy, betrothal, and initiation (11).

Van Gennep also recognized that rites of passage might be mingled with other rites (e.g., rites of protection for the mother during pregnancy, the child at birth [1960, 45], or for the survivors at death [193]). He recognized as well that the identification of the stages of certain rites was not always clear-cut and, on occasion, he questioned his own interpretation (1960, 45). In one instance, he claimed that his stages were discernible in ceremonies of social transition everywhere (18) but retracted this claim of universality in another (161). Nevertheless, what van Gennep proposed, despite his hedging, was a law about the structure of such rituals: a tripartite structure that would be marked by symbols *appropriate* to separation, marginality, and incorporation, respectively. Otherwise, without some restrictions on what the symbols for the particular stages should look like, there is a danger that the law might assert only that a rite has a beginning, a middle, and an end (Gluckman 1962, 9).[11]

Many have made use of van Gennep's notion of rite of passage (e.g., Hollman 1974; Edwards 1996; Coulbrooke 2002; Merten 2005), and some have even elaborated on it (e.g., Turner 1969, 94–130). While there has been discussion of the applicability of his law to specific rituals and to different types of rituals (e.g., Pentikäinen 1979; Honko 1979), there does not seem to have been an attempt to systematically determine the scope of his law; to identify counter-examples; to operationalize the stages of the ritual so they might be unambiguously defined; to identify the conditions under which the expansion and contraction of phases of the ritual occur; to proscriptively identify the types of symbols appropriate to each ritual phase; or to assess the degree to which the phases characterize social passages in societies with secular rather than magico-religious world-views (Gluckman 1962, 36–37; Anttonen 1995). As with Olrik's laws of folk narrative, folklorists have not been spurred to systematically assess van Gennep's law of ritual passage, although, like Olrik's laws, it too was proposed more than a century ago.

A fourth law of folklore concerns superstition. The use of the term *superstition* is deliberate. It is not to be confused with *folk belief* (a term with as many, if not more, problems than *superstition*) even though a superstition is a subcategory of folk belief.[12] I employ a narrow conception of superstition: it is a proposition about a specific relationship between a cause and effect or a sign and its referent (Dundes 1961, 28). In other words, a superstition is itself a species of law—albeit a law that is not generally tested (although it is frequently affirmed anecdotally). What counts as a superstition in this formulation is not something that is merely *known*, or even something that is *believed*, but something that is, at least occasionally, *acted* upon.[13] The action may be positive, such as throwing salt over one's shoulder, or it may be negative, such as avoiding stepping on cracks in a sidewalk or delaying an undertaking on what is deemed an inauspicious day. Furthermore, a superstition is an isolated proposition—it is not part of an explicit and integrated system of propositions (Lesser 1931, 620; Jahoda 1971, 13; Campbell 1996, 156). While the term *superstition* used by early English folklorists originally indexed differences in the beliefs of distinct social classes, the kinds of things I am calling *superstition*—both social and individual—are characteristic of all social classes.

The law of superstition ultimately derives from an observation made by Bronislaw Malinowski about fishing magic in the Trobriand Islands:

> It is most significant that in lagoon fishing where man can rely completely upon his knowledge and skill, magic does not exist, while in the open-sea fishing, full of danger and uncertainty, there is extensive magical ritual to secure safety and good results (Malinowski 1954 [1948]:31).

Malinowski had noted that Trobriand Islanders had a significant body of technical—even scientific—knowledge. When, however, an enterprise was risky and its outcome highly uncertain—when technology alone could not reasonably ensure a positive result—magic and superstition were invoked. Malinowski's observation has been corroborated elsewhere. Texas bay fishing involves fewer superstitions than riskier gulf fishing (Mullen 1969, 218). New England fishermen in a southern coastal town had numerous superstitions, while textile mill workers from the same town had almost none (Poggie and Gersuny 1972, 142). Water-witching (dowsing) was practiced in a western New Mexico town where the water table was variable and uncertain but practiced far less in a similar town in the Texas Panhandle where it was regular (Vogt 1952, 181). Baseball superstitions clustered around the uncertainties of pitching and hitting but rarely around the more governable practices of fielding (Gmelch 2001 [1971], 294).

Malinowski theorized his observations about fishing and other forms of Trobriand magic. Without the technical means to ensure safety and success in the realization of critical objectives, anxiety is generated and displaced into magical practice. Magic begins where practical knowledge ends. It is a form of wish fulfillment that relieves tensions generated by the anxiety-provoking tasks confronting both the individual and society (Malinowski 1937 [1931], 4:639).

It is important to note that it is not folklorists who primarily have been interested in superstition. A considerable literature has been produced by philosophers (e.g., Bush 1932; Kantor 1932), psychologists (e.g., Levitt 1952; Scheibe and Sarbin 1965; Jahoda 1971; Vyse 1997; Rudski and Edwards 2007; Damisch, Stoberock, and Mussweiler 2010), anthropologists and sociologists (e.g., Lesser 1931; Jarvis 1980; Campbell 1996), economists and management researchers (e.g., Tsang 2004; Ng, Chong, and Du 2010; Kramer and Block 2011; Hirshleifer, Jian, and Zhang 2018), and even biologists (e.g., Foster and Kokko 2009; Abbot and Sherratt 2011). And most of them cite Malinowski's observation on Trobriand fishing magic as the foundation of their research.

A second theory of superstition, emerging from an entirely different kind of data, complements rather than challenges the theory promoted by Malinowski. In his experimental work with pigeons, B. F. Skinner discovered that reinforcements—food—introduced independently of a pigeon's behavior nevertheless engendered the repetition of certain behaviors on the part of pigeons that were prior and proximate to the instance of reinforcement and that subsequently proved stable over time. Skinner labeled these behaviors "superstitions" (the quotation marks were Skinner's [Skinner 1948]). In other words, repetitive behaviors that seem to be directed toward producing a particular outcome can result from an accidental behavior that is fortuitously reinforced. In the human world, any relatively successful outcome of a superstitious action might serve to reinforce the practice or avoidance. Returning safely from a fishing expedition with even a modest catch might serve to reinforce behaviors enacted to promote its success. Extinguishing a superstition might prove more difficult, as repeated and unequivocal failure would probably be necessary.[14] The fear, however, that eliminating even a seemingly failed practice might result in an even worse outcome might work against a superstition's elimination (e.g., Rudski and Edwards 2007, 401). There is some evidence that superstitious behaviors with no impact on objective conditions in the world can improve task performance and thus prove to be self-reinforcing (Dudley 1999; Damisch, Stoberock, and Mussweiler 2010).

Thus, we can formulate the following law: When technology and expertise prove insufficient to ensure the positive outcome of an important enterprise, superstition—both individual and communal—will proliferate.[15] The more uncertain the outcome and the higher the risk to the wealth, safety, or reputation of the participants in the enterprise, the more superstitions will be employed, or the more elaborate they will become, or the more stable the superstitions will prove over time. Conversely, as technical mastery increases and serves to reduce uncertainty and risk, superstitious behaviors will diminish or disappear. Furthermore, superstitions will be maintained and even multiply when they are of relatively low cost—that is, when they demand only modest investments of time, effort, or material resources (Vyse 1997, 75, 195).[16]

This law of superstition is one derived from a theory (Malinowski's theory) rather than one that began with a broad empirical generalization based on a large amount of data. Not all laws begin or end as empirical generalizations. In fact, a real law must eventually connect to other laws and theories—that is, it must participate in a larger scientific structure (Kaplan 1964, 92).

The four laws discussed here are not the only ones that have emerged from folkloristic inquiry. There are James G. Frazer's laws of sympathetic magic (1925, 11–20); Walter Anderson's law of self-correction (1923, 399); E. Sydney Hartland's law on supernatural accounts of the founding of churches (Hartland in Dorson 1968a, 232); Linda Dégh and Andrew Vázsonyi's law of multi-conduit transmission (1975); Michael Owen Jones's formula for the creation of a folk hero (1971); Dan Ben-Amos's proposition that the briefer and more stable a folklore text, the more it depends on context for its meaning (Ben-Amos 1993, 213); Mary Douglas's dictum that joking can appear only when there is a joke in the social structure (1968, 366); Katherine Luomala's laws of the dramatis personae in the Polynesian Māui cycle of myths (1980); Vladimir Propp's law of folktale syntax (1968); Iona and Peter Opie's principle that the most popular customs are the ones destined for extinction (1980, 70–71);[17] Henry Glassie's contention that a shift in domestic architecture from openness and asymmetry to self-contained and symmetrical forms presages a period of great political upheaval (1975, 190–193; 1982, 398–401); and Dorothy Noyes and Roger Abrahams's four-stage development of national tradition from local calendar custom (1999). There are yet others.

The point is not whether any of the laws discussed above are correct, although none, upon first inspection, would seem abysmally wrongheaded. The real question is why these laws proposed over the past century have been neglected. Why have they not been assiduously investigated, challenged, constrained, reformulated, or even—after deliberate and critical review—decisively cast aside? Even this last possibility—the rejection of a law following a systematic evaluation—is nowhere recorded in the folkloristic literature. What has happened to convince folklorists that nothing can be true beyond their observation of an individual case?[18]

Laws, hypotheses, and theories are the kinds of formulations that are likely to show us when and how we are mistaken. They are unambiguous (or at least less ambiguous than most of our current interpretive procedures). They require some explicit definition of terms. They point to the kinds of data that can serve to validate or invalidate them. They can operate as a check on our own fertile imaginations as well as on our sense that our interventions will necessarily result in good outcomes if they are well-meant. They can serve to encourage folklorists working with disparate materials, in disparate areas, and with disparate social groups to contribute to a set of common concerns.

We do not simply formulate laws so that we might declare our work finished. Laws direct attention to new observations, new facts, facts previously overlooked, and facts yet to be encountered. In that process, laws are formulated and reformulated to account for old as well as new observations. New theories are proposed to account for the laws. These in turn generate hypotheses that are subjected to test in a search for a better understanding of what we observe in our field research (Kuznar 1997, 68–79). The formulation of laws is not the endpoint of inquiry. Rather, the formulation of laws is a stimulus to research. And it is the proposal of laws—not ethnographic description—that establishes directions for further inquiry (Kaplan 1964, 88). Ethnographic description in the absence of laws, theories, and hypotheses leads only to more ethnographic description; broader, deeper, and more fine-grained perhaps, but still only a grasping at a particular without concern for a more general human condition. The pursuit of laws presumes that human behavior is not always, or even essentially, local, insular, or idiosyncratic. In the pursuit of laws, as Dorothy Noyes observes, time will no doubt pass us by. But it may ultimately prove to be time very well spent.

To Explain Tradition

It was always a beautiful scene, the dance on New Year's Eve, which had been
kept up by the family tradition as nearly in the old fashion as inexorable
change would allow.

—George Eliot, *Daniel Deronda*

Tradition was a central term in the field of folklore even before the term *folklore*
itself was coined. The popular antiquarians, folklore's predecessors, regarded tradition as the central feature of their concern. *Tradition* is the very first word in
John Brand's general preface in *Observations on Popular Antiquities*, in which he
claimed that ceremonies and superstitions from time immemorial, though erased
from the written record, were preserved in the oral tradition of the people (Brand
1777, iii–iv). When W. J. Thoms coined the word *folklore* in 1846, he intended it as
a label for those seemingly "trifling and insignificant" traditions that might form
the basis for a reconstruction of ancient British mythology and religion, a reconstruction that Jacob Grimm had managed to accomplish for German heathenism
in his *Deutsche Mythologie* published in 1835 (Thoms in Dorson 1968a, 52–54).
Tradition and *oral tradition* have remained keywords in the definition of folklore
ever since (Brunvand 1998, 12–13; Feintuch 1995, 392; Bronner 1998, 5).

Yet *tradition* is problematic in folkloristics. When Dan Ben-Amos reviewed
the usage of the term in American folkloristics, he found that folklorists did not
think much about it. It was understood as involving "handing down" but was variously and only vaguely defined (1984, 97–98).[1] Indeed, Ben-Amos identified at
least seven different senses in which the term had been employed: as *lore, canon,
process, mass, culture, langue,* and *performance* (104–123). Ben-Amos concluded
that none of these senses was more proper or adequate than any other, and the

https://doi.org/10.7330/9781646425198.c009   137

term was merely a metaphor to guide folklorists in their dealing with an "inchoate world of experiences and ideas" (124).

Process, however, is more basic than the other senses of the term *tradition*. Folklorists have focused their attention on such things as tales, legends, ballads, riddles, proverbs, charms, costumes, and the like, but these are the products of tradition. *It is process that makes product*, and the process of tradition is one of cultural reproduction: the reproduction, in whole or in part, of previous ideas, practices, and objects (Oring 2012b, 220–224; 2013, 25–26). In the case of oral tradition, it is the reproduction of elements of past ideas and practices resident in the memories and actions of living people. Tradition, therefore, is essentially about continuities ("Final Discussion" 1983, 236; Georges and Jones 1995, 1). The tales, songs, and proverbs that folklorists study are believed to have been repeatedly reproduced overtime.

Tradition research, consequently, is both historical and prospective. This notion, in part, answers the question of the difference between tradition and culture, and it resolves the conundrum that all tradition is culture but not all culture is tradition ("Final Discussion" 1983, 235). When folklorists analyze some particular practice but ignore its situation in and through time, they are focusing on a cultural practice and not a tradition per se, even if they might call that practice a *tradition*. Folklorists often call what they study *traditions*. A proverb, belief, tale, or song may have deep roots in the past. But if that historical connection is not of concern to the folklorist, a concept of tradition really plays little part in the inquiry. If that proverb, belief, tale, or song is not in some sense being considered in a lineage of reproductions, what is being attended to is a cultural behavior. When, however, a cultural practice is approached with a concern for its past or potential future relations through time, a concept of tradition moves to the forefront.[2]

Folklorists—and the general public as well—tend to allot to the word *tradition* a positive value ("Final Discussion" 1983, 234; Salomonsson 2000, 199). Consequently, to call something a *tradition* is in some sense to endorse and enshrine it as part of a valuable legacy.[3] This is largely a consequence of the field's Romantic origins. This presumption has distorted folklorists' studies of traditions emphasizing those that are reflective of community industry, endurance, resilience, and artistry. Accordingly, many folklorists have undertaken to conserve, publicize, and foster the traditions of particular groups (e.g., Baron and Spitzer 1992, 1–3; Feintuch 1988, 1–6). This stance, however, has diverted attention away from traditions that inculcate, support, and perpetuate racist, sexist, classist, and sectarian ideologies and the prejudice, discriminatory practices, and violence that often follow from them.

It should be clear that the process of tradition, the process of cultural reproduction, cannot be restricted to those aspects of culture in which the folklorist happens to be interested. Unless certain forms, behaviors, ideas, and objects are created *ex nihilo*, everything is to some extent the outcome of a reproductive process. Architecture, fine art, opera, ballet, corporate structure, website design, scientific laboratory methods and equipment, and civil and criminal codes of law all reproduce significant aspects of past practices, products, ideas, and designs. As has long been noted, "There is nothing new under the sun" (Eccles. 1:9). Folklorists, however, have only been interested in a select range of traditional products. Consequently, the study of tradition is a problem for a wider array of disciplines than folklore, but folklore is in a position to contribute significantly to this broader inquiry (Oring 2012b, 220–224, 231–235).

The kinds of traditions upon which folklorists focused were those that had been disrupted, were in decline, or were dying. That was part of folklore's Romantic remit. Initially, these traditions were rural; those of peasants and yeoman farmers that had been unsettled by revolutions in technology, transportation, and communication. Later folklorists would turn to other traditions, even industrial ones (e.g., Green 1978; Frisch 1998), that seemed to be fading or were situated in groups that were undergoing dislocation and social disintegration. Consequently, folkloristics has been criticized for being fixated on a dying and disappearing subject. That fixation, it has been claimed, dooms the discipline itself, like its subject, to death and disappearance. To remain relevant, folklorists needed to find a truly contemporary subject (Ben-Amos 1971, 14; Kirshenblatt-Gimblett 1998, 300–302; Bauman and Briggs 2003, 306). The study of tradition, however, is a truly contemporary subject. The contemporary can only be defined in terms of what is maintained from the past, what is marginalized, and what is replaced. The old and the new are mutually constitutive. Folkloristics would make a major contribution to the understanding of society if it could explain the persistence, the marginalization, the death, and the revival of cultural ideas and practices (Oring 1998, 330–333; 2012b, 233–234).

THE QUESTION OF TRADITION

To be concerned with a process of cultural reproduction is to direct attention to the question of how and why a practice succeeds or fails in being reproduced. It calls for the identification of those forces that abet and inhibit the reproduction of the past. Yet the question of how and why past forms, ideas, texts, objects, and practices endure is a critical question that folklorists have for the most part ignored. The English Victorian/Edwardian folklorists realized, just before they themselves disappeared from the intellectual landscape, that they had failed to address some very basic questions: "What is the modus operandi of tradition" (Jacobs 1893, 293); "How and why do survivals survive" (Marret 1920, 3); and why should a tradition "flourish in one place and not in another" (Burne 1910, 32)? These questions are still with us (Nicolaisen 1990, 42; uí Ógáin 2000, 539). I believe it would prove of inestimable value were folkloristics able to answer such questions. A folkloristic approach to tradition should describe, analyze, and theorize the continuity, marginalization, disappearance, and revival of traditions (Oring 1998, 333; 2012, 234).

Folklorists of a century ago would have been entirely comfortable entertaining such questions. Evolutionists, historic-geographic scholars, and functionalists viewed folklore as operating within a world of forces. But later engagement of the field of folklore with matters of structure, meaning, and performance directed attention away from such concerns. The orientations were primarily synchronic and avoided explanations in terms of causes and effects.[4] Structure became a central concern in the 1950s and 1960s and performance since the 1970s. The search for meaning coalesced in folklore studies only in the mid-1980s (Dégh 1983; Honko 1984; Holbek 1985) although it clearly had antecedents (e.g., Dundes 1965). The interpreters of folklore meanings undoubtedly believed that they were also contributing to an understanding of the vicissitudes of tradition. Traditions were maintained because they were *meaningful*. (Calame-Griaule et al. 1983, 154). A tradition would disappear when it was no longer meaningful (Catarella 1994, 474). While the proposition seems plausible enough, it only begs the question: How and why do traditions that were meaningful lose their meaning? Furthermore, is meaning the only criterion that determines whether a practice lives or dies? Do meaningful practices never die, and do meaningless ones never survive? In any event, in the course of a switch from a concern to explain folklore to a characterization of its formal and semantic properties, to interpretations of its messages, and to a description of the dynamics of its performance, the question of the maintenance, marginalization, disappearance, and revival of the past was largely forgotten.

If tradition is fundamentally about continuities, folkloristics has invested much of its capital in the discussion of change. And indeed, change is part of the fabric of our universe. Nothing is exactly as it was a moment before. But rather than recognize tradition and change as inescapably interrelated, tradition would come to be defined solely in terms of change. "Tradition is change" was a catchphrase touted by some folklorists ("Final Discussion" 1983, 183, 236; Klein and Widbom 1994). Alan Dundes defined folklore not in terms of orality or traditionality but in terms of change and variation (Dundes and Pagter 1975, xvii), and there were those who followed his lead. Folklore (the ballad) "exists through change and is defined by its variability. . . . The only stable element is change" (Catarella 1994, 472, 474). "Constant change . . . is viewed here as a central fact of existence for folklore, and . . . I accept it as a defining feature that grows out of context, performance, attitude, cultural tastes," wrote Barre Toelken (1996, 7). That change is a "fact of existence" of folklore, as Toelken stated, I would readily acknowledge. That it is a "defining feature," however, I would question, for if everything is forever undergoing change, it is hard to see how change can be the defining feature of anything.

Folklorists put an emphasis on change because the particular traditions in which they take an interest constantly undergo change in large and small ways. Change is impossible to avoid. Nevertheless, what folklorists might have been trying to accomplish in casting tradition as change is the upending of the impression that the objects of their studies are static, bygone, passively acquired, naïve, unimprovable, unoriginal, fragmented, and—accordingly—inconsequential (Upton 1993, 11–12). By putting the word *change* at the center of their enterprise, folkloristics can be made to appear vibrant, dynamic, and contemporary (e.g., Ortutay 1959, 191). I believe that folkloristics is vibrant, dynamic, and contemporary even without making change its signature, let alone its defining, concern. Yet, without being rooted in a notion of continuity, without explicit recognition of forms, behaviors, ideas, and objects as reproductions of previous forms, behaviors, ideas, and objects, there is no way to identify anything as traditional. Change is what happens to particular practices as they are reproduced and passed on. Cultural reproduction is what defines a behavior as a tradition.[5]

Folklorists, of course, have taken quite a bit of interest in change. But their perspectives on change are not all of a piece. They have conceptualized change in at least four different ways: as degeneration, adaptation, evolution, and innovation. *Degeneration* occurs when there is a perception of loss, whether of content, structure, style, or meaning, as an expression is transmitted through time. *Adaptation* characterizes changes in content, structure, style, and sense as an oral narrative, song, or practice responds to new physical, cultural, and social environments. *Evolution* describes the emergence of one form or state out of another and the means by which this is accomplished. *Innovation* refers to the creative changes that are made in the course of reproduction by individual performers. Three caveats need to be kept in mind with respect to these distinctions. First, change is change. Change is the perceived differences between one expression and another from one moment to another. Degeneration, adaptation, evolution, and innovation are not kinds of change. They represent four different *conceptions* of change. Second, these different conceptions might be applied to the very same changes. In other words, the same change might be regarded as one or another type. For example, a change that might be perceived as an innovation might also be perceived as an adaptation, an evolution, or a degeneration. Third, these conceptions are related, although not strictly related, to different periods. Different conceptions tended to be emphasized at different times in the historical arc of folkloristic inquiry.

DEGENERATION

Degeneration is most associated with the idea that over time change has wrought the deterioration of something that was once alive, pure, and whole. Degeneration is linked with the idea that folklore is a relic, a fragment of past belief and practice. This conception was central to two different approaches to folklore. One focused on folklore as a survival of a savage philosophy that over time had lost its coherence and consequently its significance. Time had served it badly, but fragments remained from which elements of that original philosophy could be glimpsed and perhaps reconstructed. Thus, if a character in a European folktale takes an animal as a husband or a wife (e.g., ATU 425B), this trait is a survival of a savage mythology; a mythology from a time in which humans believed themselves kin to animals and descended from them (Lang 1884, liv–lvii). The other approach was that of romantic nationalism. Johann Gottfried von Herder believed the folksong in the mouths of peasants preserved elements of the poetry created by the ancient founders of the nation (Wilson 1973, 825–828). To the extent that aboriginal poetry changed over time in the mouths of the folk, it necessarily degenerated.

Folklore was, at first, presumed to be ancient and, consequently, a reflection of those past peoples who produced it and not the myriads of individuals who reproduced it. Thomas Percy published his *Reliques of Ancient English Poetry* with the understanding that these ballads and verses could "display the peculiar manners and customs of former times" (Percy 1966 [1886, 1775], 1:8).[6] Similarly, Arvid August Aufzelius published *Svenska Folkvisor från Forntiden* (Swedish songs from ancient times) in the very same year that the Grimms were publishing the first volume of their collection of Märchens (Klein and Widbom 1994, 18). The Brothers Grimm saw the tales that they compiled as part of the nation's folk poetry, which they considered basic to the recovery of the true nature of the German people even more purely, "more vigorously," than folksongs (Zipes 2014, xxiii; Ward 1981 [1816–18], 1:2). Finnish scholars published the oral poetry they collected in the nineteenth and twentieth centuries in volumes of *Suomen Kansan Vanhat Runot* (Ancient poems of the Finnish people).

When something authentic, coherent, and whole is believed to be situated in the past and is regarded as handed down through a chain of transmission—particularly, but not exclusively, through oral transmission—there is no way that that authenticity, coherence, and wholeness can be sustained.[7] Change, *any change*, causes some kind of deterioration of the original. A reproduction, a reproduction of a reproduction, and a reproduction of a reproduction of a reproduction can only result in deviation; a corruption of what was held to be perfect in the past.[8]

That is why the Brothers Grimm were so keen to emphasize the utter fidelity of Frau Viehmann's narration of her tales. "Her memory kept a firm hold of all the sagas. . . . She told her stories thoughtfully, accurately, and with wonderful vividness. . . . Anyone who holds that tradition is so easily falsified and carelessly preserved . . . ought to have heard how closely she always kept to the story, and how zealous she was for its accuracy." The folk, according to the Grimms, "leave the content of [their] tales just as they found them" (Ward 1981 [1816–1818] 1:4). Furthermore, the Grimms themselves underscored the scrupulousness of their own transcriptions: "Our first aim in collecting these stories is exactness and truth. We have added nothing of our own, have embellished no incident or feature of the story, have given its substance just as we ourselves have received it" (Hunt 1884, 1:iii–iv). Yet the Grimms were fully aware that the tales they collected could be found in different versions in numerous other sources—after all, they published extensive comparative notes to their tales (Hunt 1884, 1:337–454; 2:373–583)—and even though they repeatedly and extensively revised and edited the tales in their collection, they nevertheless claimed the faithfulness of the tales to an ancient past, for without a faithful chain of transmission, little of value from the past could ever have been preserved.

Folklorists came to recognize, register, and describe the various kinds of changes that oral traditions undergo. Tales and songs in oral transmission, for example, become localized, universalized, lyricized, or dramatized (Burns 1970; Krohn 1971 [1926], 79–98). Personal and cultural values exert their influence (Burns 1970; Abrahams and Foss 1968, 17; Krohn 1971, 64–70). Bowdlerization, in which certain disturbing words and images are suppressed prior to or in the act of performance, may be the result of deliberate or unconscious processes (Abrahams and Foss 1968, 24–29).[9]

Some of the principles informing such changes were first identified by the psychologist Frederic C. Bartlett in his experiments on the memory, selection, and transmission of narrative materials (1920). These include familiarization; rationalization; dominance; the importance of visual imagery; the intensification of relations of opposition, similarity, and subjection; and a curious "persistence of the trivial"—that is, some trivial element that influences other parts of a story (1920, 33, 45).[10] Linguistic and metrical constructions also exerted their influence (Rubin 1995). This last was also addressed by Julius Krohn, who even noted the possibility of spontaneous creativity (1971 [1926], 83–86, 92).[11]

The malleability of memory and the numerous versions and variants of a tale, song, or custom forced scholars to confront the question of the fidelity of oral transmission. If the original form of a tradition had changed—had deteriorated—in the course of its communication, it would have to be reconstructed. The versions and variants would provide the clues for such reconstruction as they allowed for the inference of an ancestral form that could generate just those versions and variants. Folklorists, consequently, set themselves the task of rooting out the corruptions by a rigorous comparison of texts distributed over time and through space in the pursuit of an archetype: the most complete, most logical, and best form of the tale or song (von Sydow 1948, 207; Krohn 1971, 59; Thompson 1977, 433–436). This was the goal of Finnish scholars in their initial attempts to identify and isolate the original elements of *Kalevala* poetry. What was eventually discovered was that the mythological elements that had been assumed to be an inheritance from an ancient Finnish folk had been borrowed from a larger store of motifs in Scandinavian and other traditions. There was no access to the lore created by an aboriginal Finnish people. Motifs and stories were borrowed and were transformed in the course of their repeated reproductions (Krohn 1971, 14). The originals were, for the most part, irretrievable.

If the depressive fact of change could not be dismissed, change itself could be reimagined. As Julius Krohn wrote, "It is after all not the material per se that is most valuable but rather its artistic transformation. . . . Even if the substance [of the *Kalevala*] has been borrowed in large part from neighbors, it has been nonetheless so independently recast, has attained such an individual Finnish character . . . that the Finnish people can with pride call this epic their own" (1971, 15). In other words, the changes wrought by transmission, rather than destroying the integrity of an ancient national poetry, could be envisioned as what actually imbued poetry with a nation's character and spirit.

ADAPTATION

Folklore no longer contained the spirit of an aboriginal folk preserved through centuries in a fixed and uncorrupted chain of transmission. Folklore was fundamentally changeable, and it was its changeability that made a song a folksong and a tale a folktale. A folksong or folktale was forever adapting to new circumstances. Cecil Sharp had argued that those who would see the transmission of a folksong as a degenerative process should likewise see the final draft of one of Beethoven's symphonies as a corruption of his very first draft (1907, 13). Clearly, however, it was the final draft that Beethoven considered the best, and that was the one that he published. Folksong, for Sharp, was a communal product; "communal in authorship and communal in that it *reflects the mind of the community*" (15, my emphasis). Likewise, what made a folksong for ballad scholar Phillips Barry was that it was subject to "communal re-creation" (Barry 1909, 76), an infinite series of individual re-creative acts (Barry 1933, 5). It did not matter who had created the song, although Barry felt it was always some talented individual. A song became a folksong as it was endlessly reworked in oral transmission. Barry was not very interested in what the song reflected of the people who sang it. He did not regard it as an ethnological document but an artistic product, and the artistic qualities of the folksong, he felt, arose and were refined in the course of its repetition and change.[12]

As early as 1865, William Allingham noted that the ballads owed much of their merit to the "siftings, shiftings, omissions, and additions of innumerable reciters. The lucky changes," he claimed, "hold, and the stupid ones fall aside" (Allingham 1872 [1865], viii). William Wells Newell, working with children's games, was more attuned to the ethnological implications of the changes wrought by tradition. Indeed, it was oral tradition that made American folklore out of what had been British folklore: "Oral repetition soon wore away traces of foreign descent" (1963 [1903], xvi). Ballad scholar Gordon Gerould reiterated Allingham's and Barry's point some years later. Ballads were the product of "the art of tradition" for "traditional impulses and traditional aptitudes acted upon it" (Gerould 1923, 24, 27). They reflected the "opinions and feelings" and "the emotional lives of ordinary people" who re-created them (Gerould 1957 [1932], 134–135) and not those of some primeval ancestors who were said to have spontaneously created them in the throes of their communal celebrations (Gummere 1959 [1907], 22). Thus came the reconceptualization of the notion of change as anathema to the preservation of the spirit of the people in folklore to a notion that change was the means by which the people imbued folklore with its spirit and transformed it into art. Old songs and tales were adapted to new communities, conditions, and tastes. In this fashion, change was rehabilitated in the field of folklore. Change itself was changed from a worry to a watchword.

The passing on of a song, tale, or custom recasts the expression in a new form or style. Traditions come into existence because they are adapted to the conditions of social life, and they disappear when those conditions are altered (Newell 1963 [1903], 12). Carl Wilhelm von Sydow's concept of the *oicotype*—borrowed from the science of botany—was based on this adaptive principle. A widely spread tradition "forms special types through isolation inside and suitability for certain culture districts" (von Sydow 1948, 243n15). Traditions may adapt in certain places and not in others. Hence the uneven distribution of tales and songs across continents (53). Such ideas had been previously proposed. Hungarian folklorist János Erdélyi recognized as early as 1847 that the change of folksongs from place to place could allow the scholar to "draw conclusions [about] . . . the morals and tastes of the people in definite areas" (quoted in Ortutay 1959, 184). Cecil Sharp also recognized that the tastes of individual communities "ultimately determine the specific characteristics of the folksongs of different nations" (1907, 29).

The notion of adaptation found favor among numerous scholars. Thus, Stanley Edgar Hyman, who never used the term *oicotype*, and might never have heard of it, described what happened to English and Scottish ballads when they migrated to the United States.[13] He noted that many of these ballads found no home in the United States at all. Those that did find their way to the New World lost their magical and supernatural motifs. Explicit sex, incest, and kin murder disappeared or were abridged. Tragedy and ominous qualities diminished while Christian, cheery, and comic elements were inserted or amplified (1957). What Hyman was proposing—whether correctly or not—was an American ballad oicotype.

Von Sydow's concept of the oicotype was the inspiration for Lauri Honko's ecological approach to folklore change. Honko identified the kinds of change that can occur in any particular physical and cultural environment. There is what he calls *milieu-morphological* change, which is the change of particular elements of a tradition to make them seem familiar in a new local landscape. For example, local flora and fauna may be substituted for animals and plants that are foreign or strange. It also involves the tying of imported traditions to particular and often unusual sites in the local landscape (1981, 19–22). There is what Honko calls *tradition-morphological* adaptation, in which new traditions conform to an already existing tradition environment. For example, foreign supernatural figures are replaced with local spirits or are absorbed into a more encompassing category like the devil. Other unfamiliar aspects of a tradition may be modified to accord with regional standards. Thus, what are perceived as the immoral behaviors of story actors may be eliminated, reduced, or otherwise normalized. Honko includes in this category the modifications that are made when a particular theme is included in a particular genre, since the expression of a theme, in his view, can change from one genre to another (23–26). *Functional* adaptation refers to the slow but ongoing social factors that rework a tradition. Macro factors may include the current spheres of interest within a community, while micro factors refer to the individual and social factors that condition a tradition in a particular performance (27–32). Finally, there is *ecotypification* itself, which is more comprehensive than the other three types of adaptation both in the concept of the environment to which the folklore is adapting as well as to the range of features that are adjusting. Different environmental zones and different occupational pursuits may reshape folk ideas and practices. And what is reshaped may extend beyond content and genre to structure, contexts, and style of performance (28–33).

Quite a few folklorists hold that adaptation not only describes a kind of change but constitutes an explanation of change as well. "Change occurs each time new variations are introduced. . . . As this process continues, each new invention is adapted gradually to the needs of the society" (Bascom 1953, 286). "Tradition lives only in individual minds as part of the adaptive process of daily life, so it exists in a steady state of change" (Glassie 1994, 252). "Creative storytellers are the ones who modernize and renew the folktale tradition to make it attractive for current consumption" (Dégh 1995, 44). "The creative impulse speaks to the fact that tradition is not and has never been something static, the most stable aspect of any tradition being its ability to change in response to changing needs" (Neulander 1998, 226). "Folklore lives through a generally selective process that ensures . . . that traditions will maintain their viability, or change so they can, or die off" (Toelken 1996, 43). "The adaptation of tradition in a specific milieu is naturally not an end in itself. Tradition is only adapted so that it can continue to exist" (Honko 1981, 32). "Proverbs do not persist or spread for their own sake, as their use and development is dependent on the adaptive environment . . . if they don't adapt they die" (Szpila 2017, 314).[14] "Artists have been able to withstand the competition of more popular forms of entertainment, such as films and television, by adapting their art form to the tastes of contemporary urban publics" (Chatterji 2016, 101). *Kuttiyattam* (Sanskrit folk theater) "is only still in existence because it has adapted to changing times. . . . Art as a dynamic, creative endeavor *is meant to change*" (Lowthorp 2020, 32, emphasis in original).

The first thing to notice about these propositions is that change and adaptation would seem to have become the sine qua non of folklore. Folklore is forever adapting and must do so in order to survive in ever-changing conditions. It would be well to pause for a moment to remember that the materials of folklore were first defined by their *failure* to adapt. They were called *survivals* (Lang 1879, vii); "processes, customs, opinions, and so forth, which have been carried on by force of habit into a new stage of society from that in which they had their original home" (Tylor 1871, 1:15). Survivals could be recognized because they made little sense. They were striking because they were out of step with the times rather than adapted to them. In fact, their meaning could only be grasped through a process of historical reconstruction. How is it folkloristics moved from a conception of folklore as maladaptive to a notion of folklore as ever adaptive without anyone calling attention to this profound transformation?

The second thing to notice is that if folklorists regularly point to instances of adaptations in song, tale, and custom, they have been less inclined to call attention to those instances in which adaptation seems to have failed to take place. For example, how is it that in a Jack tale collected in the Appalachian Mountains of

North Carolina, the protagonist Jack gets employed by a *king* to rid his kingdom of a unicorn, a boar, and a lion? True, the king behaves like any wealthy land-owner in the region (he opens his own front door), but he is still a king and has a *court* (even if that court only assembles around the "courthouse" [Hicks 1963]). No other element suggests anything but an American-backwoods setting for the tale. How was this element of the tale not adapted to the Appalachian landscape as well? How is it that lawyer jokes in India have lawyers arguing before juries even though juries have not existed in India for more than a century (Galanter 2005, 254)? Why does a ballad collected from West Virginia to Wyoming continue to be sung about a "Boston Burglar" or does an American sing about deportation to "Botany Bay" when the transportation of convicts to Australia was officially ended in 1868, and when no American miscreant was ever transported there in any event (Laws 1957, 174–175).[15] The ballad "The Lake of Ponchartrain"—a lake located in Louisiana—adapts to the American western landscape by replacing "the lake of the Ponchartrain" with "the lake of the Poncho Plains"—even if that phrase does not make a great deal of sense—but remains "the lake of the Ponchartrain" in a Michigan version of the song. In fact, American ballads often prefer to maintain nonsensical phrasings rather than adapt to local landscapes and practices (Laws 1964, 74–75). Why is a song that is otherwise known as "The Banks of the Ohio" sung about the River Dee in southern Michigan, although there seems to be no River Dee in Michigan (Gardner and Chickering 1939, 80)?[16] These are admittedly small instances (although there are many others) that perhaps may be explained away case by case, but the major point is that folklorists have not closely examined the numerous exceptions to the oft-cited principle that folklore invariably adapts to its physical and cultural environment.

The third thing should be more than noticed. There are good reasons to inter-rogate the oft-repeated principle that adaptive change is what allows folklore to survive. How does one determine which changes promote survival and which do not? Does a change, even one that is consciously wrought in order to adapt a tra-dition to its environment, necessarily succeed? What should one conclude when several variants of a particular form of folklore—an older form and a modified, newer form—seem to be happily coexisting and equally thriving? What should one conclude when a newly changed song or tale reverts to its previous form in later performances?

Last, and most important, while on the surface it seems perfectly reasonable that folklore forms survive by adapting to changing conditions, it is reasonable only because the proposition masks a tautology: what survives has adapted, and what has adapted survives.[17] The tautologous nature of these propositions is per-haps most obvious in the formulation: "Those variations will alone survive which commend themselves to other singers and narrators and are imitated by them" (Sharp 1907, 11). But what could survival mean for a song, tale, or anything else except that other singers, narrators, or practitioners choose to reproduce them? By *definition*, survival means being reproduced. The two terms—adaptation and survival—are not independently defined. What has adapted survives, and what has survived has adapted. Claiming that change is an adaptation that ensures survival is like claiming that bachelors should prove to be unmarried and then discovering that the hypothesis is repeatedly and everywhere confirmed.

To make a claim about the survival of traditions that would be legitimate, several things would have to happen. (1) One would have to examine traditions that survived and those that have died out and show *how* and *why* the changes they underwent or their resistance to change contributed to their continuation or extinction. (2) What exactly it is that survives or is extinguished needs to be specified. Ultimately, it is not a question of whether the particular opening line of a ballad is "I was brought up in London town" or "I was born and brought up in Boston, boys" changes or is maintained; it is whether the song that follows that first line survives. Survival or extinction should concern some song, tale, or practice as a whole.[18] If change is a determinant of survival, one needs to be clear about what it is that is surviving and identify the changes that make survival probable or unlikely.[19] (3) The question of survival and extinction can only be addressed over a stretch of time, a period in which it is possible to observe versions and variants actually surviving and disappearing. In the short term, pure happenstance may account for the extinction of a variant and have no relation to the nature of the tradition in question. Ultimately, the frequent claims that the survival of a folk tradition can be attributed to adaptive changes and that adaptation is the key to survival is fraught with problems, problems that have not been fully identified let alone resolved.

EVOLUTION

A distinction needs to be drawn between definitions of evolution and theories of evolution. The term *evolution* has several senses. The most basic is that a present state of existence arises from some previous state. This state could be the state of a biological population; the state of a society; the state of a particular institution; the state of a tale, song, or ritual; or the state of human consciousness itself. Unless one holds that something can come from nothing, we are all evolutionists in this basic sense of the term.

A more precise sense of *evolution* is that one state is a transformation of a previous state (Harris 1968, 25). Evolution is about changes in *form* over time. Thus, a series of reproductions might not be considered evolutionary unless a change in form was the result. A history may be said to describe a connected series of events, but it would not necessarily represent evolutionary change (White 1949, 229–230).

The word *evolution* comes from the Latin *evolvere*, meaning "to unroll."[20] Things that are unrolled necessarily have a backward and forward direction. Whatever is changing moves away from its original state, configuration, or position. The claim that evolution should not be confused with *progress* (Pimple 1996, 236) is problematic. The word *progress* comes from Latin roots that mean "to walk forward," and while those steps forward might not necessarily signify an advance along some scale of virtues (Dawkins 1986, 216–217)—after all, war has evolved in terms of its capacity to destroy lives, environments, and cultures—a notion of forward and backward is deeply implicated in the sense of *evolution* as a term.[21]

If a large molecule is gradually broken into its smaller constituent molecules, which later recombine to form the original large molecule, with the cycle repeating *ad infinitum*, would this process be evolutionary? The same might be said of a social organization that repeatedly cycled through a phase of political unification under a chief and then fragmented into an array of autonomous and opposed lineages to be once again united under a leader. Could a process of oscillation be considered evolutionary?

The answer to this question is both yes and no. It depends upon whether one is speaking of *general* or *specific* evolution. If a species adapts over time to changing environmental conditions and then changes back as those conditions revert to their original state, the result would be considered evolution (Dawkins 1986, 178–179), but only in the specific sense of the term. Specific evolution refers to the change of a species or cultural system as it responds to a particular environment. This change is fundamentally local and contextual. General evolution refers to the emergence of higher forms of biological and cultural life as a result of such specific evolutionary adaptations, but it is not anchored in any of those local adaptations. It charts an overall direction in the plethora of local adaptive changes (Sahlins and Service 1960, 12–44). Oscillation would be evolution in the specific sense of repeated adaptation to local conditions, but it would not constitute evolution in the general sense.

Folklorists have regarded the notion of evolution with a degree of repugnance (Pimple 1996, 236). Evolution did hold a place in the theorizing of the Victorian and Edwardian folklorists in the late nineteenth and early twentieth centuries, but this statement requires severe amendment. Evolution dominated anthropological theories of culture at that time. Culture evolved, and in the process bits and pieces of earlier beliefs and rituals were carried into later cultural stages.

These bits and pieces came to be labeled *folklore*. Under this evolutionary conception, however, the materials of folklore themselves were not evolving. They were merely surviving. They were no longer parts, as they once had been, of a coherent and meaningful religio-philosophical system. For some reason, folklorists today seem to regard that Victorian/Edwardian evolutionary theory as Darwinian (e.g., Ellis 2003a, 91). It was not. Absent concepts of variation, competition, and natural selection, an evolutionary theory is not Darwinian. In fact, in the preface to the second edition of *Primitive Culture*, Edward B. Tylor felt he had to explain why he had not mentioned Charles Darwin or Herbert Spencer in the first edition of his work: "The absence of particular reference is accounted by the present work . . . coming scarcely into contact of detail with the previous works of these eminent philosophers" (Tylor 1873, 1:xvi). Tylor was not dissembling. Tylor's evolution was progressive and was predicated upon a belief that a continuous and natural increase in human intelligence and morality accounted for the steady move from savagery through barbarism to civilization. He was influenced by the evolutionary philosophies of Auguste Comte and Nicolas de Condorcet, not Darwin. For Tylor, nothing was competing, and nothing was adapting. Relative fitness in relation to an environment never entered the picture.

If the term *evolution* is not used merely as a synonym for change over time, then the term implies that change is informed by some principle. For Tylor, that principle was an increasing rationality and morality (1871, 2:327, 405–406). For Herbert Spencer, the principle was increasing aggregation, differentiation of structure and function, integration of parts, and a consequent increase in complexity (Spencer 1860). For Leslie White, it was an increasing control of energy (1949, 363–393). For Daniel C. Dennett, it was increasing design (1995, 71).[22] Interestingly, although the notion of progress—what I would call *direction*—has been repeatedly rejected in anthropological science, neither Tylor, nor Spencer, nor White was wrong from an empirical point of view. Human societies began as minimally differentiated, low energy, and, as far as we can tell, supernaturally oriented. Today most societies are complex, high energy, and scientifically oriented. This does not mean that all societies, if left to their own devices, would naturally develop into highly complex, highly technological, scientific societies. It means only that the minimally differentiated, low energy, supernaturally oriented types of society were historically prior, that complex, high energy, and scientifically oriented societies appeared much later, and that the latter somehow developed from one or more of the former. It parallels the recognition in the biological world that single-cell organisms preceded the development of multicellular organisms, which preceded those with differentiated parts and specialized functions. These statements about the order of emergence of societies and cultures do not seem false. Whether these statements are merely grossly descriptive or identify genuine principles upon which predictions can be grounded is another matter. Consequently, the question of whether evolution can be a useful theory for folklore or culture more generally would seem to remain open.

Darwinian evolution identified no guiding principle. Darwin identified no underlying direction for change. He called his 1871 book *The Descent of Man*, not *The Ascent of Man*.[23] What he identified was not a direction but a *mechanism*—natural selection. Darwin did believe that later forms had a competitive advantage over and were responsible for the extinction of proximate ancestral forms, but he did not argue they were in any sense "superior" or "advanced" according to some scale of virtues (Darwin 2008 [1859], 330–331). These later forms, in the course of time, were also destined to be superseded. Nevertheless, Darwin maintained that life unrolls—that is, there was an order to the emergence of species, and once gone, species did not reappear.

Darwinian evolution does hold some small place in the history of folklore theory. Cecil Sharp's model of folk-song change was explicitly evolutionary and Darwinian. Evolution, according to Sharp, is predicated upon three principles: continuity, variation, and selection. A song enters the repertoires of different singers. It undergoes considerable variation. Most change is unconscious, but it can also be the result of deliberate invention (1907, 23). The variations are then selected according to the tastes of the community. Variations that appeal only to individuals will disappear (29).

Axel Olrik promoted a similar perspective with respect to narrative. There is a "struggle for existence" between folk narratives. There are numerous forces—psychological, ecological, and literary—promoting change in the course of narrative transmission (Olrik 1992 [1921], 65–89). Selection will take place and those narratives that are most imaginative and have clear and definite plots will receive preference. Those with unclear plots or which contain conflicting ideas will consequently die out. The result is a richer and more artistic narrative and the raising of "the spiritual level of the narrative world" (63).

Both Sharp and Olrik were largely concerned with the aesthetic development of folklore over time. Aesthetics is a problematic criterion as there is likely a discrepancy between the aesthetic principles of the scholar and those of the singers and narrators they are studying. If selection is operating on the basis of tastes, it should only be on the basis of the preferences of tradition bearers and not folklorists. It would depend, in other words, upon folk-aesthetic criteria. Even ignoring this problem, after so many transmissions over the course of centuries, these songs and narratives should have achieved a perfected form. Unless the aesthetic standards of the singers and narrators markedly change, the songs and tales should reach a level from where there was no room for further development. In any event, neither Sharp's nor Olrik's explicit evolutionary commitments led to any major research programs in folkloristics. There never was, nor is there currently, an evolutionary school in folkloristics.[24]

The disinterest in and the repugnance of later folklorists for theories of evolution was not rooted in any rational analysis. It was largely a reaction to the moral implications of progressive theories emanating from a nineteenth-century, colonial superpower. There is, nevertheless, reason to interrogate the analogy between biological and cultural evolution in empirical rather than moral terms. There are significant differences between the two (see chapter 6). In the biological realm, the Darwinian mechanism proved the solution to a major problem. When Darwin proposed his theory explaining the origin of species as a consequence of random variation and natural selection, his theory brought about a sea change in the understanding of life on the planet. Before Darwin, no explanation could be given for the variety of life forms and the strong resemblances among them, nor could an account be given, in purely material terms, for the elegance of their design. What constituted explanation before Darwin was reference to an intelligent designer who created each and every living being "according to its kind" (Gen. 1:21, 24). Before Darwin, even closet atheists had to acknowledge that God must have been responsible for creation. Darwin's theory showed how living forms could arise from other living forms, why there were detailed and significant resemblances among them, and how there could be the appearance of design in the absence of a designer. Material forces—random variation and natural selection—rather than supernatural forces could account for the variety, the homologies, and the elegant designs.

In the area of culture, however, a theory of evolution is considerably less revolutionary. There was never a necessity to demonstrate that ideas and behaviors were anything other than the products of other human ideas and behaviors. If a pagan society suddenly became Christian, the change could be attributed to the actions of missionaries promoting Christian ritual and doctrine. God might be thanked for having aided the missionaries in their endeavors, but the explanation for the change did not require an invocation of the supernatural. That new ideas and behaviors could be adopted and old ideas and behaviors given up was not a mystery. Ideas were related to one another and gave rise to new ideas. Everyone accepted that an elegant design in culture could be attributed to human intention and ingenuity. It was understood that people could remember, forget, imagine, invent, and choose.

When compared with cultural change, biological change is depressingly slow. By virtue of its embodiment in living organisms, the rate of biological change is constrained. Transmission is also constrained since, for the most part, it can occur only vertically. Biological inheritance is from parent to offspring.[25] Perhaps it is true, as Richard Dawkins maintains, that it is genes that are ultimately selected in the evolutionary process (1976, 12). Nevertheless, it is the organism that the genes create that directly interacts with the environment. It is only the relative fitness of the organism in a particular environment that gives it an advantage in reproduction (even if that advantage is simultaneously an advantage for its genes as well). But that organism must prove relatively stable over time, otherwise the advantage conferred by some random mutation would have no opportunity to be selected. Any particular trait—even a detrimental one—might survive in the short term, if only by sheer good luck, and a beneficial trait might be extinguished through an equal measure of bad luck. A beneficial trait, however, is one that confers an advantage that can endure over the long term. In each generation, it enhances the reproductive viability of that organism relative to those organisms without the trait. Over time, the population with the trait comes to outnumber and supplant the population of those without it. If an organism varied wildly, with a variety of different traits appearing and disappearing in successive generations—blinking on and blinking off, so to speak—selection could not operate. There would be no feature or features of the organism that could be selected for. Reproduction that favored a particular trait could not occur. There would be populations of organisms with widely varying traits whose nature and distribution changed in every generation. There would be continual change but no basis for the establishment of new species.

Such constraints do not apply to cultural reproduction. Transmission can be both horizontal and vertical (vertically up as well as down). Anyone can potentially be the recipient of an idea. In the biological world, selection operates on the organism. Lacking the constraints imposed by corporeality, cultural ideas and their expressions can and do vary significantly from generation to generation, that is, from reproduction to reproduction. The ballad, the tale, the dance, and the ritual are not so much replicated as re-created. A tale, for example, might, all within the space of a single transmission, gain motifs; lose motifs; drop, add, or invert plot functions; or combine with another tale entirely. The texture of a tale—its diction, meter, rhyme, alliteration (Dundes 1964)—might vary from performance to performance. This is even more true of genres like legend and joke, which have fewer textural constraints than other forms.[26] In fact, a received joke might be passed on as a legend or a legend as a joke in the course of a single transmission (Kapferer 1993; Evans 2018). Under such continuously changing conditions, what traits could be selected so that they would ultimately come to characterize a new form? Cecil Sharp recognized this problem over a century ago. He emphasized that a basic continuity in song reproduction was essential to the process of evolution. "Insistence on the type must be the rule and variation the exception. Otherwise, types would be so quickly changed and multiplied that their relationship to one another would be obscured, their genealogies concealed, and order would give place to chaos" (Sharp 1907, 16).

Biological evolutionists are more concerned to identify the particular advantage an organism acquires as a result of a mutation (even if they often have to guess at what that advantage might be). Cultural evolutionists rarely require that a cultural trait be scrutinized in terms of its contribution to the survival of the individuals that adopt it. Nor is the failure of a group to adopt a trait shown to result in that group's extinction. The success of a cultural trait is often reckoned in terms of its own proliferation, which is to say, the success of a trait is reckoned in terms of its own success (Dawkins 1976, 207–208).[27]

The mechanism that propels Darwinian evolution is differential reproduction. Some living forms in an environment reproduce less and, consequently, are extinguished over time by those that out-reproduce them. The identification of this mechanism resolved an enormous problem in the life sciences in the mid-nineteenth century. But differential survival and extinction are not the answer to the question of tradition, they stand at the very core of what needs to be explained: why do some traditions survive while others disappear?

INNOVATION

Another conceptualization of change erupted into folkloristic consciousness with a study of a completely different problem—the authorship of the Homeric epics. Were these poems oral or literary productions? Were they created by a single author or compiled and edited from the works of several authors? If they were oral, how to account for the preservation of the epics and the fantastic memories of their poets (Lord 1965, 7–12)? Milman Parry and Albert Lord took themselves to Yugoslavia to record and analyze a still functioning oral epic tradition. They discovered that such epics were *oral formulaic compositions* generated in the act of singing but produced from traditional poetic meters, formulas, themes (i.e., episodes), and plots. The epic singers were at once both the composers and the performers. They were not merely the carriers of a tradition—although they were that—but artists making and remaking the tradition as they performed (13). And although the singers often claimed to be able to reproduce a song heard only once, or to repeat a song that they had previously sung word for word and line for line, mechanical recordings demonstrated that there was considerable variability in what they produced, although all were recognizable versions of the same story and employing similar formulas (26–29, 69–70, 72–77, 236–241).[28]

Parry and Lord's work deepened the sense of an individual performer as the source of contemporary artistic creativity. There was no degeneration from a pure, inspired, ancient original. Parry and Lord's vision was more than a realization that some epics were art or that some epics were more artful than others; the oral epic was a composition in the moment of performance. Each epic performance was the creative accomplishment of an individual singer. True, the singer was working with metrical units, formulas, themes, and story lines that had been learned from previous singers, but the individual performance was the result of the singer com-posing a song in response to the exigencies of the moment through the filter of his own aesthetic preferences (see Başgöz 1975).

Of course, the notion that the forms of folklore were artistic was old. In the eigh-teenth century, Herder had acclaimed folk poetry for its ability to inspire a vibrant national art (Clark 1955, 253). The Grimms saw their Märchens as part of that repository of folk poetry. In the nineteenth and early twentieth centuries, ballad scholars argued over the aesthetic merits of what were perceived to be old and new ballads and whether that merit, or the lack thereof, was the result of their trans-mission through oral or printed channels. However, the push to place art and per-formance at the center of the folklore enterprise arose only in the mid-twentieth century. Only then did folklore come to be *defined* as an artistic product. William Bascom proposed that folklore was "verbal art"; a creative act situated in an inter-action between a performer and an audience (1949; 1955, 248–250). In the 1960s and 1970s, Roger Abrahams (1968, 143–145; 1977, 83), Dell Hymes (1971, 45; 1981, 81), Dan Ben-Amos (1971), and Richard Bauman (1975, 1977) were the foremost, if not the only (see Jansen 1957; Ortutay 1959, 181, 190), promoters of this reconceptu-alization of folklore. Their joint premise was: (1) folklore performance was a soci-olinguistic event that demanded a comprehensive grasp of the context in which the communication took place, and (2) folklore was viewed not merely as a com-munication but an "artistic communication in small groups" (Ben-Amos 1971, 13). Change that occurred in the course of folklore transmission was to be perceived "as a result of deliberate, intentional . . . choices introduced by the individual artist whose creative genius is not content with mere imitative repetition" (Nicolaisen 1990, 45). This realignment of the folklore project had considerable influence both within and outside the field of folklore (Rudy 2002). Bauman defined the notion of performance as "the assumption of responsibility to an audience for a display of communicative competence" (1975, 293; 1977, 11). In other words, art, in some sense, is constituted by performance rather than the other way around.

There are changes that can be regarded as creative or innovative, emerging in the moment of performance (or even before). But there are things not to like about the notion of creativity or innovation. Pointing to creativity is like attributing things to God; it puts a stop to all further questioning. Creativity becomes a prime mover. There is no getting behind it. It stands as a force beyond which there is no appeal. If creativity itself could be analyzed, broken into psychological and social parts and processes with their mechanisms laid bare, it would no longer be creativity but something that could be elucidated, a result of specifiable, determinative forces. The appeal to creativity is much like the Romantics' appeals to genius; something that simply is and lies beyond rational or material explanation.[29] We can discuss creativity from now till doomsday without learning anything about tradition as a process other than to say that cultural reproduction sometimes occurs in unanticipated, interesting, and perhaps appealing ways. But if we want to answer the question "How is it possible for a viable and vital folk tradition to continue over a span of centuries without diminution" (Nicolaisen 1990, 42), the concept of innovation or creativity seems likely to prove woefully insufficient.[30]

This is why "performance theorists" eschew the problem of tradition altogether. For them, tradition is a trope; it is a reference to the past invoked in the course of a performance (Bauman 2004, 25–28, 147). Richard Bauman calls this not *tradition* but *traditionalization*, a term employed by Dell Hymes to refer to "what people do to keep a sense of traditionalized identity alive."[31] The traditional only exists when someone invokes it, when "an effort to traditionalize has brought it into being" (Bauman 1975, 354). In other words, traditionalization is a discursive act that may or may not have real-world referents.[32] There is no allusion to actions, forces, or causes. It is talk, and while talk can itself be a cause (although no one has as yet specified what kinds of talk necessarily engender material effects), it is only one cause among many.

I have nothing against the close study of performances. Ethnography is, after all, the basis for everything folklorists do. The actions of people engaged in singing songs, telling tales, posing riddles, or uttering charms is where the folkloristic project begins. A focus on artistic creativity grants the folklorist a sense of wonder and admiration at the products of individual performers and a respect for their abilities as well as a respect for the various communities in which those abilities are nurtured. It allows for the delineation of the principles operating in an individual's or group's aesthetics expression (e.g., Hymes 1981b). But what the study of performances has given us to date is microscopic analyses of particular events that do not seem to speak to some of the larger questions in the study of tradition (also see Limón 1977, 48).

All in all, the conceptions of change held by folklorists have not been particularly helpful in explaining either change or the continuity of traditions. What has been offered has been more in the nature of description than explanation. The changes that have been conceptualized—degradation, adaptation, evolution, innovation—characterize, rather than explain, change, and they do not address the continuity of tradition: what it is that makes a tradition a tradition in the first place. I believe Lauri Honko erred in suggesting that the question of continuity was the least problematic or fruitful for folklore research (2013, 325). For the problem of tradition continuity is one with the problem of tradition change. Those traditions that are stable are subject to the very same array of forces that promote change in other traditions. So why are some past practices eliminated or transformed when conditions change while others are hardly altered at all? For those traditions that endure, what is the source of their stability, their resistance?[33]

We are deceived if we believe that traditions continue through some kind of inertia. A tradition needs to be reproduced both within a generation and between generations. Tradition is a matter of action, of doing. If a tradition continues, it is because there are forces that keep people acting in the same manner as before. It may be that these are the same forces that previously operated. It is also possible that a new set of forces has come into existence that nevertheless serves to maintain the tradition in something akin to its previous trajectory. The point is that forces are always operating, both in the maintenance of traditions *and* in their transformation. There is no situation in which forces are not in operation. Tradition should not be conceived as some passive space into which innovations diffuse (Rogers 1995). All traditions were once innovations. To understand traditions, how and why they thrive or perish, the folklorist needs to identify and understand the conditions that keep them in place. Where there was once a field of study that addressed social and cultural change, folklorists need to confront the question of social and cultural *unchange*.

ADDRESSING THE QUESTION

To try and get at answers to these kinds of questions, it might be best to start with both microscopic and macroscopic approaches. In fact, there already are any number of propositions as to what causes the extinction of traditional ideas, expressions, and practices: industrialization, printed and electronic communication, urbanization, rapid transportation, state-subsidized education, wage employment, missionizing, and all the other interrelated social changes that fragmented rural economic, social, and intellectual life. The question is how these kinds of social changes *specifically* operate to obliterate or abet the kinds of traditions in which folklorists are interested. One way to start to answer such questions is through targeted ethnographies of areas undergoing social, ideological, technological, economic, and political change with a focus on the specific influence of such changes on traditional practices, that is, detailing the processes by which changes weaken or enhance those practices.[34] Such ethnographies would not be engendered by interest in a particular community or a particular tradition but by the framing of a particular question: what specific effects do new forces have on oral traditions and how are these effects achieved? Of course, this kind of research is by no means new. It first became a concern in research (generally under the term *acculturation*) as anthropologists recognized that their attempts to observe and reconstruct the state of "primitive" cultures led them to ignore the great transformations that were unfolding before their eyes as a result of contact with more technologically and socially powerful societies (Herskovits 1937, 263–264).[35]

Comparative ethnographies might allow for the identification of the kinds of traditions that are most resistant to the forces of acculturation across space and time and the means by which this resistance is successfully realized. Such ethnographies would also examine why a tradition persists in one place while a similar tradition seems to be disappearing in another. Such comparisons are not unknown to folklorists, but they are, for the most part, rare.[36]

Another approach to the question of tradition emerges from what Dan Sperber has called an "epidemiology of representations" (Sperber 1996, 25–27). Human cultural ideas and behaviors exist as mental representations and as the products or effects of those representations. The basic question posed by an epidemiological approach is, "Why are some representations more successful than others in a given human population?" In order to answer such a question, the distribution of various representations has to be explored (49). What mechanisms account for such a distribution? What conditions favor the spread of particular representations and what conditions limit them? What conditions would result in their demise? Ultimately, the questions that are being asked are the very same ones being asked about tradition. Why and under what circumstances are certain traditions successfully reproduced while others are extinguished?

An epidemiological approach is not merely concerned with mapping of distributions (although mapping should not be overlooked). The approach is both psychological and ecological. There is an effort to identify the psychological dispositions and ecological conditions that cause representations to appear, spread, split, merge, change, and die (Sperber 1996, 83). For example, Sperber identifies memorability, repetition (i.e., Walter Anderson's law of self-correction), changing cultural background, incentives to recall and perform, and story attractiveness as factors that affect the reproduction and transformation of a mythic narrative (94–95). He is concerned to identify *attractors*: factors that bias microtransformations of a representation in a particular direction (112).

An attractor is not a material thing. It is often a psychological disposition; a tendency or bias to act in a certain way (or in the avoidance of other ways). There are social biases that favor the reproduction of the behaviors of prestigious indi-viduals and those that favor reproduction of what a majority of people are doing (Linton 1940, 473; Herskovits 1945, 169; Boyd and Richerson 1985, 10; Rogers 1995, 18, 27–28). There are indications that information of a certain type is more likely to be reproduced: information that seems mysterious (Sperber 1996, 90) or counter-intuitive (Stubbersfield and Tehrani 2013), disgusting (Heath, Bell, and Sternberg 2001; Nichols 2002), morally positive (Stubbersfield et al. 2019), fear inducing and salacious (Best and Bogle 2014, 47–58, 66–68), amusing (Stubbersfield, Teharni, and Flynn 2018), or promoting sociability and survival (Stubbersfield et al. 2015). An attractor could also be an external force demanding compliance; that is, an explicit directive to behave in a certain way so as to avoid punishment (e.g., Morin 2016, 146).[37]

Cultural epidemiology is open to close ethnological investigation as medical epidemiology would be open to the investigation of group behavior and patterns of social interaction. Olivier Morin is more concerned with the spread of tradition at a higher level of abstraction. He focuses on the structure of diffusion chains and what sustains them over time and space. He does not believe that the stability of tradition is chiefly dependent upon memorability and faithful reproduction. Rather, it is the frequency of transmission, redundancy (receiving transmissions from multiple sources), and the proliferation of divergent chains of transmission that predict tradition longevity.[38] Quantity of transmission trumps quality (Morin 2016, 124–125, 128–132). Therefore, the stability of a tradition heavily depends upon the level of accessibility of the members of a population—their contact with greater or lesser numbers of people. Some populations can engage in more frequent transmission than others. Accessibility, consequently, is shaped in large part by population densities, settlement patterns, generational turnover, commu-nicative and storage technologies (art, writing, print, analog and digital recording), and institutional arrangements (137–138).

For a robust tradition, there must be abundant and repairable chains of dif-fusion (Morin 2016, 122). Diffusion or transmission chains can be described as *extended* over distances of time and space, *short* in the smaller number of trans-mission nodes (i.e., transmitters) in the chain, *wide* in the number of chains radi-ating from a few individuals, *narrow* if there are only a few parallel chains, and *compact* when there is a larger number of nodes through which a tradition is transmitted in a given distance. Narrow chains are like knotted ropes, wide chains are like macramé. Thus, a long, narrow, and compact chain may cover signifi-cant distances, but it does not proliferate very much and should prove unstable over time. Accessible populations will display a wide variety of diffusion chains, while the chains in less accessible populations will tend to be restricted. Wide or extended chains will tend to be short, and long chains compact and narrow. With even less accessibility, long chains will be compact and narrow (138–140).[39]

The success of a tradition depends primarily on its prevalence in a population. The most prevalent are most likely to be retransmitted as they are most available (Morin 2016, 141). Attractors are important as well, but restricted and general attractors are to be distinguished. Restricted attractors are local, specific to a particular sociocultural or physical setting. General attractors span a wide variety of settings and circumstances and consequently are likely to be psychological in nature. They should cause traditions to diffuse more easily because of their wider appeal (146–147). Distinguishing between general and restricted attractors is not simple, as the effects of local restricted attractors can mask the effects of more general attractors. Consequently, general attractors become visible with extended, narrow, and compact diffusion chains, which are established in many individuals over long distances. The transmission is not exposed to the bias of a few individuals, and it is transmitted through a variety of sociocultural and environmental milieux (163–164).

Those folklorists in the first half of the twentieth century that employed a historic-geographic methodology were engaged, to a certain extent, in epidemiological studies. They were concerned with the distribution of a folklore form through time and across space. However, they were primarily engaged in trying to identify a Patient Zero—that is, with the reconstruction of an archetype for a tale, song, or gesture—but less concerned with trying to establish which subtypes succeeded at the expense of others, where they succeeded, and, most importantly, how and why.

More than other folklorists, Bill Ellis has been thinking epidemiologically. After the attack on the World Trade Center in New York City on September 11, 2001, he mined Internet data in an effort to see when jokes about the event emerged, which were most popular, and whether there was some rationale for the sequence of their appearance. He reported that there was an initial latent period in the week following the attack when any small efforts at humor were severely condemned. Then the humor began to appear in waves that could be distinguished in date, origin, tone, and subject matter. Certain jokes that arose in the United Kingdom soon after the event could not successfully be transmitted to the United States because of cultural and linguistic barriers. Ellis's approach to the question of the spread of jokes was novel for its use of time-stamped data and the ability to follow humor on both joke message boards and online forums that had nothing to do with humor (Ellis 2003b).

Even more sensitive to epidemiological conceptions was Ellis's discussion of the spread of urban legends. Exploring the analogy between biological viruses that infect the body and ideas or memes that infect the mind (Dawkins 1976, 203–215), Ellis began to consider legends as both infectious agents and a potent part of an immune response to such infections. Certainly, a virus composed of a strand of nucleic acid can infect an individual, reproduce, spread to an entire population, to eventually become dormant or die out completely. Many of those infected produce antibodies that remain in the body and create resistance to further infection. Ellis thought that legends might act in a similar way. They could infect the mind, but they also trigger debates about their plausibility and veracity. They can generate "anti-legends" as well: stories that challenge or ridicule the beliefs motivating the legend (Dégh and Vázsonyi 1976, 112–113). Ellis sees the debates and the anti-legends as informational antibodies reflexively deployed by the brain as part of a natural immune response to infections by packets of alien information (Ellis 2003a, 85).

Others have made some inroads into the question of distribution. Joel Best and Kathleen A. Bogle explore the dissemination of urban legends/rumors of teen sexual activities—specifically about shag bracelets and rainbow parties—in the first decade of the twenty-first century.[40] Their study did not and could not follow chains of oral transmission and was largely limited to online research. They amassed, however, a corpus of about twenty-five hundred media accounts—books, newspapers, pamphlets, television programs, talk shows—as well as online comments posted on various websites concerning such activities. The great majority of these materials could be assigned dates, and media reports could be geographically situated as well. What they found was (1) the relatively sparse mentions of these sexual practices in online discussions increased dramatically when media reports appeared about them, and the discussions likewise diminished when media coverage declined. (2) The legend/rumors came in waves peaking and almost disappearing, then peaking again several years later. (3) Media coverage of the purported sexual practices was first concentrated in the United States with eventual spread to Canada, the United Kingdom, Australia, and Ireland. Media coverage was not equally distributed in other English-speaking countries, however. Reports in the United Kingdom and Ireland, for example, grew substantially in the second wave, whereas reports in the United States decreased significantly. Overall, however, there were two peaks with a deep valley between them. (4) The researchers were able to identify variants of the legends, some of which were long- and others short-lived with some variants being associated with a particular country (Best and Bogle 2014, 21–44).

A third approach to the question of why traditions are maintained or disappear is experiment. Most folklorists seem to imagine that experiments are procedures carried out in laboratories by people in white coats with precision instruments wielding an array of statistical methods (Noyes 2019, 181). While a good number of experimentalists probably do conform to this image, the conception is far too narrow. An experiment is simply a *controlled and systematic observation*. It is an observation that is deliberate, purposive, and capable of producing results that are contrary to wishes or expectations. It is an observation that should be—at least conceptually—repeatable, and the results of the observation should be intersubjective; that is, there should be agreement by different observers as to what has been observed (Kaplan 1964, 126–128). The results of the observation should be capable of generating, as well as testing, hypotheses about the world.

There are various kinds of experiments: heuristic experiments, exploratory experiments, boundary experiments, simulation experiments, nomological experiments, crucial experiments, and pilot studies (see Kaplan 1964, 148–152). And experiments can be performed using first-hand ethnographic observations, published ethnographic accounts, archival records, maps, archeological data, surveys, tests, cross-cultural statistical data, and data produced under laboratory conditions. The crucial element of an experiment is a *design* that leads to a specific and previously unknown observation.

Designs can include natural experiments where a dramatic change in a social group allows for considering that specific change to be an independent variable whose effects can then be discerned on other beliefs and practices (Pelto and Pelto 1978, 272–273). Field experiments can be constructed in which the change is actually brought about by the researcher as when, for example, a new item of technology is introduced where it had not previously been known (273–274). Groups or situations that differ across a narrow range of factors may allow for a two-case comparison, so that a difference in beliefs or behavior can be hypothesized to stem from those factors of difference. For example, the Nupe and the Gwari of Nigeria are similar in many respects except that women in Nupe society have considerable economic and social power, and witchcraft accusations among the Nupe are directed largely at women. Witchcraft accusations among the Gwari reflect no gender bias. The Korongo and Mesakin of the Nuba Mountains in Sudan are also similar societies, but the Mesakin have three age classes while the Korongo have six. Consequently, the passage to old age is more gradual among the Korongo and better accepted than it is among the Mesakin. The Korongo have no reported witchcraft beliefs. The Mesakin are dominated by such beliefs, and accusations are mainly directed by mothers' brothers at their sisters' sons who claim inheritance gifts that highlight the retirement of their uncles from societal affairs (Nadel 1952). There can be more broadly based cross-cultural statistical comparisons to try and discern whether two factors covary across a range of different cultures such as the presence and length of postpartum sexual taboos varying with tropical climate, poor nutrition, supervision of female labor, polygyny, and the presence of unilineal descent groups (Pelto and Pelto 1978, 259–260; Saucier 1972).

In the past, there was something of a tradition of experiment in folklore (e.g., Anderson 1951, 1956; Schier 1955; Goldstein 1967; Başgöz 1975; Dégh and Vázsony 1975; Labrie-Bouthillier 1977; Burns and Burns 1976; Poggie and Gersuny 1972; Oring 1978; Smith 1974, 1975, 1978, 1986) if not a particularly robust one. Most, but not all, of the experiments were variations of the experiment by Bartlett on folklore recall and transmission (1920). Because an experiment is no more than a special kind of observation, it combines easily with both ethnographic and epidemiological approaches to the question of tradition maintenance and extinction.

For example, Olivier Morin was interested in testing the idea that children's culture was capable of sustaining traditions with a longevity comparable to that of adult traditions (Morin 2016, 252). Children's culture has its own independent trajectory. Games, game formulas, and play rules are transmitted from child to child largely independent of adult supervision or interference. A generation in a child's play group turns over in about seven years. In that interval, the personnel in the group have been replaced. Assuming fifty years, a low figure, for generational turnover in a normal human population, seven generations of children's play groups and their traditions have passed. Children's traditions should be exceedingly fragile and decay and die out sooner than others, sooner certainly than the traditions of adults (199).

To test this hypothesis, Morin looked to see which of the 217 games mentioned in François Rabelais's *La vie très horrifique du grand Gargantua, père de Pantagruel*, first published in 1534, survived to be named or described in both earlier and later French sources. The list had to be narrowed down to 103 games, and the methodology of the investigation is somewhat complex. Nevertheless, Morin discovered that children's games are, on average, at least as long-lived as those games played by both adults and children, and last considerably longer than those solely played by adults (Morin 2016, 261–266). Morin believed that children's game traditions are stable over the long term because of repetition and redundancy: they are repeated over and over, and they are learned from various performers through various performances. Furthermore, these traditions proliferate: they spread along radiating diffusion chains and are not dependent for their survival on any single one.

CODA

What follows is a concrete illustration of the kind of questions that I am asking about tradition. It concerns some counting-out rhymes that children employ in choosing an *It* for a game or in choosing up sides for teams. Cognitive psychologist David C. Rubin, in his book *Memory in Oral Tradition* (1995), shows how such rhymes can remain stable over many generations of children. A counting-out rhyme is used to count people, and it must be recognizable for children to accept its results as valid. Consequently, counting-out involves repetition, alliteration, and assonance in addition to rhyme and a regular meter because their poetics make them memorable and constrain within narrow limits the possibilities of their variation over time. Thus, in a rhyme like *Eenie meenie miney mo / catch a tiger by the toe / if he hollers let him go / eenie meenie miney mo*, what is caught—in this case, a tiger—in the second line can only be replaced by a two syllable word, and it has to be something that has toes or at least something that can be described as having feet, and indeed, virtually all variants of the second line of the rhyme adhere to this principle so that on occasion monkey, rabbit, piggie, and froggie have been found in the place of tiger (240–241).[41] While the poetics of the verse allows Rubin to explain the stability of rhymes, he is at a loss to explain how *Eenie Meenie Miney Mo* came to replace a different rhyme in the counting-out repertoire of children. Before *Eenie Meenie Miney Mo* became dominant, another rhyme seems to have held pride of place among English-speaking children: *Onery, twoery, tickery, teven / alabone, crackabone, ten and eleven / Tweedleum, twadleum, twenty-one.*[42] Rubin noted the increase in meaningful words and phrases in *Eenie Meenie* over *Onery Twoery*, but this merely describes a difference and does not explain why one rhyme should have replaced the other in children's repertoires (247–250). In fact, a comparison of common English counting-out rhymes with rare counting-out rhymes showed no significant difference in their proportions of meaningful and meaningless words (231–232). And nonsense words in a counting-out rhyme might seem more magical and thus more suitable to what is essentially a divinatory procedure.[43] Children do alter texts so they make sense, but they also accept and maintain nonsense (Bauer and Bauer 2007, 188).

Carola Ekrem noticed something similar in the children's rhymes of Finland Swedes. The rhyme *Äppel päppel pirum parum puff / kråkan satt på tallekvist / hon sat ett hon sa tu / ut skall du vara nu* (Äppel päppel pirum parum puff / the crow sat on a pine branch / she said one she said two / and out you go now) has flourished for over a century both among Swedish- and Finnish-speaking children in Finland. Yet the rhyme *Kalle Lång fick en gång / höra på en vacker sång / ding dång ding dång / ut med dig för denna gång* (Kalle Lång did one time / listen to a beautiful song / Ding dong, ding dong / and out you go this time) lost much of its popularity. Ekrem notes that the most popular rhymes were increasingly "action rhymes," which probably means that nonsense phrases are replaced by meaningful phrases describing actions; an observation not out of keeping with Rubin's comment about *Eenie Meenie Miney Mo* (Ekrem 2000, 293–295; Rubin 1995, 249). But again, Ekrem's observation is simply that. It is descriptive but not explanatory. No reason is given as to why more sensible and action-based rhymes should replace nonsensical ones, nor would these observations precisely explain the continued popularity of *Äppel Päppel* or the decline of *Kalle Lång*.

So why are certain children's rhymes long-lived, and why do these long-lived rhymes come to be replaced by new ones? Is there a general trend to replace nonsense rhymes with more meaningful ones? If so, how does one account for this trajectory? And what part would this tendency play in formulating an explanation? Both *Onery Twoery* and *Kalle Lång* were stable prior to their decline. Neither would appear to have challenged children's memories or behaviors. So, what happened?

One might think the example of children's rhyme is somehow trivial. It is not. In fact, it might be argued that if folklorists are unable to account for stability and change in children's rhymes, they are unlikely to be able to account for stability or change in anything else.[44] Furthermore, why traditions are maintained and discarded, although a major question, need not require a major answer. Answers can, and probably should at first, be small, local, partial, and tentative. But whatever answers are proposed, they should also be somehow testable. They should move from interpretation to evidence-based explanation (Oring 2019c, 144–147). Only then will folkloristics begin to make a major contribution to understanding the forces that give rise to traditions, give them shape, and determine their fates. Only then will our inquiries begin to resemble the "Science of Tradition" that was imagined in the earliest period of folklore's history (E. Sidney Hartland quoted in Dorson 1968b, 243).

Of course, why traditions survive or die in particular times and places is not the only question that can be asked about them. Folklorists also pay attention to emic notions of continuity and change in traditions. Informants can provide their own descriptions of change, articulate reasons for change, and describe the means by which they believe change occurs. How and when individuals invoke the past—traditionalization—are part of a study of tradition; or one should say, the rhetoric of tradition. Likewise, the meanings of traditions are open to both etic and emic analysis. The role of traditions in maintaining individual and cultural identity and group cohesiveness (and divisiveness) are another matter of concern. But I would contend that the question of how and why traditions persist or die out is one that is embedded in the very meaning of the word *tradition*, a word composed from Latin roots meaning handing across or handing down. It is a question that folklorists need to address in a substantial way if they are to continue to employ the word *tradition* as a part of the definition of their enterprise.

Afterword

> Doubt is not a pleasant condition, but certainty is an absurd one.
> —Francis-Marie Arouet de Voltaire, letter to Frederick II of Prussia

Although the essays in this volume were composed individually (except for chapters 6 and 7), there are substantive relationships between them. Chapters 1, 2, and 3 are concerned with the interpretation of jokes. Chapter 1 offers an interpretation of anecdotes about J. Golden Kimball and suggests a species of consolation they might have provided to those who told and listened to them. Interpretation, however, poses a problem. Just over a half-century ago, Alan Dundes declared that it was not sufficient for folklorists to simply collect folklore; they had to interpret it as well (Dundes 1965), and folklorists followed Dundes's injunction with, dare I say, almost religious enthusiasm. I have become leery of interpretations, however (Oring 2019c, 144–146). In taking an interpretive approach to a corpus of jokes, or to any folklore texts or practices for that matter, how does one decide whether the interpretation is correct? After all, it is not as though folklorists were interpreting a novel, short story, or poem. The interpretation of those literary genres generally depends upon enlarging our response to, and appreciation of, the work in question. Unless the interpretation is one restricted to the motivations or intentions of the author (Hirsch 1967, 25, 207; Palmer 1969, 86), there is really no basis for declaring any one or another interpretation correct. In the absence of some obvious misreading of the text, an interpretation is likely to be deemed successful if it addresses prominent aspects of the text, is comprehensive, coherent, subtle, and edifying. But with folklore the matter is different.

https://doi.org/10.7330/9781646425198.c010   167

Folklorists should not merely be providing compelling readings of texts. In their interpretations, folklorists claim to be identifying meanings that are in fact being *conveyed* in the course of a folkloric communication. Consequently, the criteria for a powerful interpretation of a literary text may not be sufficient for the satisfactory interpretation of a folkloric one. Folkloristic interpretations must go further and demonstrate that the meanings of texts are actually—even if unconsciously—communicated. Are J. Golden Kimball stories told because they allow their tellers and hearers to indulge in minor swearing and the vicarious enactment of minor sins in order to relieve the pressures imposed by a taxing religious regime? Do J. Golden Kimball stories serve as some sort of philosophical commentary on the effort to work out one's salvation as a flawed human being and perhaps inspire hope? Are J. Golden Kimball stories simply stories with nothing more than transient humorous value? Do J. Golden Kimball stories serve some other ends entirely or perhaps no significant ends at all?

Only armed with hypotheses about what these stories might be doing can folklorists examine the specific tellers, audiences, and telling situations in search of evidence that would support one or another of them. In other words, situations of performance would serve as testing grounds for hypotheses rather than being considered as self-contained events requiring only close description and analysis.

There is, of course, oral literary criticism that might lend to or take support from a particular hypothesis (Dundes 1966). Oral literary criticism can prove valuable, but in many instances it is difficult to collect, and it is data that needs to be carefully evaluated. William A. Wilson suggested that Mormon missionary pranks, jokes, and humorous folk speech helped the young missionaries survive in the course of their difficult and sometimes depressing battle for converts (2006b, 211). I also encountered former Soviet citizens who claimed that political jokes about the regime helped them to survive (Oring 2004, 215–216). There is even a book, *It Kept Us Alive: Humor in the Holocaust* (Ostrower 2014), that maintains, as the title states, that humor was critical to prisoner survival during the Holocaust. But can we really accept that those who died in the Nazi camps were the ones who lacked humor and those who lived were the ones who could create or appreciate it? Were there really few humorless survivors and no dead comedians? Undoubtedly, those survivors who engaged in humorous activity in the camps felt—*in retrospect*—that humor was significant in helping them to endure. But is it not just as likely, or perhaps more likely, that those who connived to get jobs in the kitchen or the hospital rather than engaging in heavy manual labor in the forests in sub-freezing temperatures, those who were able to cadge or steal a little bit more bread or soup for themselves, those who managed in some fashion to entertain their Nazi overlords, or those who were just plain lucky were perhaps more likely to survive than those who made witticisms or composed or sang comic songs about their circumstances? So, what people say about their jokes or other lore is pertinent data, but data that folklorists should be careful in accepting at face value.

So, how is one to determine whether the messages that are recovered from a text or corpus of texts are the ones actually intended and actually received by those participating in the communication? Perhaps what we need is to go at the question widdershins. Instead of collecting the jokes and then positing meanings and functions for them, we might explore what J. Golden jokes might index. That is to say, folklorists should identify groups of people who tell, appreciate, and seek out J. Golden Kimball stories; groups of people who tolerate J. Golden Kimball stories; and groups of people who avoid and condemn the stories altogether in order to see whether any differences between these populations are discernable. Folklorists would look for differences between these groups in their social relationships; economic status; education; and degrees of religious faith, practice, and church participation. Then folklorists would not be trying to posit a meaning for the jokes but would be initiating a search for possible correlations between the presence and absence of joke telling and joke appreciation with other social factors. Suspected correlations could then be subjected to more formal testing.[1] That is how the investigation of J. Golden Kimball jokes—or an investigation of any joke tradition—might proceed. It is not that interpretation is without value but that establishing correlations might support or contradict a particular interpretation of a joke or joke corpus.

Chapter 2, "Three *Jewish* Jokes," is likewise concerned with the matter of interpretation. The basic question is how a joke is assigned to be a "Jewish" joke, or for that matter, a Scottish, German, Polish, or Japanese one. The Jewish joke literature—both scholarly and popular—is replete with such assignments. Most often, the assignment is made on the basis of joke content: characters, settings, or situations. Thus, a joke is often regarded as Jewish if the protagonist is identified as a Jew; manifests physical, behavioral, or psychological traits considered Jewish; the setting is prototypically Jewish; or the situation is regarded as common to Jewish experience. But what makes a joke a joke is not its content but its structure, and a structure may remain constant with its content significantly altered. The fact that many jokes that are called Jewish appear in other corpuses without any reference to Jewish characters, settings, or situations greatly complicates the matter of joke interpretation.

During World War I, a Jew was asked, "Why don't you go to war?" He replied, "God! I don't know a single person among the enemy army, and they don't know me, so how could enmity exist between us?" This is the kind of joke that might be considered Jewish because of the Jews' supposed aversion to physical violence (Telushkin 1992, 65).[2] In fact, I don't know that this ever was a Jewish joke. I simply inserted the figure of a Jew during World War I into a joke from the joke collection of Obeyd-e Zakani, a fourteenth-century Persian poet (Javadi 2008, 91). His text simply refers to a soldier. It would not surprise me, however, if a variant of this joke did show up in some collection of jokes as being quintessentially Jewish.

It is not difficult to imagine how a repertoire of jokes might crystallize around particular national, ethnic, religious, occupational, geographical, or local groups. The groups tend to be characterized with certain traits—negative and/or positive— by both those inside and those outside the group. The jokes of outsiders about the group may be taken up by those inside, and jokes created inside the group may be told by those outside. But it is not necessary for completely new jokes to be created. Jokes from almost any source that focus on these traits may be transformed and adapted to the group in question. So, jokes and anecdotes with broad distribution might be adopted and adapted by Jews to what they view as their psychosocial condition. Perhaps we need to think that such jokes are not so much *expressions* of the group as something *impressed* upon it. Perhaps it is not that the character of the group can be read out of the jokes so much as perceived or imagined aspects of character are the basis for impressing certain jokes onto the group in the first place.

Chapter 3 revisits a neighborhood that folklorists have not tenanted for some time. The length of that time can be measured by the fact that such jokes were seen to need explanation rather than interpretation; that is, the engagement of folklorists with such jokes preceded the interpretive turn in folkloristics. It is somewhat peculiar that folklorists were willing to latch on to a psychoanalytic perspective with respect to these jokes, since they largely rejected that perspective for practically all other forms of folklore.[3]

For folklorists, psychoanalytic perspectives really served a means of interpretation because folklorists never tried to ascertain whether the effects claimed for sexual joking were ever realized in fact. As psychoanalytic theory was fundamentally a sexual theory, and as the contents of the jokes they were dealing with were sexual, the shoe seemed to fit. The theory, however, was never scrutinized in the light of ethnographic data. Nor could folklorists establish any sort of difference between sexual and non-sexual joking other than to register that the former employed sexual descriptions or allusions while the latter did not. The presumption was that jokes expressed and relieved tensions: sexual jokes expressed and relieved sexual tensions; political jokes, political tensions; ethnic jokes, ethnic tensions; mother-in-law jokes, kinship tensions. What could be simpler? More specifically, on the premise that sexual jokes were meant solely to expose and/

or disparage females (a premise that does not accord with the sample of sexual jokes in Legman, analyzed in the chapter), sexual jokes were treated either as the equivalents of sexual solicitations or assaults. They were a means of harassment.[4]

Almost three decades ago, I was struck by a report in the press of an incident of sexual joking in the American military. At a dinner for cadets and their guests at the U.S. Coast Guard Academy in New London, Connecticut, in 1995, Captain Ernie Blanchard told the following three jokes:

> [I saw] a cadet's fiancée wearing a brooch featuring maritime signal flags. She said the flags meant, "I love you." They really said, "Permission granted to lay alongside."
>
> Referring to his old friend Captain Patrick Stillman, the commandant of the cadets, Blanchard said, "On Stillman's wedding night, the captain told his bride she could do anything she wanted. So she immediately went to sleep."
>
> [And there was the one about] the cadet who wondered why his fiancée was wolfing down a costly meal at a fancy restaurant when she never ate like that at home. She replied . . . "that her mother didn't want to sleep with her."[5]

Looking at the first joke, the incongruity lies in translating a declaration of love into a terminology about the disposition of naval vessels. The incongruity is not dissimilar to the example in chapter 4 of the deceased woman who is likened to a postal package. The incongruity is appropriate because such a disposition, "laying alongside," is also applicable to sexual relations between two individuals. But the appropriateness is spurious because, even though love often implies sex, a public declaration of love is not a public announcement of a sexual relation. If the joke has a message, it would seem to be that sex underlies love, although declarations of love and references to sexual acts are usually assigned to separate spheres of discourse.

The joke about Captain Stillman and his bride is front loaded for a sexual outcome. The outcome is incongruously denied, but it is appropriate since the bride is offered the opportunity to do *anything* she wants. The bride chooses sleep, although this would be a spurious choice on a wedding night when a marriage is traditionally assumed to be consummated. The joke is somewhat similar to a joke about a man walking down the street who is approached by a beautiful young woman who says, "I will do anything" for thirty dollars—So, I had her paint my house. (Not all jokes move from a presumption of innocence to a revelation of an underlying sexual theme. Some, such as this one, move in the opposite direction.) If there is a message in Blanchard's joke, it is that Captain Stillman was not appealing or exciting enough to keep his bride interested on her wedding night.

The third joke, like the first, speaks to the sexual underpinnings of romantic relations between individuals. It is incongruous that the woman who always ate modestly in her mother's home suddenly becomes a big eater when in an expensive restaurant with her fiancé. The incongruity is appropriate since what her mother wanted from her and what her fiancé expected from her were entirely different. She was going to get something in exchange for what she was expected to give. The appropriateness is spurious since marriage is not traditionally viewed as a cost accounting of exchanged goods and services (i.e., good food for good sex). If there is a message in the joke it is a that marriage can be viewed as a quid pro quo, and if someone is required to give something, that person might expect to get something in return.

I would argue that there is nothing particularly sexist about these jokes. They all allude to sex. Sex, however, is not explicitly referred to, let alone graphically described. If the jokes contain messages, they would seem to be: (1) underneath love there is sex, (2) a husband is not sufficiently attractive or exciting to keep his bride awake on her wedding night, and (3) a woman entering a marriage sees it as an economic arrangement, which it is,[6] and consequently, she expects something tangible and up front for the sex that she will be expected to provide.

Captain Blanchard told these jokes during dessert before launching into his speech on tales of Coast Guard glory. He introduced them as slightly risqué; that they perhaps skirted the boundaries of political correctness. A group of women present at the dinner complained about Blanchard's poor taste. Stillman called Blanchard to formally express the academy's displeasure with his performance. Blanchard sent a letter of apology. But a group of women pressured the Coast Guard to launch a criminal investigation into the jokes. Instructors at the academy maintained that Blanchard needed to be punished if gender equality was to be taken seriously. Colleagues began to avoid him. A female political science teacher at the academy said, "All the sexual jokes he told were typical 'male power' jokes and involved males doing it to females." Blanchard offered to resign his post if the Coast Guard would give up its investigation, but he was turned down. Fearing a court martial could leave him and his family without a pension, he committed suicide, leaving behind a wife and two teenage children (Thompson 1996).[7]

Told in a public venue in an after-dinner speech, it would be difficult to reckon Blanchard's jokes as constituting sexual harassment. It would be even more difficult to characterize the jokes as being about "male power." In the first joke, a male is *given permission* to "lay alongside." In the second joke, the male is rebuffed by a bride who would rather go to sleep than have sex with him. In the third joke, the woman recognizes that marriage will involve sex, for which she expects something in return up front. If these are expressions of "male power," that term seems devoid of any real-world referents. In none of these jokes do males "do it" to females. In fact, none of these characters even express an interest in "doing it" to females. They are about as far from displays of male power as a sexual joke is likely to be. If the argument that any mention of or allusion to sex in the presence of females is a form of harassment, or that females are necessarily embarrassed and made uncomfortable by any allusion to sex by a male, then there is a tacit admission that females must be protected against any and all references to matters sexual, even in the most unthreatening of settings. In that case, contemporary society should be seen as essentially Victorian in its orientation. Women can never really be equal.[8]

The question is not whether a sexual joke, or an ethnic joke for that matter, can be used to harass. It can.[9] But it would greatly depend on the nature of the joke, the character of the teller, the person to whom it is told, and the circumstances of its telling. A problem arises when the telling of a joke with some sexual content automatically is presumed to define an instance of harassment. Joking—even sexual, practical, and put-down—can prove an important component of group camaraderie (Bradney 1957; Terrion and Ashforth 2002). The chilling of joke-telling and joking behavior can have detrimental effects on workplace culture (Marsh 2015, 129–133). The willingness of individuals to good-naturedly accept jokes made at their expense can greatly contribute to the creation of an environment in which people are content to work.[10]

One reliable indicator of whether joking is mean-spirited is whether it is repeatedly directed at only a single individual or group or distributed evenly across the social spectrum.[11] Even hazing, which is often defined as involving abusive or humiliating behavior—thus lacking the ameliorating effects of a joke structure—is ultimately designed to turn newcomers to an organization into social equals. Hazing is a peer-making behavior. *All* members of the group have gone through the same hazing process. Another reliable indicator of whether joking is intended as play or ill-treatment is whether it is reciprocal. Play is rooted in reciprocity (Burns 1978, 28). Those who expect others to good-naturedly accept their joking must be prepared to accept similar kinds of joking in return.

Andrew Sykes studied joking relationships in a printing works with over a thousand employees in Glasgow, Scotland. Obscene banter was exchanged between old and young men and between old men and old women (old being someone who was married or over the age of about 25). Old women and young men could engage in such banter, but it was understood that the old women were the initiators of such exchanges. There was no physical contact or horseplay between them. Old men, however, could engage in obscene banter, physical contact, and horseplay with the young women if it was conducted in a joking manner. The young women never objected and often "led the men on." Any serious attempt on the part of the old men to engage in sexual touching was heavily censured by young and old men and women alike.

The interactions between the young men and young women proceeded solely in terms of joking. Conversation by the young men would fall into thinly disguised suggestive remarks. The women would pretend to be shocked, not to understand, or they would make insulting or suggestive responses of their own. The remarks of the men were never obscene, nor were they permitted to make serious reference to sexual matters. Any public attempt to engage in the physical touching of a young woman was condemned by all the women. Serious physical sexual activities were known to go on in private—in storerooms and other out-of-the-way places—but this knowledge shocked no one.

Gross obscene remarks and behavior by old men to young women signaled that serious sexual relations between them were tabooed. Suggestive exchanges between young men and young women indicated that serious sexual interactions might be possible. If a young woman wanted to signal that she was unavailable for serious sexual encounters, she publicly adopted the obscene register of an old woman (Sykes 1966).

What is significant about the above example is that workplace relations are subtle and complex. They require the effort of an ethnographer to tease them out. Obscene joking, rather than proving to be sexually arousing or threatening among the Glaswegian workers, served to signal the opposite: that serious sexual intent or availability was absent. Furthermore, workplaces often have their own means of identifying, assessing, and condemning social breaches. Legislative codes and bureaucratic procedures imposed from the outside are unlikely to capture the subtleties of the cultures they endeavor to regulate. They can seem very much like the imposition of a colonial administration on a local culture.

Chapters 4 and 5 do not deal with the content of humor but its structure. The problem with a mere reliance on content, is that there is a tendency—a strong tendency—to regard a joke about Jews, Blacks, Poles, lawyers, mothers-in-law, communism, capitalism, or the police, as attacks upon or forms of abuse of said categories of persons, occupations, ideologies, or institutions. After all, it would seem that, at the very least, a joke is "making light of" such persons, ideologies, or institutions. It would seem important, however, for anyone attempting an interpretation of a joke to have some grasp of how jokes make something "light." That is, they should have a clear sense of what is incongruous, how it is appropriate, why it is spurious, and what message, if any, might be gleaned from such an analysis.

The epigraph of chapter 4—that a sense of humor is merely commonsense dancing—would seem to be very far from the truth. As delightful as the aphorism sounds, despite who first said it (William James, Clive James, or someone else altogether), and despite the numerous posters that have been copied and sold proclaiming it, humor and jokes are not kinds of common sense. Humor depends upon violations of common sense. Jokes are profoundly rooted in illogic and highly dubious judgments and associations. The "sense" they betray seems closer to that underlying magical spells and religious rituals than the sense that characterizes analytic thought. Humor depends upon incongruities—incongruities that can only be reconciled by utterly spurious means. Because jokes are, in essence, *doubly* incongruous, they cannot be regarded as a substitute for rational argument. People may be amused, but they should not be persuaded by a joke.

Chapter 5 is a critique of a particular computational approach to the recognition and production of humor. Recognition is far more difficult than production. To produce a humorous expression, a computer need only generate something incongruous that is at the same time spuriously appropriate. This might even be done by generating random combinations of words and expressions from disparate domains until something humorous fortuitously emerges. One such Twitter bot (a bit of software that performs some repetitive task online) involves mashing up newspaper headlines so that a particular character from one headline is conjoined with a particular action from another. For example, "Miss Universe Attacks Northeast Nigerian City; Dozens Killed" or "Donald Trump Trying to Bring Nintendo Entertainment System Back to Life" (Veale 2021, 52–53) are incongruous in that Miss Universe never attacked or could attack anything in Nigeria (although Boko Haram did), and Nintendo, not Donald Trump, might have expressed some interest in reviving the old entertainment system. They are at the same time appropriate because they have the format of news headlines and might look like news if they possibly could be true. This appropriateness is spurious because one can rarely create legitimate news by the random or haphazard combination of noun and verb phrases of distinct headlines. In most instances, anyone reading them would immediately deduce the spuriousness underlying their composition and thus their humor. Indeed, people go to the platform to find such mashups knowing they are mashups. Furthermore, many mashups do not necessarily evoke amusement. They may too closely approximate real news, prove puzzling, or be dismissed as the result of simple typographical errors. "US Ambassador to Donald Trump Defends Response to Gaza Protests"; "Weekly Poll: Meghan Markle—Hot or Not?"; or "Qualcomm is Ready for Tesla, Inc. and its Biometric Upgrade," might require some focused attention to sense their artificiality—if their artificiality is noted at all ("Two Headlines" May 15–17, 2018).

The mashup of two headlines is a rather crude way for a computer to generate humor. It would not be very different than cutting out headlines from newspapers, cutting them in half at the verb, dropping them on the floor, mixing them up, and taping them together as they are haphazardly picked up. (Indeed, this seems to have been the inspiration for the bot in the first place.) Mashups may result in humor, but it is a method of brute force, and it is likely to result in numerous non-humorous outputs.

The first programs to generate humorous expressions were developed in the last decade of the twentieth century. JAPE (Joke Appreciation and Production Engine) was one that could produce punning riddles of the sort: "What do you get when you cross a sheep and a kangaroo?—A woolly jumper [i.e., a sweater in British English]" (Binstead and Richie 1994, 1997). The program is based on a lexicon of homophones, which are semantically and syntactically indexed and conjoined in a noun phrase (adjective + noun). Trading on the ambiguity of the noun in the phrase, a restricted number of riddle questions are constructed (e.g., "What do you get when you cross a ___ with a ___?"; "What do you call a ___?"). While the output of this program generated mostly poor jokes—by the programmers' own admission and the ratings of judges—the output was usually recognized as a joke, and on occasion produced jokes that raters claimed they had previously heard or approximated punning riddles in a children's joke book. This program was sensitive to both syntax and semantics.

Contrasted with the top-down and symbolic approach to humor generation employed by JAPE, there is a bottom-up statistical approach. An automated statistical analysis of a large corpus of English texts can gauge the most likely and least likely words to appear in a phrase. For example, the next word in the sequence "had a hard day at the ___" is most likely to be "office," while "track," "roulette table" and "theater" are considerably less likely. Thus, the probabilities of each of these words can be computed. The likelihood of "orifice" filling out the phrase would be close to zero, but the phonetic distance between "office" and "orifice" can also be measured by a machine. Thus, "orifice," which has a near zero probability in the phrase would result in an incongruity but one that can be made appropriate by virtue of its phonetic resemblance to a high-probability word choice. The whole phrase "hard day at the orifice" can be motivated by a set-up such as "the dentist was in a bad mood because. . . ." But this last task depends upon a computer recognizing the dual *senses* of the pun, an undertaking in which computers are still weak although not totally inept (Veale 2021, 149–168).

Tony Veale's *Your Wit Is My Command: Building AIs with a Sense of Humor* (2021) describes the various ways that computer scientists have approached the problem of humor generation and identification, primarily from a statistical point of view. The great advantage of the statistical approach, it seems to me, is its modularity; the ability to search very large data sets of text and to filter results through a variety of analytic programs. For example, millions of words of text can be mechanically perused, lexicons of puns and synonyms can likewise be scrutinized, and even the presence of emotion-laden words can be identified (Veale 2021, 159, 187). Each of these individual operations can be conjoined. Algorithms can then be tested on databases of text and databases of joke texts. The statistical point of view has produced results, not through a powerful insight into the nature of humor but rather through an amalgamation of weaker generalizations that nevertheless serve to get something done—pun recognition, irony detection, or cartoon caption evaluation. The results are promising if not yet earthshaking. Computers do not seem ready to handle most of the kinds of jokes that folklorists are likely to find themselves confronting. Nevertheless, some small steps have been made. There is no reason to presume that larger steps might not be taken in the future.

It might at first seem that the last four chapters in this volume have nothing to do with the first five. In fact, these chapters derive from the reexamination and interrogation of the interpretive mood in folklore studies. They constitute a search for alternative modes of sensemaking. Chapters 6 and 7 are a critical survey of Richard Dawkins's definition of the *meme* and the science of memetics that arose in its wake. The memetics program is Darwinian, and while I believe culture evolves, and while I am not, in principle, opposed to a Darwinian theory of cultural evolution, I think the demonstration of a Darwinian dynamic in culture is wanting, even if it makes a great deal of sense. Ideas and practices are in competition, and only the fittest survive. But the crucial point is to define fitness independently of survival. It is not sufficient to claim that whatever is fit survives and that whatever survives must necessarily be fit. The fitness of any particular idea or practice must be evidenced. That fitness must be established with respect to the period of time in which the idea or practice has emerged and becomes dominant. Conversely, it must also be shown how ideas and practices that are losing their purchase in a society are no longer fit in their current context. Only then can a Darwinian theory of cultural evolution be worth entertaining.

Memetics did constitute something of a fad in the last decade of the twentieth century and the first decade of the twenty-first. A bevy of books and essays were published in that period. That fad has certainly passed. But the interest in memetics has not been extinguished (nor am I interested in extinguishing it). Exploring the applicability of memes to such things as rhetoric or witchcraft belief is still going on (Tindale 2017; Boudry 2018). The philosopher Daniel C. Dennett, who has been a strong advocate of memetic arguments since the 1990s, claims to be planning one more book to make his case (2013, 274). The object of chapters 6 and 7 is to point out what folklorists (and others) need to be asking before they succumb to a Darwinian account of folklore and culture.

The question that memetics poses as to how and why certain ideas and practices spread at the expense of others—an epidemiological approach—holds promise.

It promotes the identification of forces that constrain and promote a particular idea or practice, whether through some quality of the idea or practice itself (a psychological attractor), aspects of the media and routes of dissemination for that idea or practice, or something about the sociocultural or physical environment that welcomes certain ideas and practices while repelling others (e.g., Barber 1941; Hill 1944). The fad of memetics may be over, but the underlying questions remain.

The search for laws, discussed in chapter 8, is another tactic in the analysis of folklore. The proposal of laws was once a stock practice in theoretical folkloristics. The notion that there may be laws operating in the sociocultural realm has seriously atrophied, in part, no doubt, to postmodern reservations about science and scientific claims (reservations that I do not share). Nevertheless, lawlike claims can be found throughout the folkloristic literature although they are rarely labeled as such, and those laws that are proposed are never assiduously explored in an effort to establish their truth, range, and limiting conditions. Laws are subject to the test of evidence in ways that interpretations usually are not (although they could and should be [Oring 2019c, 146–147]).

One of my early publications in folklore concerned the status of explanation in folkloristics (Oring 1976).[12] I return to the matter in chapter 9. I believe that explanation is one of the chief tasks of folkloristics. Interpretation is valuable to the extent that it contributes to the task of explanation, but all too often it remains an enterprise largely isolated from goings-on in the real world. The interpretations that are promoted may seem plausible or ingenious, but they are almost never tested. The single most important question that can be asked about an interpretation of a folklore expression or practice—once it is determined that the interpretation is coherent, comprehensive, and cogent—is: If this interpretation is true, what else would have to be true in the real world (and is it)? And what might obtain in the real world that would indicate the interpretation is mistaken? It is not that interpretation cannot be made to serve the object of explanation, but it almost never is. Interpretation is usually self-affirming. The relation between *hermeneutic* and *hermetic* is not only phonological and mythological, but substantive. Interpretation tends to be a hermetically sealed enterprise.

The question posed by Joseph Jacobs in 1893, "What is the modus operandi of tradition?" is one of the grand questions of folkloristics (237). The related but subsidiary questions concerning the recall and transmission of traditions was seriously engaged for a time by folklorists before the inquiry was abandoned and largely left to scholars in other disciplines—today, most notably, to cognitive psychologists.

The break with diachronic concerns in folkloristics was engendered by the development of functionalism and then structuralism. The break was extended first in the move to interpretation and then the study of performance. More recently, folkloristics, again under influences of trends in other disciplines, has taken a critical turn, an essentially emancipatory undertaking that aims to identify the hidden and destructive forces underlying Western institutions and practices—sexism, racism, xenophobia, colonialism, capitalism, the neoliberal order—and to explore the extent to which folklore serves to promote or resist them. Beyond critique, there are those who see the role of the discipline as the pursuit of social justice, advocacy, and intervention on behalf of the stigmatized, marginalized, and oppressed (Mills 2020). Some time ago, I registered my reaction to these moves (Oring 2006a; Oring 2006b). I would merely reiterate that as a mode of inquiry, the premises and the conclusions are pretty much known in advance. It is only the connections between them that remain to be teased out.

Folklore scholarship has not kept its eye upon, let alone resolved, its traditional questions. Perhaps worse, there has been no clear statement of what the central questions of folklore research are. There has been some talk of late of a need for "big ideas" in folklore.[13] I am not opposed to big ideas, although I must confess I have yet to see any. But I would prefer to start with *big questions*; intellectual questions about those beliefs, practices, products, and groups that constitute the subject matter of the discipline. Big questions do not necessarily require big ideas or big answers, at least not at first. Answers may accumulate and modify each other. From little answers mighty ideas may grow. The miscellaneous nature of folklore work might crystallize around such questions and give folklorists a sense of both purpose and identity and perhaps result in some real accomplishment. If the questions are big enough, much of the work that folklorists do will likely speak—directly or tangentially—to them. Folklorists may, consequently, find themselves speaking to and debating with one another. From where I sit, that would prove an entirely agreeable state of affairs.

Notes

CHAPTER 1: THE CONSOLATIONS OF HUMOR

1. My colleague Christie Davies (1990, 2002, 2011) and I agreed on this point.

2. This notion persists even though the hydraulic metaphor on which it is based has long been rejected in the psychological sciences.

3. Also, because it involves an "understanding test," which may also provoke an emotional reaction (Sacks 1974, 350)

4. For example, Lee (1964) and Kimball (1999, 2002).

5. The language may be saltier in oral versions than in published ones (Eliason 2007, 48).

CHAPTER 2: THREE *JEWISH* JOKES

1. Unless Spalding's version was itself influenced by Sholem Aleichem's story.

2. Uther also includes Type 1284A: *White Man Made to Believe He is Black* and 1284B: *Man Needs Patch on Pants to Recognize Himself* (originally 1531B in Aarne-Thompson) and 1284C: "You, Or, Your Brother?" Only Type 1284A is in Aarne-Thompson.

3. Druyanow includes a version of Type 1284B (Motif J2012.6) in his joke collection that has more of a Jewish ambience. It is a story about a Chelmite who feels obliged to go to the bath-house on Sabbath eve but is worried that he won't recognize himself once he takes off his clothes. Consequently, he ties a thread around his leg so he will recognize himself. He loses the thread and doesn't know who he is (1963, 2:21–22, joke #1061). There are non-Jewish versions of this joke as well (e.g., Marzolph 1992, 2:227). Indeed, the Chelm stories themselves derive from non-Jewish predecessors (see Von Bernuth 2016).

4. A question that does need to be addressed with respect to the Jewish and non-Jewish versions of Type 1284 is why the non-Jewish versions tend to depend on a *trick* played on an unsuspecting victim whereas the Jewish versions appear to hinge on an *error* made by the protagonist.

5. Before the advent of printing, these were hand-written manuscripts of the Talmud and extremely valuable.

6. The Talmud is composed of both the Mishnah and the Gemara, the latter being a discussion of the questions, opinions, and legal principles presented in the Mishnah.

7. Cray also includes a version ATU 924 in his collection of American-Jewish jokes and is fully aware of its worldwide distribution (1964, 342–343).

8. In an account in the Talmud of disputations before Alexander the Great between the Jews and Africans, Egyptians, and descendants of Ishmael, Gabiah ben Psisa puts himself forward as a disputant with the argument that if he is defeated, they have merely defeated an ignoramus, but if he should prove victorious, it would be the laws of Moses that prevailed (*Sanhedrin* 91a). He is chosen, but his arguments are both learned and to the point. He is no fool.

9. It would, however, be easy enough to read the triumph of the fool as evidence of God's favor. God works for the preservation of the Jewish community through a simpleton, and He humiliates its adversaries who do not even recognize they have been defeated by a fool.

10. Although answering a question with a question was included (Nevo 1991, 254).

11. Israeli folklorists have been interested in the distinctiveness of Jewish *tales* (e.g., Meir 1979; Hasan-Rokem 1982; Yassif 1986; 2009, 58–59) and Dov Noy even attempted to formulate some rules of oicotypification (1971, 173–177), but these rules cannot be easily applied to jokes.

12. This text begins a sermon that the rabbi of a Reform congregation in California delivered on Yom Kippur in 2007. Following the presentation of the joke, the rabbi continued his sermon, stating that he very much liked the joke, but he actually would direct a troubled member of his congregation to "specific texts" in the Torah, the Prophets, *Pirke Avot* [Ethics of the Fathers], and Talmudic and Hasidic texts. As noted above, the rabbi's text of the joke is very similar to other texts.

13. Actually two "sites" are the actual pages of self-published books (Brenner 2010, 99–100; Rabeeya 2004, 23).

14. Minor variations can creep into a text even when it has been copied and pasted (Oring 2012a, 103–104).

15. I do not think the number of texts one finds on the Internet or the percentage of Jewish versus non-Jewish texts is significant.

16. It would be possible if the Prophets and Writings were included.

17. A similar situation would seem to obtain with respect to Sephardic humor. Although the figure Joha (Juha, Goha, Giufà, Hodja Nasreddin) appears in Arab, Turkish, Persian, Balkan, and even Italian folklore, when a collection of tales translated from Ladino (Judaeo-Spanish) appeared in 2003, it was titled *Folktales of Joha: Jewish Trickster* (Koén-Sarano 2003). How, given the long and widespread tradition of such tales in the Middle East and beyond, Joha managed to become a "Jewish" trickster, is a question that merits an answer. Even a cursory examination of the 267 tales in the book—without comparing them to collections of Arab, Turkish, and Persian Joha tales—reveals that some 15 percent of them are international folktales or jokes that appear in joke books, indeed Jewish joke books, in Europe and the United States. One text, in fact, is from the talmudic tractate *Nedarim* 66b (116–117), and three of the jokes were in the repertoire of Sigmund Freud (Koén-Sarano 2003, 131–132, 205, 238–239). A reviewer of this collection stated, "Joha has deep Jewish meaning. The laugh and the cheerful approach to life represents a core religious belief" (Mushabac 2003, 37). It is a core religious belief that a Jew experiences joy in the study of the Torah and in the fulfillment of the commandments. I don't know it to be a core belief in the approach to everyday life. In any event, given that the Joha tales are widely known, it would seem that a cheerful approach to life would characterize a very wide range of Middle Eastern societies.

CHAPTER 3: WHATEVER BECAME OF THE DIRTY JOKE?

1. The matter is somewhat different when one searches for "sex + humor" in the psychological databases. In the experimental psychological literature on sexual joking, however, one usually does not encounter dirty jokes. Such jokes may be employed in the experiments, but they are rarely described (see p. 43).

2. What constitutes a "dirty" or "obscene" joke is not entirely clear. I seem to recall a joke I heard as a child: "Do you want to hear a dirty joke?—Yes—A boy fell into a puddle of muddy water." (I cannot swear to its exact phrasing, but the overall structure is correct.) This "folk critique" of the dirty joke is essentially spot on. Such jokes are classified by their content, which portrays or alludes to things dirty. The joke further indicates that not any kind of dirt suffices to make a joke dirty. Clothes and bodies covered with mud do not qualify. The basic assumption is that a dirty joke concerns itself with sexual or scatological matters. But the breadth of the sexual and scatological in jokes is broad and ranges from graphic description (e.g., Legman 1975, 418–419) to subtle allusion (e.g., Legman 1968, 49–50).

3. While Morreall recognizes that, in Freud's view, laughter discharges superfluous energy used to *repress* sexual feelings and thoughts, he immediately claims that sexual jokes, like dreams, serve as a safety valve for the expression of such forbidden feelings and thoughts (1987, 111).

4. A more important collection appears in Carol Mitchell's PhD dissertation (1976). Her collection comprises 1,507 jokes collected from known sources both male and female. Forty percent of the collection she classifies as obscene.

5. An idea that he seems to have gotten from Martha Wolfenstein (1978, 52).

6. Legman, of course, was not the first to establish a connection between jokes and neurosis. Freud suggested that the determinants of the joke-work might not be all that distant from those of neurotic illness (1960, 8:142); but he viewed the joke-work as related to the techniques of the joke and not to its content. Martin Grotjahn saw inveterate jokers as sadistic (1957, 44), and Otto Fenichel regarded jokes as attempts to get relief from guilt, relief being obtained by getting the audience to participate in the guilt-inducing act (1945, 165). Edmund Bergler thought that jokes were created to defend against an internal adversary and regarded laughter as an attempt to outdistance one's own psychic masochism (1956, 61). Although Ludwig Eidelberg saw some analogies between jokes and neurotic symptoms, he did not consider them to be identical (Eidelberg 1945, 45–46, 49–58).

7. I only chose texts that were jokes and in italics. I chose the first complete joke on the page. If there was no joke on the page, I skipped ten pages and looked for a joke until I found one. In the few cases in which the number pointed to a page with no joke at the end of the volume, I skipped ten pages back until I found one.

8. Also noted by Burns with Burns (1976, 28).

9. For what it is worth, 13 percent of the tales in Vance Randolph's *Pissing in the Snow and Other Ozark Folktales* were collected from females (1965, 41–42, 43–44, 45–46, 49–50, 73–74, 92, 102–103, 125–126, 130–131, 140–141, 148–149, 176–177, 187–188). Also see Mitchell (1977, 1985) on jokes that women both tell and appreciate.

10. Rayna Green also noted the variety of bawdy materials that appeared in Vance Randolph's *Pissing in the Snow and Other Ozark Folktales* although more impressionistically (Green 1976, 20–22).

11. There have been many attempts to experimentally induce such tensions (see p. 41).

12. A "nonsense" joke is, presumably, a joke that has no overt sexual or aggressive component; what Freud would have called an "innocent" [*harmlose*] joke (Freud 1960, 8:90–96).

13. I was unable to find this image on the Internet, but there are a number of cartoon parodies of it (see "Darken my Door" 2020).

14. Curiously, he did not relate this preference to his own possible latent aggressiveness.

15. For other concerns about the choice of humorous test materials see Burns with Burns (1976, 29–31).

16. The descriptions by Leary are largely of adolescents, and they are rarely of canned sexual jokes. They are valuable, nonetheless.

17. Among folklorists, only Mitchell has made any attempt to systematically compare jokes told by males and females (1977, 1985). She has also explored those jokes that are more appreciated by one gender or the other (1977), although also see Lundell (1993). Psychologists have experimentally investigated differences between male and female humor preferences for quite some time (e.g., More and Roberts 1957; Cantor 1976; Herzog and Hager 1995; Greengross 2020).

18. Even the stringing out of sexual and scatological scenes can be apprehended as art. See the film *The Aristocrats* by Penn Jillette and Paul Provenza, in which professional comedians all perform their version of the same joke (2005). Also see a review of this film in *Journal of American Folklore* (Oring 2007, 500–501).

CHAPTER 4: INCONGRUOUS, APPROPRIATE, SPURIOUS

1. For traditional versus modern notions regarding a name, compare Trachtenberg (1961, 79–103) with Levitt and Dubner (2005, 179–204).

2. Graeme Ritchie believes that I do not regard my appropriate incongruity perspective as being a form of incongruity resolution because of my dubiousness over the requirement that the perception of an incongruity necessarily precedes the recognition of its resolution (2009, 12), that is, whether the recognition of an incongruity must precede the detection of its appropriateness. My differences with incongruity-resolution theory are rooted in the notion of the term *resolution* (discussed on p. 52 in this essay). Nevertheless, I certainly recognize the close relation of my perspective with incongruity-resolution theory.

3. "What has been said of the cause of laughter does not amount to an exact description, far less to a logical definition: there being innumerable combinations of congruity and inconsistency, or relation and contrariety, of likeness and dissimilitude, which are not ludicrous at all. If we could ascertain the peculiarities of these, we should be able to characterize with more accuracy the general nature of the ludicrous combination" (Beattie 1779, 324).

4. Computational linguists sometimes recognize this as well. See Rayz (2017, 172).

5. For more detailed critiques of these theories see Oring (2016, 1–100).

6. Attardo and Raskin, however, do cite previous sources—Elie Auboin and Avner Ziv—in their discussion (1991, 307, 337–338n8).

7. "*Lorsque nous écrivons qu'un double sens, une assimilation fautive, une erreur de jugement . . . sont acceptés ou justifiés, il ne peut, bien entendu s'agir que d'une acceptation conditionelle et temporaire, sujette à revision immediate; d'une justification superficielle et nullement absolu qui voile un instant l'absurdité du jugement, du raisonnemen, de l'acte, mais laisse subsister le double caractère indispensable au contraste comique.*"

8. In their punning-riddle-generating computer program JAPE, Kim Binstead and Graeme Ritchie included a post-production checking module to ensure that such riddles as "What do you call a cylindrical drink container? A Coke can" were suppressed (1997, 52–53).

9. The technical report was referred to in a single postscript in an essay about the use of sex and aggression in attempts to create—not merely to evaluate—humor (Nevo and Nevo 1983, 194). The title of the report led me to the article published in 1988. Curiously, the authors seem to have misunderstood the thrust of Navon's argument, seeing his notion of "virtually inappropriate" as a special case of incongruity (193).

10. Where I differ from Navon is in his characterization of a joke as being a "story" (1988, 208) with a protagonist (211). Many of the texts analyzed below would not conform to this description although I consider them jokes.

11. Tony Veale has added the thought experiment to this list (2012, 145).

12. I have discussed the problem that metaphors pose elsewhere (Oring 1995; 2003, 5–6, 51; 2016, 35–39, 46, 50–54).

13. The nature of the reality of mathematics—as something discovered or invented—is debated in a series of essays in Polkinghorne 2011.

14. This raises the question of whether the problems proposed in mathematics textbooks should be considered problems or puzzles since the answers have previously been worked out and are usually published in the back of the book.

15. It may be that Schiller's language is the problem and that his view actually accords with my exposition since there are instances where he seems to indicate that it is the question that is artificial in its deliberate attempt to disguise the configuration necessary for an appropriate solution (1938, 225).

16. Schiller believes the laughter in response to jokes results from the "joy of reasoning" and the escape from the embarrassment of failing to understand (1938, 226). I am skeptical of this interpretation. While joy does accompany many forms of play, particularly physical play, the response to jokes seems qualitatively different. Amusement seems different from joy. Furthermore, there is the distinction between the "a-ha" that accompanies the intellectual solution of a problem or puzzle and the "ha-ha" that is a reaction to a joke. The "a-ha" might follow a joke that has to be explained or that takes a long time to figure out.

17. There is a Polish joke about a Pole and a Frenchman who are hunting together when they come across a beautiful, naked woman sitting on the path through the woods. The Frenchman runs over and starts making love, and says to her feverishly, "Are you game? Are you game?" She says, "Oh, yes, I'm game." And the Pole shot her.

18. My own surname, Oring, might also work, but because the word "ring" is contained within the name, it would not prove to be very funny. Little in the way of a reconceptualization of terms or concepts would be required. See Oring (2003, 8).

19. Some linguists might deny this text the status of a joke because there is no semantic connection between the literal and figurative domains (see Hempelmann 2004, 337; Oring 2019a, 162n9). I disagree and consider this a joke.

20. I first encountered a form of this joke in an article on cannibalism by, I believe, Paul Krassner in *The Realist*: "If the good Lord hadn't meant us to be cannibals, he wouldn't have made us out of meat."

21. The prohibition may stem from religious, economic, medical, environmental, or moral concerns. Cross-culturally, most food taboos concern the eating of meat (Simoons 1994).

22. See, for example, Socrates's idea about the naming of the body and soul (Plato 1998, 30).

23. This would also serve to falsify the theory of joking proposed by Hurley, Dennett, and Adams that humor is predicated on the discovery of a false belief (2011). The revelation that a driver lacks the license to operate the vehicle she is driving does not create humor. See Oring (2016, 81–100) for a critique of this position.

24. One reviewer of the manuscript for this book from the United Kingdom offered a completely different reading of this joke. To quote: " 'So the barman gave her one' was an appropriate incongruity because 'giving her one' is already an expression for sex that makes it . . . more explicit, like he 'gave her one up the ass.' Collins Dictionary gives a British English definition for 'give someone one' as 'to have sex with someone.' "

I can see how the expression "gave her one" could have a sexual meaning, although I am not sure that that meaning is as salient in American as British English. Nevertheless, the reviewer's reading of the joke seems plausible. The woman asked for a double entendre and the barman "gave her one"—sex—so that the barman's response is itself the double entendre she requested. Still, I do not think that this was the meaning intended by the editors of the book from which the example was drawn. The joke appears in a section titled "Bar Jokes." Of the seventy-six jokes in this section this would be the only real sexual joke. There is the section "Adults Only Jokes," which seems to be where sexual jokes are largely confined. As a joke depends on the *perception* of an appropriate incongruity, it is possible for there to be two different perceptions of a single text. I perceived a joke and explained the structure of the joke that I saw. The reviewer perceived a very different joke.

25. This joke is included in one of the earliest jokebooks and would seem to be at least fifteen hundred years old (Baldwin 1983, 29; Beard 2014, 185).

26. This shows that simply mentioning "dirty words" is not in itself the source of humor and thereby contests the claim that humor is the result of the release of and relief from repressed thoughts.

CHAPTER 5: OVERLAPS, OPPOSITIONS, AND ONTOLOGIES

1. Proposition 3 is not part of the formal description of a joke-carrying text, but since it is the only proposition that identifies how an opposition is made compatible, I include it as part of the main hypothesis. It seems reasonable as script overlap reappears in the theory's most recent instantiations (e.g., Raskin, Hempelmann, and Taylor 2009, 301).

2. Carla Canestrari and Ivana Bianchi (2013) have discussed the notion of contraries in humor. I do not believe jokes depend on oppositions; only on conceptual differences, some of which can be categorized as oppositions.

3. Ritchie has raised the problem of whether, according to SSTH and GTVH, a script has to be tied to a lexical term in the joke text (Ritchie 2004, 72–73).

4. The Duke of Wellington was famous for his pithy statements and aphorisms, the most famous perhaps being "Up guards, and at 'em" ("Quotes" 1999–2017).

5. It would be instructive to learn what percentage of jokes actually employs overlapping scripts, as illustrated by the patient/lover joke, to create humor. The exercise should be easy enough to perform through a random selection of jokes from a large number of joke books.

6. Problematic only when starting from a conceptualization of a joke in terms of compatibly opposed scripts. It is not a problem from the perspective of a joke as embodying an appropriate incongruity.

7. I have indicated elsewhere why I find the term *resolution* somewhat problematic (Oring 2003, 2; also Forabosco 1992, 59).

8. John C. Paolillo (1998) examines logical mechanisms in Gary Larson's *Far Side* cartoons, but as his mechanisms are included in Attardo, Hempelmann, and Di Maio (2002), they are not presented separately.

9. Garden-path is not a genuine logical mechanism. It does not identify the *means* by which incongruities are made appropriate. Garden-path is rather a *joke strategy*. It describes where an incongruity is created within a joke and made appropriate. It is to be distinguished from the strategies of red light and crossroads (Dynel 2012).

10. Christian Hempelmann (2004, 387) does not consider such jokes to be jokes but a kind of "word play" because there is no relationship of opposition between the categories connected by the pun—in this case, *needles* and *needs*. As indicated above, I do not regard most jokes as organized around true oppositions. I understand that knock-knock jokes often link categories only by sound with no deeper semantic relations in evidence, but I do not see why such texts should be excluded from the category of jokes. Perhaps they should only be excluded from the category of "good jokes."

11. This would seem to be the crux of Victor Raskin's criticism of the appropriate incongruity perspective. Appropriate incongruity is post hoc (2011, 224). After the fact, an incongruity and its appropriateness in a humorous text can always be found. It is not clear, however, that SSTH and GTVH do not suffer from the same deficiency. Yet, if the appropriate incongruity perspective is capable of pointing to misanalyses of jokes by other theories, it is hardly "vacuous" (228).

12. Since SSTH and GTVH have been around for decades, I am not quite sure why "formalizing and tightening up definitions and reformulating some basic tenets of the theory" should only now be necessary (Raskin 2017, 18).

13. Unlike what IBM seems to have done with chess program Deep Blue in their match with Gary Kasparov (Jayanti 2005).

CHAPTER 6: MEMETICS AND FOLKLORISTICS: THE THEORY

1. Dawkins first published his book *The Selfish Gene* in 1976. It has gone through several editions. The thirtieth anniversary edition (2006) includes two additional chapters plus endnotes that were not in the first edition but were included in a 1989 edition. The 2006 edition is the one I am citing in this essay.

2. This is the example of what Dawkins calls "negative replication" (as in photographic "negative"), but the copying could have been more direct and "positive" with each segment of the original chain attracting a molecule identical to itself before splitting apart (2006, 13–14).

3. Genes often work in concert with one another in determining a phenotype, and there may be master genes that turn other genes on and off. Only rarely do genes seem to operate in isolation in determining a specific phenotypic trait. Furthermore, the environment for a gene is other genes and not only genes on the same chromosome (Dawkins 2006, 24, 37–39, 84–85).

4. In asexual reproduction or in sexual reproduction where there is no crossing over, chromosomes are faithfully reproduced for innumerable generations. According to Dawkins's definition, the entire chromosome would then constitute a gene (Dawkins 2006, 43).

5. A question that Dawkins raises but does not successfully answer is why sexual reproduction ever arose in the first place since it is a means of reproduction that necessarily leads to the reproduction of only half an organism's genes. He tries to answer the question by claiming that there may be a gene for sexual reproduction that selfishly reproduces itself. This, however, is merely a wild guess and seems like special pleading (Dawkins 2008, 44).

6. Dawkins recognizes his tautological tendencies on a number of occasions (2006, 33, 44, 86).

7. Furthermore, Dawkins sometimes seems willing to overlook contrary evidence in favor of selfish gene theory. He also is ready to posit explanations that apply in one case but not in another. In discussing the monogamous pairing of kittiwakes where both partners seem to do equal work in caring for offspring—on the surface contrary to his theorizing—Dawkins states: "Here we must suppose some evolutionary counter-pressure has been at work" (2006, 147). While his notion of kin selection depends upon close kin being able to identify one another (99–100), Dawkins does not seem bothered that slave ants cannot recognize that they are working for a queen to which they are totally unrelated (177–180). He regularly suggests that species must almost necessarily evolve countermeasures to recognize deceit or a healthy potential mate (157–162), but fungi-cultivating ants don't seem to be able to evolve stomachs that can process dead leaves directly (180). And then there is that comment about there being a selfish gene for sexual reproduction (see note 5).

8. Darwin was no lover of the concept of species. He found it vague and without any clear boundaries (Darwin 2008, 46–47, 53–54). He knew nothing of genes but might have found the idea that genes are the unit of selection compelling.

9. They sometimes reinforce one another, however (Dawkins 2006, 198).

10. They are not *entirely* independent. A meme that kills off the population in whose brains it has taken up residence will prove self-limiting.

11. This latter formulation is Dawkins's own.

12. Michael Drout holds that it is "the essential logical pattern, character, etc." of the story (2002, 56 n38). But what is that exactly?

13. Leave aside for the moment the enormous number of memes that are not easy to imitate and persist only because of the laborious efforts of a few—for example, the scores mastered by musicians, the liturgies mastered by clergy, the epics mastered by oral poets.

14. The selective advantage of novelty versus ideational coherence should merit some discussion and clarification. How much novelty is acceptable to a complex of already established memes?

15. Brodie links some meme success to the human genome, and Blackmore seems open to this possibility as well (1996, 41). Memes tied to danger, food, and sex are likely to prove successful, and the advertising and entertainment industries would seem to bear this out. Food, sex, and danger may provide the emotional charge that makes any associated meme memorable, but Brodie considers these to be memes in themselves (1996, 89). Blackmore does not consider perceptions necessarily to be memes (1999, 43), and Distin does not consider emotions or beliefs to be memes but *responses* to memes (2005, 63, 169).

16. The terminology is derived from Daniel Dennett (Blackmore 1999, 155). There is certainly some analogy here with Carl von Sydow's notion of the active and passive bearers of tradition (von Sydow 1948).

17. Consider two similar commercial products that are promoted in the same media with equal advertising budgets. Why should only one of them succeed?

18. Dawkins is willing to acknowledge that the evolution of language may not be guided by natural selection. What other aspects of culture might escape selective forces? "'*Dans des cas pareils, ce n'est que le premier pas qui coute.*' The rest is easy" (In these cases, it is only the first step that matters. The rest is easy; Freud 1955, 18: 193). The great Darwinist, Stephen Jay Gould, regards cultural evolution as Lamarckian rather than Darwinian (Gould 1991, 65). Nevertheless, he also suggests that stories develop according to Darwinian principles (244).

19. See Paul Gauthier (1990) for a critique of Weismann's experiment.

20. I admired the work by Peter and Daphne Grant on the adaptation of finches in the Galapagos Islands as described by Jonathan Weiner in *The Beak of the Finch* (1995). I now wonder, however, whether the changes to the finches' beaks were the result of genetic variations and natural selection or were epigenetic changes.

21. The Darwinian hypothesis would go out the window in cultural evolution in the same way that it would go out the window in biological evolution were it to be demonstrated that some species were actually the result of special creation.

22. Monica Foote observes that one person's product may become the next person's instructions (2007, 36). Aunger notes this as well (2002, 58). Foote is right to be suspicious of those who dismiss a Lamarckian concept of cultural evolution.

23. Darwin also offered a hypothesis for the relations between species in the same order and orders in the same class. He provided a historical understanding of Linnaeus's taxonomy.

24. Of course, we do not know where new ideas in the human brain come from and whether ideas that are transmitted are neurologically identical formations in the brain of the source and the receiver. But identical information can be conveyed even if the methods of encoding and storing that information vary (Jeffreys 2000, 233). Joe Davis encoded a Goethe poem and a map of the Milky Way in the DNA of a bacterium (Nadis 2013, 54). Aunger's entire book is devoted to theorizing the neurological underpinnings of memetics (2002).

25. Blackmore claims that memetics provides a "simple and obvious" explanation for the catchiness of the tunes in your head, but she does not explain the catchiness of any tune (1999, 56).

26. What abets or impedes the spread of particular types or items of folklore is an important question. An epidemiology of folklore is a worthwhile enterprise (Ellis 2003a, 84–86). To some extent, the historic-geographic study of folktales was essentially epidemiological, but the scholars were focused initially on recreating the *Urform* of a tale—that is, finding the equivalent of Patient Zero. Their ability to identify conditions, channels, and vectors was crude. The peregrinations of tales were sufficiently distant in time to make the identifications of such factors inexact or conjectural. Nevertheless, folklorists were and continue to be interested in conduits, transmission, and oicotypes.

27. Dawkins tries to avoid the word "fitness" in his book because he feels it puts too much emphasis on the perspective of the individual (2006, 137). I am not sure I understand this since one could talk about the fitness of genes—the ability of genes to produce organisms that successfully reproduce in a particular environment.

28. In discussing "good" genes, Dawkins states that they are the genes that survive in the gene pool, and that this proposition is not a fact or theory but a tautology. He then says that the "interesting question is what makes a gene good" (2006, 68).

29. "New 'mutants' . . . that are better at spreading will become more numerous" (Dawkins 1993, 20).

30. Suspicion that Distin's program might fail is aroused at the outset when she avoids setting out to demonstrate whether memetics is true or explains anything but proposes instead to examine "whether memetics could be true" (2005, 4).

31. The word "meme" is older and more widespread than the word "memetic," but because of its similarity to the French word *même* ("same," "self," "likewise"), it could not be used in Edmonds's bibliographic searches.

32. I do not know whether Edmonds realized that his article was being published in the final volume of the journal.

CHAPTER 7: MEMETICS AND FOLKLORISTICS: THE APPLICATIONS

1. It is the first published reference. Bill Ellis's discussion of contemporary legends was first presented in a conference paper in 1983. It was not published, however, until twenty years later.

2. There is some equivocation in her position as she thinks that Lamarckian selection may be more appropriate to understanding the evolution of folklore (Foote 2007, 36–37).

3. Zipes, however, is often restating arguments and materials from the book.

4. The problem with this approach is obvious. Memes do not have to be shown to be beneficial; they are beneficial by definition.

5. How avoiding the transgression of other bodies—violence—relates to an evolutionary argument is difficult to fathom. Evolution is about competition for food, sex, and shelter within particular environmental niches. Violence is a part of the natural order. If Zipes is suggesting that human evolution is a matter of moral evolution he would seem closer to the Marquis de Condorcet than Darwin.

6. Zipes actually quotes Dawkins that a meme seeks only its own advantage, but he does not recognize or does not register the difference between this and his own position. He attends only to the selfishness of memes and maintains, as Dawkins does, that humans have the power to choose the memes with which they operate (2006, 23).

7. Whatever one thinks of psychoanalytic approaches, they seem to make more sense of this material than a memetic and evolutionary approach.

8. He does seem to say that. He acknowledges that "The Frog Prince" meme does not exist in every culture, but he believes that every culture has narrative discourse about courtship, sexual

preference, and mating. It is likely that every culture talks about and tells stories about mating, but what has that to do with why *fairy tales* endure? Clearly such discourses need not be codified in fairy tale form and clearly they exist outside the frame of the fairy tale. So what does the fairy tale do? This is the old problem of functional equivalents that plagued functionalist explanations in mid-twentieth-century anthropology (Jarvie 1968, 198).

9. As Zipes himself seems to recognize (2006, 2).

10. The distinction between these two concepts escapes me. Why isn't a meme a packet of information that manipulates its host?

11. Dawkins could see certain viruses, at least in the computer realm, as potentially beneficial, particularly if they could be used to ward off viruses of a more insidious nature (1993, 16).

12. This criticism is somewhat unfair in that science is a part of culture, and culture is cumulative. There are scientific methods, and there is the knowledge that these methods produce. While some, or even much, of scientific knowledge may eventually be modified or overthrown, science cannot be constantly starting from scratch. One cannot abandon students in a chemistry laboratory, for example, and expect them to rediscover the periodic table. They have to be *taught* the periodic table. On the other hand, much of what takes place in chemistry laboratory classes is often what was once called "cookbook chemistry." Students were not taught how to hypothesize and test so much as they were taught to follow directions to known outcomes. Nevertheless, science seems no less a memeplex than religion, whether one prefers one or the other.

13. Witness, for example, the damage done by the routine surgeries performed on children with hypertrophy of the tonsils in the first half of the twentieth century. More than twenty percent of patients experienced post-surgical complications and thousands of deaths resulted from what is now considered a self-limiting condition (Gross 1966, 100–105).

14. This is simply a mathematical calculation: $20^8 = 25,600,000,000$. Dividing this figure by the total world population in 1994 would probably yield the 4.5 billion figure. However, millions of people do not read or write or have access to mail or computers, so they could neither receive nor transmit the letter. The number of letters received by each person should be substantially higher for this reason. People, however, send out the letters within the same social networks. Consequently, the same people would receive them again and again and would likely not retransmit them.

15. Ellis is critical, however, of Goodenough's and Dawkins's failure to refer to any of the scholarly literature on chain letters. He argues that their suggestion that making two copies rather than twenty might actually have restricted the spread of the chain letter even more. The more quickly a computer virus spreads, Ellis argues, the more likely it is to draw attention to itself. Precautions will be taken and counter-measures enacted. Likewise, a biological virus that quickly kills its hosts may die of its own success (Dawkins 1993, 15; Ellis 2003a, 81). Of course, if a legend spreads in the same manner as a biological virus, even if that infection should prove self-limiting, this would seem a substantiation, rather than a criticism, of the epidemiological model. After all, biological infections are also self-limiting.

16. Something similar would seem to obtain in the reaction of liberal media to the extremes of right-wing radio and television content. Rather than counter their assumptions and claims with reasoned rebuttal, television shows like *The Daily Show* and *The Colbert Report* turn those claims into farce.

17. It is surprising that Ellis did not identify books by folklorists that include discussion of the stolen kidney legend (e.g., Brunvand 1993, 149–154; Bennett 2005, 199–211; Campion-Vincent 2005, 24–29, 156–159). These books too might "neutralize" the belief, although they might also serve as a source of future infection.

18. Nevertheless, Ellis is comfortable in characterizing pieces of folklore as forms of resistance or immune responses. Should this not be as problematic as assigning meanings to legends?

19. In any event, what may need to be determined is a very narrow range in the personalities of individuals and groups; issues that arouse anxieties, for example (Bangerter and Heath 2004).

20. Dawkins shows that animal altruism is manifested primarily between kin—actually, between parents and their offspring—and that this is evidence for gene selfishness. Since the young grow up in the proximity of their parents, any expenditure by parents on behalf of their offspring might be attributed to propinquity rather than gene selfishness. The whole matter depends on whether altruistic behavior is directed to kin of differing genetic distances according to the degree of their relatedness (see Dawkins 2006, 90–94). So, the fact that legends might spread to close friends and relatives may only have to do with propinquity—who is likely to be around most of the time—rather than effecting any return benefits.

21. Pimple and Ellis both seem to have some issues with the nineteenth-century evolutionary theory used by folklorists and state or imply that this theory damaged the field of folklore. Pimple refers to the "specter" of unilinear cultural evolution (1996, 236), and Ellis refers to "old fashioned pseudo-Darwinian" cultural evolution (2003a, 91). First, cultural evolution was unilinear in the sense that the history of mankind reveals a development from what was termed "savagery" to "barbarism," to "civilization"—not the other way round—with each *stage* growing out of the previous one. These stages had fairly precise definitions. It does not mean that if left to themselves each and every society would eventually become Victorian England. Nevertheless, Western European societies in the nineteenth century did represent the height of human technological, social, and even intellectual complexity (which is not to say that complexity equals goodness). Second, evolutionary theory was not the exclusive province of folklore studies—it was shared by anthropology, sociology, literature, and other disciplines—none of which seem to have been impaired by their prior evolutionary tendencies. Third, evolutionary theory in folklore studies was never "pseudo-Darwinian"; it was never Darwinian at all. It was progressive and made no use of natural selection, which is what distinguishes a Darwinian perspective (Oring 2012b, 174).

22. It might be fruitful to compare the spread of computer viruses with computer-mediated legends. The legend is computer-mediated, but it is also human-mediated in a way a computer virus is not. That is to say, a person receiving a legend in an email has to decide whether to pass it on and whether to emend it. The interposition of a human agent between a legend and its copy might spread very differently than a computer virus that does not depend on human agency.

23. There were other reasons for choosing disgust. Not only were other emotions harder to operationalize, but previous discussions of the emotional attraction of legends and rumors often depended upon the claim that *preexisting* emotions—anxieties—are aroused that contribute to their dissemination. Disgust is not a preexisting emotion but is aroused by a specific stimulus.

24. Of course, making a claim is not the same as the demonstration of that claim.

25. Heath, Bell, and Sternberg also show that there is something of an inverse relationship between disgust and truth. Stories rated higher in levels of disgust were also rated lower in plausibility (2001, 1036). Thus, higher levels of disgust may dampen the enthusiasm for passing on a legend because of a sense that it is less likely to be true.

26. Heath, Bell, and Sternberg rightly point out that "selection only works in general [and] not that it always produces an optimum on each dimension of selection" (2001, 1037). But the question is not whether legends would necessarily be in some optimum state of disgust but why less disgusting variants would continue to coexist with the disgusting ones. Darwinian evolution is not fundamentally about improvement; it is about survival and extinction.

27. Is there perhaps something about the experimental environment that favors certain story choices?

28. Richard Dawkins would argue that the disgust memes are simply using human consciousness to reproduce themselves. (This is discussed in chapter 6.)

29. There are a few things about the experiments that I have questions about. Although I am neither an experimentalist nor a statistician, I was bothered by some of the categories of emotional

reaction employed in the first experiment. Disgust, joy, anger, sadness, fear, and contempt do seem to be emotional reactions (although the definition of an emotion is not straightforward). But why is *interest* an emotional reaction? Interest seems cognitive rather than emotional. Although some emotion-arousing stimuli may also prove interesting, mean interest varied hardly at all in subjects' responses to low, medium, and high disgust legends (Heath, Bell, and Sternberg 2001, 1036).

In the third experiment, Heath et al. survey popular urban legend websites to see whether legends with more disgust motifs are more likely to be found. But since the seventy-six legends that form the database for their experiments were taken from popular legend websites in the first place, it is not clear to me that any finding of these legends on popular websites is likely to be meaningful. Even though they show that the more disgust motifs they contain correlate with their appearance on a greater number of websites, it seems to me that they are using material that has already been demonstrated to be popular as it appeared on these websites in the first place. For some reason, they did not measure the popularity of the thirty-six non-disgust legends that they included in their data set of 112 legends that were employed in the first experiment. The popularity of those non-disgust legends on websites might have provided a revealing comparison. Furthermore, are legend websites a valid representation of legend popularity? Websites often serve as repositories, and once a legend is listed on a site, it is not clear what the basis is for removing it. So legends may persist for long periods of time in digital space after they cease being, or perhaps never were, current in oral or social space.

30. This etic quality is belied by the *justificatio* since people consciously justify their behavior (see pp. 118–119).

31. See the film *Whose Is This Song?* For a preview, go to http://www.der.org/films/whose-is-this-song.html.

32. On the other hand, one meme might spoil the entire bunch. Perhaps nothing dealt as much of a blow to racist ideologies in the United States than the idea that the Nazis, whom America fought in World War II, were racists.

33. Drout would reject this argument because he aims for a purely materialistic explanation of tradition.

34. The "Riming poem" is in the Exeter Book and the poem "Höfuðlausn" in Egill's saga.

35. See the chain of userpicks cited by Monica Foote (2007) of the "bunny with a pancake on its head." It eventually is transformed into "Snape (from the *Harry Potter* films) with a pancake on his head" and "Jesus with a pancake on His head." What would be left of this meme should it morph into "Jesus with a frisbee on his shoulder"?

36. Drout certainly recognizes the difference between evolutionary and revolutionary change. He regards the influence of the Scandinavian settlement on the English language as *evolutionary* but the influence of the Norman Conquest on the language as *revolutionary* (2006b, 81).

37. Leslie White (1949, 146–189) made this point many years ago. It is surprising to find that none of the anthropological "neo-evolutionists" of the mid-twentieth century are cited by memeticists. So much for tradition. Curiously, the memeticists slip intention and the soul back into the language—if not the rationale—of memetics in what they call the "memes' eye view" (Blackmore 1999, 37–52; Drout 2006a, 17, 175).

38. To hear Drout's excellent readings of the Anglo-Saxon literature go to http://acadblogs.wheatoncollege.edu/mdrout/.

39. This raises questions about the replication of unwritten memes—that is, of folklore.

40. What would have been the result of Constantine converting to Judaism rather than Christianity?

41. Drout argues that the social structure of the monastery creates an environment favorable to such memes, so that he is trying to have it both ways. On the one hand, the Benedictine monastery is an insular and resistant memeplex. On the other, when it is not resistant to change, it is a favorable environment in which certain other memes can propagate: "The very stasis brought

about by the monasteries' strict adherence to the *Rule of St. Benedict* and the *Regularis Concordia* caused them to fulfill an important adaptive niche in the culture" (2006a, 154). The adoption of these inheritance functions by the monasteries, however, does not indicate stasis but change.

CHAPTER 8: FOUR LAWS OF FOLKLORE

1. Appearances can be deceiving, however, and proposed laws are always open to challenge, revision, and possible abandonment.

2. They do not hold at the subatomic level. They may not even hold at the macroatomic level. Space probes Pioneer 10 and Pioneer 11 launched in 1972 and 1973 are off course, and despite a review of all the data, the deviation has no clear explanation. MOND (modified Newtonian dynamics), which suggests that gravity is a bit stronger across vast distances, has been invoked to explain the anomaly. MOND, however, was not proposed to explain the trajectories of the Pioneer spacecrafts but rather to deal with the issue of dark matter (Brooks 2008, 29–31, 43). That Newton's gravitational constant might not be uniform over large distances was already suggested by Friedrich Wilhelm Bessel (1784–1846) in the nineteenth century (Levenson 2016, 34).

An eccentricity in the orbit of Mercury led Urbain Jean Joseph Le Verrier, using Newton's laws, to predict the existence of a small planet or a cluster of asteroids between Mercury and the sun. A planet was later observed by a number of amateur and professional astronomers. It was appropriately named Vulcan. More systematic searches, however, failed to reproduce the observations. In 1915, when Albert Einstein explained the anomaly in Mercury's orbit, the hypothetical planet was banished from the solar system, and Newton's laws became a generalization within the theory of general relativity (Levenson 2016, xi–xii; 69–78, 169–172). A debate is now going on about the presence of "Planet Nine" some fifty-six billion miles from the sun that would solve some other orbital anomalies of objects in the Kuiper Belt ("A Whole New World" 2019).

3. Coffin acknowledges that Anglo-American ballads can be collected with complete plots, but those variants that focus on the emotional core are the most artful (1957, 211). Artfulness is, of course, a highly subjective criterion for characterizing or predicting folksong change in transmission.

4. Coffin specifically cites "Geordie" (Child #209; Child 1965, 3:127); the Sir Walter Scott "Twa Corbies" (Child #26; Scott 1803, 3:239–242; Child 1965, 1:256); the Thomas Percy "Sir Patrick Spens" and "Edward" (Child #59; Child #13; Percy 1966 [1886], 1:98–99, 83–84); the Charles Mackie-William Mcmath "Lord Randal" (Child #12; Child 1965, 1:157–158); and the American ballad "Charles Guiteau" (Laws 1964, 181 Type E11). In *The British Traditional Ballad in North America* (1963, 9), Coffin also mentions "The Death of Queen Jane" (Child #170), "The Elfin Knight" (Child #6), "The Cherry Tree Carol" (Child #54), and the "Little Lizzie" fragments (Child #226) as adhering to this principle.

5. Jokes, however, are rarely narratives (see Oring 2016, 147–164).

6. Katherine Luomala suggested that this law be renamed the law of ritual number so that it might be more generally applied (Luomala 1980, 367).

7. In his comparison of oral and printed supernatural narratives, Larry Danielson characterizes some of Olrik's laws as stylistic rather than structural (1979, 133–134). I agree with him that the law of three is structural, but I think that the law of contrast and the law of two to a scene are structural as well; they pertain, however, to the structure of scene, not to the structure of the narrative as a whole.

8. Danielson has compared ghost stories from oral and vernacular printed sources. The printed sources, however, usually report oral accounts of supernatural occurrences (1979, 133). They are not fictional creations and would not serve as an assessment of the applicability of Olrik's laws to literary texts.

9. That was the year Olrik published his essay "Epische Gesetze der Volksdictung," although Olrik had presented his laws in an address to historians in Berlin in 1908 as well as in a paper in *Dansker Studier* (Olrik 1965, 131n1).

10. Van Gennep was even inclined to call the stages of a rite of passage a *law* but was dissuaded and used the word "schema" instead. He later used the word "law" in *La Formation des legends* but apologized for it (Zumwalt 1988, 31).

11. Symbols of death and rebirth might be appropriate to rites of transition. Purifications and the cutting of hair might be appropriate to rites of separation, and naming or renaming (or the symbolic performance of some activity appropriate to the new status) to rites of incorporation (van Gennep 1960, 20–24, 53–54; Honko 1979, 374).

12. The term *superstition* originally held no pejorative meaning. It meant "surviving" and designated a surviving belief or practice. As the Roman Catholic Church came to regard superstitions as survivals of pagan practice, they were deemed sinful (Belmont 2005 [1982], 164–166).

13. It is possible, however, to have action in the absence of belief (see Campbell 1996).

14. Even then, the particulars of the practice might be extinguished while the form might remain intact. It was not uncommon for baseball players during a winning streak to wear the same articles of clothing again and again without allowing them to be cleaned. When they encountered a losing streak, the team might go out and buy a whole new set of clothes. The particular articles of clothing were changed but not the form of the superstition (Gmelch 2001 [1971], 298).

15. Folklorists have not investigated individual superstitions—those initiated and practiced by solitary individuals—although they would seem relevant to the understanding of communal superstitions.

16. This is not to suggest that there are no high-cost superstitions. See the elaborate ritual of baseball player Wade Boggs, for example (Vyse 1997, 3–4).

17. In the same essay, the Opies suggest that the stability of tradition is always deceptive (Opie and Opie 1980, 72), that customs feed on their own commemoration (71), and that credulity prospers in an age of disillusionment (73).

18. Undoubtedly, postmodernism plays a part, but even before the advent of postmodernism, these laws were not assiduously explored.

CHAPTER 9: TO EXPLAIN TRADITION

1. A conference held in Liperi, Finland in 1981 illustrates the point. The conference topic was "Trends in Nordic Tradition Research," and the participants addressed themselves to trends in traditional social organizations, customs, beliefs, material culture, prose narratives, and folksongs. Only in the concluding general session of the conference, however, did someone think to ask, "What is tradition?" ("Final Discussion" 1983, 233). One might think it curious that this question was raised only after everything transpired rather than as the conference was being conceptualized and organized.

2. Lauri Honko would resolve the conundrum of culture versus tradition dilemma in a different fashion. He reserves *culture* for an integrated organization of elements (Honko 2013, 306). But what he is referring to is really not culture but *a culture*, or what is sometimes called a *cultural system*. *Culture* does not always or even usually imply an organized system. See, for example, Edward B. Tylor's work *Primitive Culture*, which put the term *culture* on the map and in which the term *culture* implies nothing about local, organized systems.

3. The notion that a tradition was something valuable goes back to Roman uses of the word *tradition* (Gross quoted in Bronner 1998, 27). Witness the reaction of animal rights activists to the Hegin's Pigeon Shoot in Central Pennsylvania, or the response of the National Endowment of the Arts Folk Arts Division and the members of the American Studies Association to the suggestion that hunting and shooting constituted traditional arts (Bronner 1998, 462–469).

4. Functionalists thought they were explaining matters in terms of cause and effect, but they tended to explain A in terms of its effects on B rather than explain B as a consequence of A (see Oring 1976).

5. Toelken is not unaware of this problem, and he attempts to resolve it by relegating folklore to those dynamic changes in artifacts and performances that are expressed in local settings apart from the institutions of the larger society (1996, 33–34).

6. Percy, however, did not see this ancient poetry as the pinnacle of poetic art. While they possessed a "pleasing simplicity," they were lacking in "higher beauties." Consequently, he included some modern verses in his volumes to "atone for the rudeness of the more obsolete poems" (Percy 1966, 1:8).

7. See Thomas Percy's comments on manuscript copies of ballad poetry (1966, 3:13).

8. Alan Dundes, in his essay "The Devolutionary Premise in Folklore Theory" (1969) argues that the notion of *Zersingen*—often translated as "sing to death" or "sing to pieces"—was yet another instance of folklorists' predisposition to see folklore as necessarily degenerating (1969, 7). But in fact, the term really related to what happened to *art poetry* with known authors when that poetry was orally transmitted. Since the original texts of the poems were known, those in oral circulation could only move further away from the originals. They would necessarily lose something in the course of their transmission. Hermann Goja, in his *Das Zersingen der Volkslieder* (1920), tried to show how art songs changed when circulating orally among Austrian soldiers in World War I. The direction of the changes, he claimed, largely had to do with the unconscious responses of soldiers to changing conditions during the war. He never indicated that the songs had deteriorated, and his translators wisely translated *Zersingen* as "alteration" rather than "sing to pieces" or "degeneration" (Goja 1964, 111).

Improvement would seem to be another conception of change that remains unanalyzed and discussed in this essay. Improvement would at first appear to be the inverse of degeneration, but this is not the case. Degeneration can describe any loss to an original song, tale, or custom whether or not the progeny of that original improves in any other way. The elements of an orally transmitted myth or custom once changed are changed forever. Absent a literary or recorded document, information from the original is forever unreclaimable (except by accident). A myth that has changed has degenerated even if it is aesthetically superior to the original. Folklorists need only consider the numerous literary versions of ballads and folktales that have been produced for a reading public and which were ignored by folklorists, if not by literary scholars, because they were not believed to reflect the voice of some folk. Improvement, furthermore, generally refers to aesthetic improvement. Any tradition may improve aesthetically even if it retains only a tenuous relation to its progenitor. Aesthetic improvement, furthermore, is always dependent on the taste and judgment of the scholar who is doing the assessing. It is rarely, if ever, an assessment of those whose traditions are being discussed. The ballad scholars often registered aesthetic improvements of ballads in the course of their transmission. It might be argued that improvement need not always be rooted in aesthetic criteria; there could be *functional* improvement where folklore changes to better fit the culture or social group in which it is found, but this is likely to be an example of adaptation.

9. In the eighteenth century, Henrik Gabriel Porthan noted that a reciter of Finnish oral poetical forms might want to conceal portions of a text that contained incantations to keep those incantations efficacious (Honko 2013, 191).

10. Dominance refers to some salient word, phrase, or event that shapes other parts of the narrative. Not all the processes identified by Bartlett have been given equal weight by folklorists. The persistence of the trivial and the influence of visual imagery seem to be less prominent in their work (although see Hymes 1981a, 144). The intensification of relations of opposition, similarity, and subjection would probably be considered by most folklorists an aspect of dramatization. Axel Olrik made contrast one of his "laws" of folk narrative (Olrik 1965 [1909], 135.)

11. Annikki Kaivola-Bregenhøj states (2000, 98) that creative change was not something considered by Krohn, although he clearly recognized it (1971, 92).

12. Barry did not believe that folksongs always improved artistically in oral tradition, although he felt that most of them did (Alvey 1973, 85).

13. Hyman was a literary critic and not a folklorist; nevertheless, his article was published in *Journal of American Folklore* and folklorist Richard M. Dorson was much taken with it (Dorson 1978, 105).

14. Actually, the Polish proverbs employed in the memes that Szpila studied must remain very much alive for the meme parodies to prove successful.

15. In fact, "the Boston Burglar" is an Americanization of "Botany Bay" but both songs were collected in southern Michigan at about the same time (Gardner and Chickering 1939, 323, 335).

16. There is a Dee Lundeen Falls in Michigan but apparently no River Dee or Dee River.

17. A similar point was made in 1912 by Arthur Balfour when addressing the inaugural banquet of the First International Eugenics Congress in London (see Blom 2008, 352).

18. A concept that in itself is problematic. Certainly, we cannot be speaking of the survival of a particular performance or even a text since these are bound to change in some small if not large ways. Should we be talking about the survival or extinction of tales in which a character named Cinderella loses her shoe at a ball, or tales that generally conform to ATU Types 510A or 510B, or tales of the persecuted heroine more generally, or magic tales, or folktales as a whole? And at what point should it be acknowledged that a series of changes ultimately results in a song or tale that no longer resembles its original so that it has failed to survive precisely because of its numerous adaptations?

19. Roma Chatterji argued that the art of the *chitrakars* of the Medinipur district of West Bengal were able to survive by adapting the images in their painted narrative scrolls to urban forms of entertainment such as public service posters, graphic novels, and comic books. The songs that accompanied the display of the scrolls in the village setting, of course, had to be dropped. Even the "traditional" village performances had lost the sacred character they once seemed to possess. The Gond-Pardhan style of folk or tribal art of Madhya Pradesh found a new home in the modern art gallery. How much adaptation or "translation" can take place before one questions whether a tradition is, in fact, being maintained? (2012, 5, 27, 63, 120).

20. Once in a seminar where we were discussing the meaning of *evolution*, I asked the students what kinds of things were unrolled. The Jewish student said, "a scroll"; the Armenian student said, "a carpet"; and the American student said, "toilet paper."

21. Darwin did not employ the word *evolution* in the first edition of *On the Origin of Species* in 1859, although he did use the word *evolved* as the last word in the book. In the 1872 edition, he used the term somewhat more liberally.

22. Increasing design occurs because new design is a result of changes to previous designs. There is, however, no simple metric for quantifying degrees of design. Dennett does not precisely define design. It is the opposite of entropy and disorder and is characteristic of life processes (1995, 70–71). Dawkins defines design as "attributes that an intelligent and knowledgeable engineer might have built into it [a living body] in order to achieve some sensible purpose." The design does not need to be optimum (1986, 21). Of course, neither Dawkins nor Dennett holds that such design requires an intelligent designer. Nevertheless, these are not particularly good definitions. Ultimately, it would seem that Dawkins, at least, would be content to define design as organizational complexity (as was proposed by Herbert Spencer) that has functional value and that was unlikely to have arisen by chance alone (Dawkins 1986, 317).

23. *The Ascent of Man* was the title of a book and of a television series written by Jacob Bronowski in the 1970s.

24. In fact, the total number of articles in folklore journals in English that employ the term *evolution* in their titles is only eighteen, and not all of those are actually about folklore change.

One, for example, is about change in the concept of folklore and the field of folkloristics. Another is about the idea of evolution in works by H. G. Wells. Most employ the word as a synonym for *history* and concern the development of a particular tune, dance, legend, or religious figure. In other words, *evolution* is not a theoretical term.

25. This is not entirely true. There is horizontal transmission even in biology, and some of a mother's cells can even be acquired from her children (Zimmer 2018, 386–389).

26. Which is why David C. Rubin (1995) considers only ballads, epics, and counting-out rhymes in his book on memory and transmission.

27. Anthropologists are more likely to see cultural innovation and spread as linked to group survival in the early history of the species; that is, in their considerations of biological and cultural co-evolution (Boyd and Richerson 2009). Twentieth-century cultural evolutionary explanations, offered by the so-called neo-evolutionists such as Leslie White, Elman Service, and Marshall Sahlins, did suggest that the group with the more advanced technology benefitted in competition with other groups. Anthropologists that regard selection for certain cultural practices and institutions focus on such institutions as monogamy (Henrich, Boyd, and Richerson 2012) or general social processes like reciprocity (Boyd and Richerson 1988), and group cooperation (Boyd and Richerson 1992). Such a perspective is virtually nonexistent in folklore studies. Folklorists do not normally argue for the contribution of a particular folktale, legend, or riddling practice to group reproductive success. Jack Zipes (2008) is an exception as he attempts to link fairy tales with group survival, but his arguments are problematic (see chapter 7).

28. The singers themselves, in fact, had no conception of word-for-word reproduction (Foley 1992, 279).

29. Leslie White regards a genius as someone who is known for making a significant discovery or invention. This discovery or invention, however, is a cultural act that can be explained in terms of the synthesis of preexisting cultural elements. If the elements are there, they will eventually be synthesized in someone's brain (White 1949, 203–205). The genius is the one who happens to synthesize it first. Tony Veale (2012) believes that creativity needs to be demystified. He holds that creativity is well within the potential of algorithm-driven computers.

30. This is contrary to Nicolaisen's intent, however, as he hopes that the creativity of the performer lies at the center of the explanation for the maintenance of traditions. In other words, he holds with those who believe that creativity produces adaptations that ensure survival. Undoubtedly some innovations do produce long-lived adaptations (E. Wilson 2017, 40). The question is, *which ones*? It seems as likely—indeed, more likely—that innovative changes would lead to the extinction of a tradition, even if they were *intended* to preserve it.

31. I do not find it helpful when a term is re-invoked to define itself.

32. While I have no problem with employing *traditionalization* as a term to label the invocation of the past in relation to present practice, I would also want to use it for the act of identifying a model for future reproduction. Following the engagement of a group of people in some activity, the proposition, "Let's make this a tradition" would also seem to be a traditionalization. Hymes further suggests that the term *traditionalization* would serve to universalize folklore's realm of discourse as it labels a universal disposition and need (1975, 354), but this should also be true of the word *tradition*. Traditions are also universal. Tradition—cultural reproduction—exists even when a reproducer fails to acknowledge it or is unaware that such reproduction is taking place.

Ehsan Estiri (2018) considers traditionalization a theory—indeed, a grand theory of folklore (15). I regard it, like performance itself, simply as a concept. Traditionalization in itself explains nothing. While it is true to traditionalize, to invoke and tell stories about the past can be used to affirm a particular ideology by claiming aspects of the past should continue to govern in the present (19), it can also be used to discredit or ridicule a past practice or belief. It also seems possible that invoking the past may make no ideological claims at all.

33. After World War II, the culture on Manus in the Admiralty Islands underwent a profound change. *The New Way* swept through the villages with the principle of the brotherhood of man, the sharing of resources, and the end to warfare. Some basic practices were precipitously abandoned. The belief in ancestral ghosts that chastised wrong behavior and protected the family against outside supernatural attack was discarded. The obsessive and aggressive pursuit of traditional forms of wealth was given up. Anger and cursing were suppressed. Strict avoidances between certain categories of kin were abolished, women were somewhat emancipated, and Western-style clothing was adopted. A new village layout was designed, new houses were built, new schools established, and communal labor organized. With all these and other momentous changes, the ribald joking between cross-cousins was maintained (Mead 1956, 46–47, 71–73, 170, 199, 207, 275–316, 318–326, 372). Whyever did that continue?

34. Jeff Titon suggests that the lined-out hymn singing of the Old Regular Baptists in Kentucky was threatened by the community's economic dependence on a declining coal industry (2015, 184). Certainly, if the economic base of a community is obliterated, the community itself may be destroyed and its traditions extinguished or fragmented. But that observation does not specifically identify the forces at work in the change of a tradition. Furthermore, although the Old Regular Baptists very much wanted to preserve their mode of hymn singing, it seems that a more direct threat to this tradition were gospel songs, which, though incorporated into the song repertoire, were compartmentalized within the church service. The community was having difficulty finding younger singers to master the ornate lining-out tunes of the old hymns (Titon 1999, 117–118, 120).

35. Anthropologists have long been interested in the change of cultures over time. But interest in the dynamics of change only really took off in the 1930s. The term *acculturation* first appears in the anthropological literature in the 1880s. An article with the term in the title appears in an anthropological journal in 1898 (McGee 1898). It only enters into dictionaries in the first decades of the twentieth century (Keesing 1973, 12). In 1935, the study of acculturation became pressing, and a memorandum was sent out to various journals stressing the need for such studies (Redfield, Linton, and Herskovits 1935a 1935b, 1936). *Acculturation* refers to change as a result of first-hand contact between groups of people. Acculturation is an aspect of *culture change*, and *assimilation* is a phase of acculturation. *Diffusion*, however, may take place with and without firsthand contact (Redfield, Linton, and Herskovits 1935a, 145–146). Although there is an emphasis in the outline on the traits presented by the donor society, it recognized that the resistance of the receiving group needed to be addressed as well (147).

I am in no way critical of what has been called "salvage anthropology." Anthropologists were interested in obtaining as many descriptions of different societies as possible so they might determine what was culturally unique, commonplace, and universal in the human condition. They were trying to reconstruct a variety of cultures before they were completely destroyed or transformed by Western civilization.

A small book was published in in 1985 titled *Contemporary Folklore and Culture Change*. It was the product of the fourth Finnish-Hungarian symposium that took place in Helsinki in 1983. While changes are described, almost none of those changes are genuinely explained. See Järvinen (1985).

36. Carla Bianco studied the transplantation of villagers from Roseto Valfortore to the United States (1974). They did not settle in the cities but founded a new community in Pennsylvania, also named Roseto. Bianco noted the differences between the Italian and American communities but did not precisely explain how the changes in the new community occurred. For example, harvest songs disappeared in Pennsylvania because the migrants were no longer engaged in agricultural work. But as the villagers regretted their loss, one wonders why they were not revived in some other musical venue—the town maintained a strong instrumental musical tradition—but left to dwindle in individual memories (1974, 31, 129). The decay of Rosetan story traditions in the United

States was attributed to the influence of television (78). She noted that Rosetans did maintain story traditions into the second generation, whereas they were quickly lost in Italian immigrant groups that had moved to cities (79). The changes are described, but not precisely.

Aili Nenola-Kallio studied the decline of the lament tradition in Karelia and Ingria. Ingrian laments were on the verge of extinction. Nineteenth-century Lutheran ministers were an important cause of decline in Ingria of wedding and funeral customs as well as the associated lament tradition. In some cases, they forced congregations to sign contracts to reform their rituals. Russian Orthodox church authorities in Karelia attempted to eliminate laments as well. They were actually forbidden by law. Nevertheless, they only managed to end the tradition in cities and among the higher social classes. The Orthodox priests in the rural areas did not concern themselves with them. Why the Lutherans were successful while the Orthodox were not is not entirely explained. But it is noted that the Ingrian customs only entered their final decline when the Lutheran communities were dispersed to different parts of the Soviet Union in the 1920s and 1930s (Nenola-Kallio 1981).

Robin Harris described the forces that precipitated the decline of the Sakha epic tradition of *olonkho* in Siberia. Language loss, Soviet policy, urbanization, education, and the spread of literacy all played a part in its decay (Harris 2017, 39–63). The impetus to revive olonkho in the twenty-first century came from the outside with its recognition by UNESCO as a "Masterpiece of the Oral and Intangible Heritage of Humanity" (33). Subsequently, olonkho became less an oral epos performed in intimate settings than a symbol of Sakha identity. State and NGO monies were invested in olonkho education, artistic productions, festivals, prize competitions, and scholarly research. Original theater pieces were composed based in part on epic plots and characters in which segments of olonkho music and poetry were embedded. It might be said that elements of the epos were framed and sacralized rather than being restored to their original styles and conditions of performance.

37. Morin identifies the Manchu dynasty's edict to the population to adopt the queue or be executed as one example (2016, 146). At various periods in their histories, Jewish, Christian, and Islamic conquerors employed similar threats to spread their religious beliefs and practices.

38. To characterize proliferation as a measure of longevity may itself be tautologous. If a chain is proliferating, what is proliferated may be long-lived by definition.

39. It would seem that certain genres are more likely to be transmitted in different chains. Lengthy and highly complex verbal material and behavioral routines may require long periods of practice: healing chants and rituals, royal genealogies, or oral epics, for example. The chains for the diffusion of such materials are likely to be narrow and short as few individuals undertake the arduous training necessary to successfully reproduce the texts and ritual behaviors. The chains for jokes, legends, and proverbs, however, would more likely prove to be wide and compact. Thus, the shape of a diffusion chain would seem, to some extent, to be a function of the kind of tradition that is being transmitted.

40. Shag bracelets were an inexpensive fashion accessory worn by girls in grade and middle schools that were composed of plastic gel beads sold in a variety of colors. The different colors were supposed to indicate the type of sexual activity that the child had performed or would be willing to engage in. If someone snapped the bracelet, the child had to perform the act in question. Rainbow parties were said to be gatherings in which girls wore different colored lipsticks and then performed fellatio on the boys, leaving a rainbow of different colors on the boys' penises (Best and Bogle 2014, 2–4). In truth, Best and Bogle are sociologists, but Best has very close ties to folklorists and folklore research.

41. The "N-word" was once the dominant term in the rhyme but was expurgated as social values changed (Rubin 1995, 238). (Curiously, references to the term even show up in the counting-out rhymes of Finland Swedes [Ekrem 2000, 293].) My own childhood experience might serve as a counterexample to Rubin's contention that there is a semantic constraint on the nature of the

replacement noun in the second line of the verse as something having toes or at least feet. In the rhyme I remember, the second line was "catch a *nickel* by the toe." A nickel, being an American five-cent coin, has no toes or feet. While the word would seem to have replaced the N-word somewhere in the rhyme's history, this was not something done by my play group. Neither I nor the other children in my group would have heard or known that word. The word *nickel*, however, was very familiar and served the rhyme even though it made no real sense. Thus, the change to *nickel* could just as easily have been a result of mishearing rather than expurgation. The use of the term *nickel* in the rhyme was also recorded in New Zealand (Bauer and Bauer 2007, 198).

42. Both *Eenie Meenie* and *Onery Twoery* also have numerous variants. See Bolton (1888, 94–100, 103–106).

43. The outcome of counting-out procedures is generally unknown to those who employ the technique, but it is, in fact, completely determined. If a child counts correctly using the same rhyme with the same number of children, the outcome will necessarily be the same. See Oring (2012, 153–166).

44. It also might be argued that children's counting-out rhymes are more insulated from the social, economic, and political forces at work in a society, and they are thus *harder* to explain. If one advances this argument, then the obligation would be to identify the kinds of traditions that are more and less integrated with other aspects of the society and the way the relationships operate. Even so, it would be hard to maintain that there could be *no* cause for changes in children's counting-out rhymes.

AFTERWORD

1. There is some evidence that the difference in the appreciation of humor by atheists and practicing Christians is, at best, "subtle." There is little distinction in the appreciation of religious humor and even somewhat blasphemous humor (Schweizer and Ott 2016, 428–429).

2. Certainly, there is no record of a Jewish aversion to physical violence in the Hebrew Bible. Under Seleucid and Roman domination, violent Jewish revolts erupted. Against the Seleucids, the Jewish revolt was successful (leaving behind the Hasmonean dynasty and the festival of Chanukkah); against Rome the various revolts proved utterly disastrous (and left the Jews without their Temple or a homeland). The aversion to violence attributed to Jews in the Diaspora is more likely a result of being minority populations in societies with no aversions to violence, so that any manifestation of violence on the part of Jews was likely to incite even more violent reprisals.

3. Alan Dundes was almost the only American folklorist who consistently employed a psychoanalytic perspective (e.g., Dundes 1997).

4. A workplace survey conducted by the Employment Law Alliance found that the most common type of sexual misconduct in the workplace was expressed in "language, jokes, and teasing" ("Employment Law Alliance Survey" 2018).

5. There was no mechanical recording of the jokes, and rumors after the event tended to increase their number and nature exponentially. But the jokes included here seem to reliably reflect the jokes that Captain Blanchard told at the event (see Vick 1997; Mills III 2019).

6. Many couples only begin to realize the extent of that economic arrangement when the marriage is in the process of being dissolved.

7. The *Time* article by Mark Thompson, which forms the basis of my description, also points to a complaint by a junior petty officer that she had been treated unfairly and called a "Jewish-American Princess." An inquiry concluded that he had harassed the woman. The details of this inquiry were not reported by *Time*, but the magazine pointed out that "she wasn't even Jewish." If she were Jewish, it *might* have been considered a slur directed against an ethnic minority, but as she was not, it might only suggest that she was spoiled and expected special treatment. The term

would have been a metaphor derived from that joke corpus. Whether American Jewish females deserve this characterization is another matter entirely.

Karl Vick followed up the case in a *Washington Post* article in July of the same year (Vick 1997). Much later, Ladson F. Mills III wrote a book on the subject (2019). Most of the book is dedicated to describing the culture of coverup in the United States Navy and Coast Guard, which the author felt was instrumental in creating the conditions for Captain Blanchard's disgrace and suicide. There is also reporting of many important details of the case—including those concerning the supposedly harassed woman—that naturally could not be addressed in the brief news articles.

8. If females in the military cannot accept a sexual joke as a joke, what will be the situation when they are shot at or ordered to kill?

9. But almost anything can, including rules against harassment.

10. On average, work makes people more miserable than any other activity (except for being sick in bed). Working with those whom one considers to be friends gives a great boost to a sense of happiness on the job (Stephens-Davidowitz 2022, 238–242).

11. Professional stand-up comedians are sensitive to this principle and vary the targets of jokes in their routines (Kravitz 1977, 295–301).

12. I suggested that functionalism in folkloristics and anthropology constituted less of an explanation than an interpretation (Oring 1976, 78–80).

13. The call was first made by Bill Ivey (2018, 4–5). Ivey's enthusiasm for the "big idea" was inspired by a *New York Times* essay by Neal Gabler (Gabler 2011). The problem, of course, is to come up with compelling big ideas.

References

Aarne, Antti, and Stith Thompson. 1964. *The Types of the Folktale*. Helsinki: Suomalainen Tiedeaketemia.

Abbot, Kevin R., and Thomas N. Sherratt. 2011. "The Evolution of Superstition through Optimal Use of Incomplete Information." *Animal Behavior* 82 (1): 85–92.

Abrahams, Roger D. 1964. *Deep Down in the Jungle: Negro Narrative Folklore from the Streets of Philadelphia*. Hatboro, PA: Folklore Associates.

Abrahams, Roger D. 1968. "Introductory Remarks to a Rhetorical Theory of Folklore." *Journal of American Folklore* 81 (320): 143–158.

Abrahams, Roger D. 1977. "An Enactment-Centered Theory of Folklore." In *Frontiers of Folklore*, ed. William R. Bascom, 79–120. Boulder, CO: Westview.

Abrahams, Roger D., and George Foss. 1968. *Anglo-American Folksong Style*. Englewood Cliffs, NJ: Prentice-Hall.

Adler, Ruth. 1998. "Shalom Aleichem's 'On Account of a Hat.'" In *Jewish Humor*, ed. Avner Ziv, 19–25. New Brunswick, NJ: Transaction.

Allen, Garland E. 1983. "The Several Faces of Darwin: Materialism in Nineteenth and Twentieth Century Evolutionary Theory." In *Evolution from Molecules to Men*, ed. D. S. Bendall, 81–102. Cambridge: Cambridge University Press.

Allingham, William, ed. 1872 (1865). *The Ballad Book: A Selection of the Choicest British Ballads*. New York: Macmillan.

Altman, Sig. 1971. *The Comic Image of the Jew: Explorations of a Pop Culture Phenomenon*. Rutherford, NJ: Farleigh Dickinson Press.

Alvey, R. Gerald. 1973. "Phillips Barry and Anglo-American Folksong Scholarship." *Journal of the Folklore Institute* 10 (1/2): 67–95.

https://doi.org/10.7330/9781646425198.c011

Anderson, Walter. 1923. *Kaiser und Abt*. Folklore Fellows Communications No. 42. Helsinki: Suomalainen Tiedeakatemia.

Anderson, Walter. 1951. *Ein volkskundliches Experiment*. Folklore Fellows Communications No. 141. Helsinki: Suomalainen Tiedeakatemia.

Anderson, Walter. 1956. *Eine neue Arbeit zur experimentellen Volkskunde*. Folklore Fellows Communications No. 168. Helsinki: Suomalainen Tiedeakatemia.

Anttonen, Pertti J. 1995. "The Rites of Passage Revisited: A New Look at van Gennep's Theory of the Ritual Process and Its Application in the Study of Finnish-Karelian Wedding Rituals." In *Folklore: Critical Concepts in Literary and Cultural Studies*, ed. Alan Dundes, Vol. 3, 178–211. London: Routledge.

Aristotle. 1991. *On Rhetoric: A Theory of Civil Discourse*. Edited and translated by George A. Kennedy. New York: Oxford University Press.

Attardo, Salvatore. 2001. *Humorous Texts: A Semantic and Pragmatic Analysis*. Berlin: Mouton de Gruyter.

Attardo, Salvatore. 2007. "Humorous Metaphors." Paper presented at the Tenth Conference of International Linguistics in Kraków, Poland, July 19, 2007.

Attardo, Salvatore. 2015. "Humorous Metaphors." In *Cognitive Linguistics and Humor Research*, ed. Gert Brône, Kurt Feyaerts, and Tony Veale, 91–110. Berlin: Walter de Gruyter.

Attardo, Salvatore, Christian F. Hempelmann, and Sarah Di Maio 2002. "Script Oppositions and Logical Mechanisms: Modeling Incongruities and Their Resolutions." *Humor: International Journal of Humor Research* 15 (1): 3–46.

Attardo, Salvatore, and Victor Raskin. 1991. "Script Theory Revis(it)ed: Joke Similarity and Joke Representation Model." *Humor: International Journal of Humor Research* 4 (3/4): 293–347.

Auboin, Elie. 1948. *Technique et psychologie du comique*. Marseille: OFEP.

Aunger, Robert. 2000. "Introduction." In *Darwinizing Culture: The Status of the Science of Memetics*, ed. Robert Aunger, 1–23. Oxford: Oxford University Press.

Aunger, Robert. 2002. *The Electric Meme: A New Theory of How We Think*. New York: The Free Press.

Ausubel, Nathan. 1948. *A Treasury of Jewish Folklore*. New York: Crown.

Baldwin, Barry, ed. 1983. *The Philogelos or Laughter-Lover*. Translated by Barry Baldwin. Amsterdam: J. C. Gieben.

Bangerter, Adrian, and Chip Heath. 2004. "The Mozart Effect: Tracking the Evolution of a Scientific Legend." *British Journal of Social Psychology* 43 (Pt 4): 605–623.

Barber, Bernard. 1941. "Acculturation and Messianic Movements." *American Sociological Review* 6 (5): 663–669.

Barnes, Daniel R. 1986. "Interpreting Urban Legends." *ARV: Scandinavian Yearbook of Folklore* 40: 67–78.

Baron, Robert A., and Rodney L. Ball. 1974. "The Aggression-Inhibiting Influence of Nonhostile Humor." *Journal of Experimental Social Psychology* 10 (1): 23–33.

Baron, Robert, and Nicholas R. Spitzer. 1992. "Introduction." In *Public Folklore*, ed. Robert Baron and Nicholas R. Spitzer, 1–14. Washington, DC: Smithsonian Institute Press.

Barry, Phillips. 1909. "Folk Music in America." *Journal of American Folklore* 22 (83): 72–81.

Barry, Phillips. 1933. "Communal Re-Creation." *Bulletin of the Folksong Society of the Northeast* 5: 4–6.

Bartlett, F. C. 1920. "Some Experiments on the Reproduction of Folk-Stories." *Folklore* 31 (1): 30–47.

Bascom, William R. 1949. "Folklore." In *Dictionary of Folklore, Mythology, and Legend*, ed. Maria Leach, 2 vols., 398–403. New York: Funk and Wagnalls.

Bascom, William R. 1953. "Folklore and Anthropology." *Journal of American Folklore* 66 (262): 283–290.

Bascom, William R. 1955. "Verbal Art." *Journal of American Folklore* 68 (269): 245–252.

Başgöz, İlhan. 1975. "The Tale Singer and His Audience." In *Folklore: Performance and Communication*, ed. Dan Ben-Amos and Kenneth S. Goldstein, 143–203. The Hague, Netherlands: Mouton.

Bauer, Laurie, and Winifred Bauer. 2007. "Playing with Tradition." *Journal of Folklore Research* 44 (2/3): 185–225.

Bauman, Richard. 1970. "The Turtles: An American Riddling Institution." *Western Folklore* 29 (1): 21–25.

Bauman, Richard. 1975. "Verbal Art as Performance." *American Anthropologist* 77 (2): 290–311.

Bauman, Richard. 1977. *Verbal Art as Performance*. Prospect Heights, IL: Waveland.

Bauman, Richard. 2004. *A World of Other's Words: Cross-Cultural Perspectives on Intertextuality*. Malden, MA: Blackwell.

Bauman, Richard, and Charles L. Briggs. 2003. *Voices of Modernity: Language Ideologies and the Politics of Inequality*. Cambridge: Cambridge University Press.

Beard, Mary. 2014. *Laughter in Ancient Rome: On Joking, Tickling, and Cracking Up*. Berkeley: University of California Press.

Beattie, James. 1779. *Essays on Poetry and Music as They Effect the Mind; On Laughter, and Ludicrous Composition; on the Usefulness of Classical Learning*. London: Edward and Charles Dilly.

Bellow, Saul, ed. 1963. *Great Jewish Short Stories*. New York, NY: Laurel.

Belmont, Nicole. (1982) 2005. "Superstition and Popular Belief." In *Folklore: Critical Concepts in Literary and Cultural Studies*, ed. Alan Dundes, Vol. 3, 163–177. London: Routledge.

Ben-Amos, Dan 1971. "Toward a Definition of Folklore in Context." *Journal of American Folklore* 84 (331): 3–15.

Ben-Amos, Dan, 1984. "The Seven Strands of Tradition: Varieties in Its Meaning in American Folklore Studies." *Journal of Folklore Research* 21 (2/3): 97–131.

Ben-Amos, Dan. 1992. "Foreword." In *Principles for Oral Narrative Research* by Axel Olrik. Translated by Kirsten Wolf and Jody Jensen, vii–xi. Bloomington: Indiana University Press.

Ben-Amos, Dan. 1993. "'Context' in Context." *Western Folklore* 52 (2/4): 209–226.

Bennett, Gillian. 2005. *Bodies: Sex, Violence, and Death in Contemporary Legend*. Jackson: University Press of Mississippi.

Bergler, Edmund. 1956. *Laughter and the Sense of Humor*. New York: Intercontinental Medical Book.

Bergson, Henri. (1900) 1956. "Laughter." In *Comedy*, ed. Wylie Sypher, 61–190. New York: Doubleday Anchor.

Berkowitz, Leonard. 1970. "Experimental Investigations of Hostility Catharsis." *Journal of Consulting and Clinical Psychology* 35 (1): 1–7.

Best, Joel, and Kathleen A. Bogle. 2014. *Kids Gone Wild: From Rainbow Parties to Sexting, Understanding the Hype over Teen Sex*. New York: New York University Press.

Bianco, Carla. 1974. *The Two Rosetos*. Bloomington: Indiana University Press.

"Biblical Interpretation." n.d. Ironic Catholic. Accessed August 31, 2015. http://www.ironiccatholic.com/2008/01/interpreting-bible-joke.html.

Binstead, Kim, and Graeme Ritchie. 1994. "An Implemented Model of Punning Riddles." Proceedings of the Twelfth National Conference on Artificial Intelligence, 633–638.

Binstead, Kim, and Graeme Ritchie. 1997. "Computational Rules for Generating Punning Riddles." *Humor: International Journal of Humor Research* 10 (1): 25–76.

Blackmore, Susan. 1999. *The Meme Machine*. Oxford: Oxford University Press.

Blank, Trevor J. 2012. "Introduction: Pattern in the Virtual Folk Culture of Computer-Mediated Communication." In *Folk Culture in the Digital Age: The Emergent Dynamics of Human Interaction*, ed. Trevor J. Blank, 1–24. Logan: Utah State University Press.

Blank, Trevor J. 2013. *The Last Laugh: Folk Humor, Celebrity Culture, and Mass-Mediated Disasters in the Digital Age*. Madison: University of Wisconsin Press.

Bloch, Maurice. 2000. "A Well-Disposed Social Anthropologist's Problem with Memes." In *Darwinizing Culture: The Status of the Science of Memetics*, ed. Robert Aunger, 189–203. Oxford: Oxford University Press.

Blom, Philipp. 2008. *The Vertigo Years: Change and Culture in the West, 1900–1914*. London: Weidenfeld and Nicolson.

Bolton, Henry Carrington. 1888. *The Counting-Out Rhymes of Children*, New York: D. Appleton.

Boudry, Maarten. 2018. "Invasion of the Mind Snatchers: On Memes and Cultural Parasites." *Revista Internacional de Filosofia* 37 (3): 111–124.

Boyd, Robert, and Peter J. Richerson. 1985. *Culture and the Evolutionary Process*. Chicago: University of Chicago Press.

Boyd, Robert, and Peter J. Richerson. 1988. "The Evolution of Reciprocity in Sizable Groups." *Journal of Theoretical Biology* 132: 337–356.

Boyd, Robert, and Peter J. Richerson. 1992. "Punishment Allows the Evolution of Cooperation (or Anything Else) in Sizeable Groups." *Ethnology and Sociobiology* 13 (3): 171–195.

Boyd, Robert, and Peter J. Richerson. 2009. "Culture and the Evolution of Human Cooperation." *Philosophical Transactions of the Royal Society B: Biological Sciences* 364 (1533): 3281–3288.

Bradney, Pamela. 1957. "The Joking Relationship in Industry." *Human Relations* 10 (2): 179–187.

Brand, John. 1777. *Observations on Popular Antiquities*. New Castle Upon Tyne, UK: T. Saint for J. Johnson.

Brenner, Norm. 2010. *The Best Medicine*. Bloomington, IN: Xlibris.

Brodie, Richard. 1996. *Virus of the Mind: The New Science of the Meme*. Seattle, WA: Integral.

Bronner, Simon J. 1988. *American Children's Folklore*. Little Rock, AK: August House.

Bronner, Simon. 1998. *Following Tradition: Folklore in the Discourse of American Culture*. Logan: Utah State University Press.

Brooks, Michael. 2008. *13 Things That Don't Make Sense: The Most Baffling Scientific Mysteries of Our Time*. New York: Doubleday.

Brown, Robert. 1963. *Explanation in Social Science*. Chicago: Aldine.

Brunvand, Jan Harold. 1993. *The Baby Train and Other Lusty Legends*. New York: W. W. Norton.

Brunvand, Jan Harold. 1998. *The Study of American Folklore*. 4th ed. New York: W. W. Norton.

Brunvand, Jan Harold. 2013. "As the Saints Go Marching By: Modern Jokelore Concerning Mormons." In *Latter Day Lore: Mormon Folklore Studies*, ed. Eric Eliason and Tom Mould, 360–368. Salt Lake City: University of Utah Press.

Burne, Charlotte S. 1910. "Presidential Address: The Value of European Folklore in the History of Culture." *Folk-Lore* 21 (1): 14–41.

Burns, Thomas A. 1970. "A Model for Textual Variation in Folksong." *Folklore Forum* 3 (2): 49–56.

Burns, Thomas A. 1978. "Fifty Seconds of Play: Expressive Interaction in Context." *Western Folklore* 37 (2): 1–29.

Burns, Thomas A., with Inger H. Burns. 1976. *Doing the Wash: An Expressive Culture and Personality Study of a Joke and Its Tellers*. Norwood, PA: Norwood Editions.

Bush, Wendell T. 1932. "Superstition and Logic." *The Journal of Philosophy* 29 (9): 236–241.

"Businessman in Trouble." 2007. *So Here is This* (blog). February 12, 2007. http:byronik.blogspot.com/2007/02/businessman-in-trouble-jewish.html.

Butwin, Joseph, and Frances Butwin. 1977. *Sholom Aleichem*. Boston: Twayne.

Byrne, Donn. 1961. "Some Inconsistencies in the Effect of Motivation Arousal on Humor Preferences." *Journal of Abnormal and Social Psychology* 62 (1): 158–160.

Calame-Griaule, Geneviève, Veronica Görög-Karady, Suzanne Platiel, Diana Rey-Hulman, and Christiane Seydou. 1983. "The Variability of Meaning and the Meaning of Variability." *Journal of Folklore Research* 20 (2/3): 153–170.

Campbell, Colin. 1996. "Half-Belief and the Paradox of Ritual Instrumental Activism." *British Journal of Sociology* 47 (1): 151–166.

Campion-Vincent, Véronique. 2005. *Organ Theft Legends*. Translated by Jacqueline Simpson. Jackson: University Press of Mississippi.

Canestrari, Carla, and Ivana Bianchi. 2013. "From Perception of Contraries to Humorous Incongruities." In *Developments in Linguistic Humor Theory*, ed. Marta Dynel, 3–24. Amsterdam: John Benjamins.

Cantor, Joanne R. 1976. "What is Funny and to Whom? The Role of Gender." *Journal of Communication* 26 (3): 164–172.

Carroll, Lewis. 1960. *The Annotated Alice: Alice's Adventures in Wonderland and Through the Looking Glass*. New York: Wings.

Catarella, Teresa. 1994. "The Study of the Orally Transmitted Ballad: Past Paradigms and a New Poetics." *Oral Tradition* 9 (2): 468–478.

"Chapter 11." 2008. *Neowin*. September 6, 2008. www.neowin.net/forum/topic/666104-joke-chapter-11/.

"Chapter Eleven." n.d. *Gospelweb*. Accessed October 24, 2022. http://www.gospelweb.net/Church Humor8/ChapterEleven.htm.

Chatterji, Roma. 2012. *Speaking with Pictures: Folk Art and the Narrative Tradition in India*. London: Routledge.

Chatterji, Roma. 2016. "Repetition, Improvisation, Tradition: Deleuzean Themes in the Folk Art of Bengal." *Cultural Analysis: An Interdisciplinary Forum on Folklore and Popular Culture*. Special issue of *Everyday Practice and Tradition*, ed. Anthony Bak Buccitelli and Casey R. Schmidt, 151: 99–127.

Child, Francis James. (1882–1906) 1965. *The English and Scottish Ballads*. 5 vols. New York: Dover.

"Chumash." n.d. Learn Religions. Accessed September 5, 2015. http://judaism.about.com/library /2_humor/bldef-joke_chumash.htm.

Clark, Robert T., Jr. 1955. *Herder: His Life and Thought*. Berkeley: University of California Press.

Clark, Ronald W. 1980. *Freud: The Man and the Cause*. New York: Random House.

"Clean Joke." n.d. Funny Clean Jokes. Accessed September 9, 2015. http://www.cleanjoke.com /humor/Chapter-11.html.

Coffin, Tristram P. 1957. "'Mary Hamilton' and the Anglo-American Ballad as an Art Form." *Journal of American Folklore* 70 (277): 208–214.

Coffin, Tristram P. 1963. *The British Traditional Ballad in North America*. Rev. ed. Philadelphia: The American Folklore Society.

Cohen, Ted. 1999. *Philosophical Thoughts on Joking Matters*. Chicago: University of Chicago Press.

Collins, R. G. 1970. "Night Thoughts in the Broad Light of Day." Review of *Rationale of the Dirty Joke* by G. Legman. *Mosaic: An Interdisciplinary Critical Journal* 3 (2): 148–155.

Coulbrooke, Star. 2002. "Women's Mid-Life Rites of Passage and 'The Goddess of Hysterectomy.'" *Western Folklore* 61 (2): 152–172.

Coulson, Seana. 2005. "What's So Funny? Conceptual Integration in Humorous Examples." University of California San Diego. http://cogsci.ucsd.edu/~coulson/funstuff/funny.html.

Cray, Ed. 1964. "The Rabbi Trickster." *Journal of American Folklore* 77 (306): 331–345.

Culler, Jonathan. 1988. "The Call of the Phoneme." In *On Puns*, ed. Jonathan Culler, 1–16. Oxford, UK: Basil Blackwell.

Damisch, Lysann, Barbara Stoberock, and Thomas Mussweiler. 2010. "Keep Your Fingers Crossed! How Superstition Improves Performance." *Psychological Science* 21 (7): 1014–1020.

Danielson, Larry. 1979. "Toward the Analysis of Vernacular Texts: The Supernatural Narrative in Oral and Popular Printed Sources." *Journal of the Folklore Institute* 16 (3): 130–154.

"Darken my Door." 2020. *Pipe and PJs*. https://pipeandpjs.wordpress.com/2020/04/11/october-1958/.

Darwin, Charles. 2008 (1859). *The Origin of Species*. New York: Bantam.

Dauber, Jeremy. 2017. *Jewish Comedy: A Serious History*. New York: W. W. Norton.

Davies, Christie. 1990. *Ethnic Humor around the World: A Comparative Analysis*. Bloomington: Indiana University Press.

Davies, Christie. 2002. *The Mirth of Nations*. New Brunswick, NJ: Transaction.

Davies, Christie. 2011. *Jokes and Targets*. Bloomington: Indiana University Press.

Davies, Stephen. 1991. *Definitions of Art*. Ithaca, NY: Cornell University Press.

Davis, Susan G. 2019. *Dirty Jokes and Bawdy Songs: The Uncensored Life of Gershon Legman*. Urbana: University of Illinois Press.

Dawkins, Richard. 1976. *The Selfish Gene*. New York: Oxford University Press.

Dawkins, Richard. 1983. "Universal Darwinism." In *Evolution from Molecules to Men*, ed. D. S. Bendall, 403–425. Cambridge: Cambridge University Press.

Dawkins, Richard. 1986. *The Blind Watchmaker*. New York: W. W. Norton.

Dawkins, Richard. 1993. "Viruses of the Mind." In *Dennett and His Critics: Demystifying Mind*, ed. B. Dahlbom, 13–27. Oxford: Blackwell.

Dawkins, Richard. 2006. *The Selfish Gene*. 30th Anniversary Edition. Oxford: Oxford University Press.

Dawkins, Richard. 2008. *The God Delusion*. Boston: Mariner.

Dégh, Linda. 1983. "Foreword: A Quest for Meaning." *Journal of Folklore Research* 20 (2/3): 145–150.

Dégh, Linda. 1995. *Narratives in Society: A Performer-Centered Study of Narration*. Folklore Fellows Communication 255. Helsinki: Suomalainen Tiedeakatemia.

Dégh, Linda, and Andrew Vázsonyi. 1975. "The Hypothesis of Multi-Conduit Transmission in Folklore." In *Folklore: Performance and Communication*, ed. Dan Ben-Amos and Kenneth S. Goldstein, 207–252. The Hague: Mouton.

Dégh, Linda, and Andrew Vázsonyi. 1976. "Legend and Belief." In *Folklore Genres*, ed. Dan Ben-Amos, 93–123. Austin: University of Texas Press.

Dennett, Daniel C. 1995. *Darwin's Dangerous Idea: Evolution and the Meanings of Life*. New York: Touchstone.

Dennett, Daniel C. 2013. *Intuition Pumps and Other Tools for Thinking*. New York: W. W. Norton.

Distin, Kate. 2005. *The Selfish Meme*. Cambridge: Cambridge University Press.

"Divine Advice." n.d. Christians Unite. Accessed October 24, 2022. http://www.christiansunite .com/Faith/Divine_Advice.shtml.

Doris, John, and Ella Fierman. 1956. "Humor and Anxiety." *Journal of Abnormal and Social Psychology* 53 (1): 59–62.

Dorson, Richard M. 1958. *Negro Folktales from Pine Bluff, Arkansas and Calvin, Michigan*. Bloomington: Indiana University Press.

Dorson, Richard M. 1968a. *Peasant Customs and Savage Myths: Selections from the British Folklorists*. 2 vols. Chicago: University of Chicago Press.

Dorson, Richard M. 1968b. *The British Folklorists: A History*. Chicago: University of Chicago Press.

Dorson, Richard M. 1978. "American Folklore vs. Folklore in America." *Journal of the Folklore Institute* 15 (2): 97–111.

Douglas, Mary. 1968. "The Social Control of Cognition: Some Factors in Joke Perception." *Man. New Series*, 3 (3): 361–376.

Drout, Michael D. C. 2006a. *How Traditions Works: A Meme-Based Cultural Poetics of the Anglo-Saxon Tenth Century*. Medieval and Renaissance Texts and Studies Volume 306. Tempe: Arizona Center for Medieval and Renaissance Studies.

Drout, Michael D. C. 2006b. *A History of the English Language: Course Guide*. The Modern Scholar. Frederick, MD: Recorded Books.

Druyanow, Alter. 1963. *Sefer ha-bedichah ve-ha-hidud* [Book of the Joke and the Witticism]. 3 vols. Tel Aviv: Dvir.

Druyanow, Alter. 2010 (1922). "Jewish Folk Humor." In *Pioneers of Jewish Ethnography and Folkloristics in Eastern Europe*, ed. Haya Bar-Itzhak, 119–156. Ljubljana: Scientific Research Centre of the Slovenian Academy of Sciences and Arts.

Dudley, R. Thomas. 1999. "The Effect of Superstitious Belief on Performance Following an Unsolvable Problem." *Personality and Individual Difference* 26 (6): 1057–1064.

Duffin, Charles. 2004. "Echoes of Authority: Audience and Formula in the Scots Ballad." In *The Singer and the Scribe: European Ballad Traditions and European Ballad Cultures*, ed. Phillip E. Bennett and Richard Firth Green, 135–153. Amsterdam: Rodopi.

Dundes, Alan. 1961. "Brown County Superstitions: The Structure of Superstition." *Midwest Folklore* 11 (1): 25–56.

Dundes, Alan. 1964. "Texture, Text, and Context." *Southern Folklore Quarterly* 28: 251–265.

Dundes, Alan. 1965. "The Study of Folklore in Literature and Culture: Identification and Interpretation." *Journal of American Folklore* 78 (308): 136–142.

Dundes, Alan. 1966. "Metafolklore and Oral Literary Criticism." *The Monist: An International Quarterly Journal of General Philosophical Inquiry* 50 (4): 505–516.

Dundes, Alan. 1969. "The Devolutionary Premise in Folklore Theory." *Journal of the Folklore Institute* 6 (1): 5–19.

Dundes, Alan. 1987. *Cracking Jokes: Studies of Sick Humor Cycles and Stereotypes*. Berkeley, CA: Ten Speed.

Dundes, Alan. 1997. *From Game to War and Other Psychoanalytic Essays on Folklore*. Lexington: University Press of Kentucky.

Dundes, Alan, and Carl R. Pagter. 1975. *Work Hard and You Shall Be Rewarded: Urban Folklore from the Paperwork Empire*. Detroit, MI: Wayne State University Press.

Dworkin, Earl S., and Jay S. Efran. 1967. "The Angered: Their Susceptibility to Varieties of Humor." *Journal of Personality and Social Psychology* 6 (2): 233–236.

Dynel, Marta. 2012. "Garden Paths, Red Lights and Crossroads: On Finding Our Way to Understanding the Cognitive Mechanisms Underlying Jokes." *Israeli Journal of Humor Research* 1 (1): 6–28.

Edmonds, Bruce. 2005. "The Revealed Poverty of the Gene-Meme Analogy—Why Memetics Per Se Has Failed to Produce Substantive Results." *Journal of Memetics: Evolutionary Models of Information Transmission*. http://jom-emit.cfpm.org/2005/vol9/edmonds_b.html.

Edwards, Thornton B. 1996. "The Sugared Almond in Modern Greek Rites of Passage." *Folklore* 107: 49–57.

Eidelberg, Ludwig. 1945. "A Contribution to the Study of Wit." *The Psychoanalytic Review* 32: 33–61.

Ekrem, Carola. 2000. "Variation and Continuity in Children's Counting-Out Rhymes." In *Thick Corpus, Organic Variation, and Textuality in Oral Tradition*, ed. Lauri Honko, 287–298. Studia Fennica 7. Helsinki: Finnish Literature Society.

Eliason, Eric A. 2007. *The J. Golden Kimball Stories*. Urbana: University of Illinois Press.

Eliason, Eric, and Tom Mould. 2013. *Latter Day Lore: Mormon Folklore Studies*. Salt Lake City: University of Utah Press.

Ellis, Bill. 2003a. *Aliens, Ghosts, and Cults: Legends We Live*. Jackson: University Press of Mississippi.

Ellis, Bill. 2003b. "Making a Big Apple Crumble: The Role of Humor in Constructing a Global Response to Disaster." In *Of Corpse: Death and Humor in Folklore and Popular Culture*, ed. Peter Narváez, 35–39. Logan: Utah State University Press.

"Employment Law Alliance Survey." 2018. *Employment Law Alliance*. March 7, 2018. https://www.ela.law/articles/employment-law-alliance-survey -takes-american-pulse-on-metoo-and-workplace-harassment-.

Esar, Evan, 1952. *The Humor of Humor*. New York: Bramhall House.

Estiri, Ehsan. 2018. "Alleviating Folkloristics Theory Anxiety: What Folklorists Can Learn from Conceptualizations of Tradition in the Anthropology of Islam." *New Directions in Folklore* 16 (1): 15–26.

Evans, Timothy H. 2018. "The Bowling Green Massacre." *Journal of American Folklore* 131 (522): 460–470.

Feintuch, Burt. 1988. "Introduction: Folklorists and the Public Sector." In *The Conservation of Culture: Folklorists and the Public Sector*, ed. Burt Feintuch, 1–16. Lexington: The University Press of Kentucky.

Feintuch, Burt. 1995. "Common Ground: Keywords for the Study of Expressive Culture." *Journal of American Folklore* 108 (430): 391–394.

Feldman, Sandor. 1941. "A Supplement to Freud's Theory of Wit." *The Psychoanalytic Review* 28: 201–217.

Fenichel, Otto. 1945. *The Psychoanalytic Theory of Neurosis*. New York: W. W. Norton.

Ferguson, Mark A., and Thomas E. Ford. 2008. "Disparagement Humor; A Theoretical and Empirical Review of Psychoanalytic, Superiority, and Social Identity Theories." *Humor: International Journal of Humor Research* 21 (3): 283–312.

Filthy Dirty Jokes: Uncensored Edition. 2005. New York: Platinum.

"Final Discussion: On the Analytic Value of the Concept of Tradition." 1983. In *Trends in Nordic Tradition Research*, ed. Lauri Honko and Pekka Laaksonen, 233–249. Studia Fennica 27. Helsinki: Suomalaisen Kirjallisuuden Seura.

"Financial Advice." n.d. *Thrifty Fun*. Accessed October 24, 2022. http://www.thriftyfun.com/tf375 98015.tip.html.

Fine, Gary Alan. 1976. "Obscene Joking Across Cultures." *Journal of Communication* 26 (3): 134–140.

Fine, Gary Alan. 1991. "Redemption Rumors and the Power of Ostension." *Journal of American Folklore* 104 (412): 179–181.

Fine, Gary Alan, and Barry O'Neill. 2010. "Policy Legends and Folklorists: Traditional Beliefs in the Public Sphere." *Journal of American Folklore* 123 (488): 150–178.

Foley, John Miles. 1992. "Word Power, Performance, and Tradition." *Journal of American Folklore* 105 (427): 275–301.

Foote, Monica. 2007. "Userpicks: Cyber Folk Art in the Early 21st Century." *Folklore Forum* 37 (1): 27–38.

Forabosco, Giovannantonio. 1992. "Cognitive Aspects of the Humor Process: The Concept of Incongruity." *Humor: International Journal of Humor Research* 5 (1/2): 45–68.

Foster, Kevin R., and Hanna Kokko. 2009. "Evolution of Superstition and Superstition-Like Behavior." *Proceedings of the Royal Society B: Biological Sciences* 276 (1654): 31–37.

Frazer, James George. 1925. *The Golden Bough: A Study in Magic and Religion*. 1 vol. abrgd. ed. New York: Macmillan.

"Fresh Start." n.d. *Aish*. Accessed October 24, 2022. http://www.aish.com/ 214266821-3/.

Freud, Sigmund, 1953–1975. *The Standard Edition of the Complete Psychological Works of Sigmund Freud*. Translated and edited by James Strachey. 24 vols. Hogarth Press and the Institute of Psycho-Analysis.

Frisch, Michael. 1998. "De-, Re-, and Post-Industrialization: Industrial Heritage as Contested Memorial Terrain." *Journal of Folklore Research* 35 (3): 241–249.

"Funny Bankruptcy." n.d. *Family Friend Jokes*. Accessed September 5, 2015. http://www.family friendjokes.com/joke/funny-bankruptcy-bible-joke.

Gabbert, Lisa. 2020. "Suffering in Medical Contexts: Laughter, Humor, and the Medical Carnivalesque." *Journal of American Folklore* 133 (527): 3–26.

Gabler, Neal. 2011. "The Elusive Big Idea." *New York Times*. August 13, 2011.

Galanter, Marc. 2005. *Lowering the Bar: Lawyer Jokes and Legal Culture*. Madison: University of Wisconsin Press.

Gardner, Emelyn Elizabeth, and Geraldine J. Chickering. 1939. *Ballads and Songs of Southern Michigan*. Ann Arbor: University of Michigan Press.

Gauthier, Paul. 1990. "Does Weismann's Experiment Constitute a Refutation of the Lamarckian Hypothesis." *Bios* 61 (1/2): 6–8.

Geddes, William R. 1957. *Nine Dayak Nights*. Melbourne: Oxford University Press.

Georges, Robert A., and Michael Owen Jones. 1995. *Folkloristics: An Introduction*. Bloomington: Indiana University Press.

Gerould, Gordon. 1923. "The Making of Ballads." *Modern Philology* 21 (1): 15–28.

Gerould, Gordon. 1957 (1932). *The Ballad of Tradition*. New York: Galaxy.

Gibb, Elias John Wilkinson, trans. 1836. *The History of the Forty Vezirs or, The Story of the Forty Morns and Eves* by Sheykh-Zāda. London: George Redway.

Giora, Rachel. 1991. "On the Cognitive Aspects of the Joke." *Journal of Pragmatics* 16 (5): 465–485.

Glassie, Henry. 1975. *Folk Housing in Middle Virginia*. Knoxville: University of Tennessee Press.

Glassie, Henry. 1982. *Passing the Time in Ballymenone: Culture and History of an Ulster Community*. Philadelphia: University of Pennsylvania Press.

Glassie, Henry. 1994. "Epilogue." In *The Spirit of Swedish Folk Art*, ed. Barbro Klein and Mats Widbom, 247–255. New York: Harry N. Abrams.

Gluckman, Max. 1962. "Les Rites de Passage." In *The Rituals of Social Relations*, ed. Max Gluckman, 1–52. Manchester: Manchester University Press.

Glucksberg, Sam, Mary R. Newsome, and Yevgeniya Goldvarg. 2001. "Inhibition of the Literal: Filtering Metaphor-Irrelevant Information during Metaphor Comprehension." *Metaphor and Symbol* 16 (3): 277–293.

Gmelch, George. (1971) 2001. "Baseball Magic." In *Magic, Witchcraft, and Religion: An Anthropological Study of the Supernatural*, ed. Arthur C. Lehman and James E. Myers, 5th ed., 293–299. Mountain View, CA: Mayfield.

Goja, Hermann. 1920. "Das Zersingen des Volkslieder: Ein Beitrag zur Psychologie der Volksdichtung." *Imago: Zeitschrift für Anwendung der Psychoanalyse auf die Geisteswissenschaften* 6 (1): 132–241.

Goja, Hermann. 1964. "The Alteration of Folksongs by Frequent Singing: A Contribution to the Psychology of Folk Poetry." Edited and translated by Sidney Axelrod and Warner Münsterberger. In *The Psychoanalytic Study of Society*, vol. 3, 111–170. New York: International Universities Press.

Goldberg, Christine. 1986. "The Construction of Folktales." *Journal of Folklore Research* 23 (2/3): 163–176.

Goldenberg, Robert. 1984. "Talmud." In *Back to the Sources: Reading the Classic Jewish Texts*, ed. Barry W. Holtz, 128–175. New York: Summit.

Goldstein, Jeffrey H., Jerry M. Suls, and Susan Anthony. 1972. "Enjoyment of Specific Types of Humor Content: Motivation or Salience?" In *The Psychology of Humor: Theoretical Perspectives and Empirical Issues*, ed. Jeffrey H. Goldstein and Paul E. McGhee, 159–171. New York: Academic Press.

Goldstein, Kenneth S. 1967. "Experimental Folklore: Laboratory vs. Field." In *Folklore International: Essays in Traditional Literature, Belief, and Custom in Honor of Wayland Debs Hand*, ed. D. K. Wilgus, 71–82. Hatboro, PA: Folklore Associates.

Goodenough, Oliver R., and Richard Dawkins. 1994. "The 'St. Jude' Mind Virus." *Nature* 371 (Sept 1): 23–24.

Gould, Stephen Jay. 1991. *Bully for Brontosaurus: Reflections in Natural History*. New York: W. W. Norton.

Green, Archie. 1978. "Industrial Lore: A Bibliographic-Semantic Query." *Western Folklore* 37 (3): 143–245.

Green, Rayna. 1976. "Introduction." In *Pissing in the Snow and Other Ozark Folktales*, by Vance Randolph, 11–30. New York: Bard.

Green, Rayna. 1977. "Magnolias Grow in Dirt: The Bawdy Lore of Southern Women." *The Radical Teacher*. Special Issue on Women's Studies in the 70s: Moving Forward 6: 26–31. Reprinted from *Southern Exposure* 6 (4).

Greengross, Gil. 2020. "Sex and Gender Differences in Humor: Introduction and Overview." *Humor: International Journal of Humor Research* 33 (2): 175–178.

Greenway, John. 1953. *American Folksongs of Protest*. Philadelphia: University of Pennsylvania Press.

Gross, Martin L. 1966. *The Doctors*. New York: Random House.

Gross, Naftoli. 1955. *Maaselech un Mesholim* [Tales and Parables]. New York: Aber.

Grotjahn, Martin. 1957. *Beyond Laughter: Humor and the Subconscious*. New York: McGraw-Hill.

Gruner, Charles R. 1978. *Understanding Laughter: The Workings of Wit and Humor*. Chicago: Nelson-Hall.

Gummere, Francis B. 1959 (1907). *The Popular Ballad*. New Yok: Dover.

Gunders, John, and Damon Brown. 2010. *The Complete Idiot's Guide to Memes*. New York: Alpha (Penguin Group).

Halkin, Hillel. 2006. "Why Jews Laugh at Themselves." *Commentary*, April, 47–54.

Hamilton, W.D. 1977. "The Play by Nature." *Science* 196 (4291): 757–759.

Harris, Marvin. 1968. *The Rise of Anthropological Theory*. New York: Thomas Y. Crowell.

Harris, Marvin. 1979. *Cultural Materialism: The Struggle for a Science of Culture*. New York: Random House.

Harris, Robin P. 2017. *Storytelling in Siberia: The Olonkho Epic in a Changing World*. Urbana: University of Illinois Press.

Hasan-Rokem, Galit. 1982. "Kheker tahalikhei temurah be-sippur ha-amami." [The study of processes of change in folk narrative]. *Mekhkere Yerushalayim be-folklor Yehudi* [Jerusalem Investigations into Jewish folklore] 3: 129–138.

Heath, Chip, and Dan Heath. 2007. *Made to Stick: Why Some Ideas Survive and Others Die*. New York: Random House.

Heath, Chip, Chris Bell, and Emily Sternberg. 2001. "Emotional Selection in Memes: The Case of Urban Legends." *Journal of Personality and Social Psychology* 81 (6): 1028–1041.

Heider, Karl. 1988. "The Rashomon Effect: When Ethnographers Disagree." *American Anthropologist* 90 (1): 73–81.

Hempelmann, Christian F. 2004. "Script Opposition and Logical Mechanism in Punning." *Humor: International Journal of Humor Research* 17 (4): 381–392.

Hempelmann, Christian, and Salvatore Attardo. 2011. "Resolutions and Their Incongruities: Further Thoughts on Logical Mechanisms." *Humor: International Journal of Humor Research* 24 (2): 125-149.

Henderson, Mark. 2010. "Murder in Winnat's Pass: Evolution of a Peak District Legend." *Folklore* 121 (3): 292–310.

Henrich, Joseph, Robert Boyd, and Peter J. Richerson. 2012. "The Puzzle of Monogamous Marriage." *Philosophical Transactions of the Royal Society B: Biological Sciences* 367 (1589): 657–669.

Herskovits, Melville J. 1937. "The Significance of the Study of Acculturation for Anthropology." *American Anthropologist* 39 (2): 259–264.

Herskovits, Melville J. 1945. "The Processes of Cultural Change." In *The Science of Man in the World Crisis*, ed. Ralph Linton, 143–170. New York: Columbia University Press.

Herzog, Thomas R., and Andrew W. Hager. 1995. "The Prediction of Preference for Sexual Cartoons." *Humor: International Journal of Humor Research* 8 (4): 385–405.

Hicks, Ray. 1963. "Big Man Jack Killed Seven at a Whack." In *Ray Hicks of Beech Mountain, North Carolina Telling Four Traditional Jack Tales*. Recorded by Sandy Paton and transcribed by Lee B. Haggerty. Side 1, track 2. Huntington, VT: Folk Legacy Records FTA-14.

Hill, W. W. 1944. "The Navaho Indians and the Ghost Dance of 1890." *American Anthropologist* 46 (4): 523–527.

Hirsch, E. D., Jr. 1967. *Validity in Interpretation*. New Haven, CT: Yale University Press.

Hirshleifer, David, Ming Jian, and Huai Zhang. 2018. "Superstition and Financial Decision Making." *Management Science* 64 (1): 235–252.

Hobbes, Thomas. 1962 (1651). *Leviathan or the Matter, Forme, and Power of a Commonwealth Ecclesiasticall and Civil*. New York: Collier.

Hofstadter, Douglas, Liane Gabor, and Salvatore Attardo. 1989. "Synopsis of the Workshop on Humor and Cognition." *Humor: International Journal of Humor Research* 2 (4): 417–440.

Holbek, Bengt. 1985. "The Many Abodes of Fata Morgana: The Quest for Meaning in Fairy Tales." *Journal of Folklore Research* 22 (1): 19–28.

Holland, Norman M. 1982. *Laughing: A Psychology of Humor*. Ithaca, NY: Cornell University Press.

Hollman, Regina E. 1974. "Ritual Opening and Individual Transformation: Rites of Passage at Esalen." *American Anthropologist* 76 (2): 265–280.

Honko, Lauri. 1979. "Theories Concerning the Ritual Process." In *Science of Religion: Studies in Methodology*, ed. Lauri Honko, 369–390. The Hague: Mouton.

Honko, Lauri. 1981. "Four Forms of Adaptation of Tradition." In *Adaptation, Change, and Decline in Oral Literature*, ed. Lauri Honko and Vilmos Voigt, 19–33. Helsinki: Suomalainen Kirjallisuuden Seura.

Honko, Lauri. 1984. "Folkloristic Studies of Meaning: An Introduction." *Arv: Scandinavian Yearbook of Folklore* 40: 35–56.

Honko, Lauri. 2013. "Traditions in the Construction of Cultural Identity." In *Theoretical Milestones: Selected Writings of Lauri Honko*, ed. Pekka Hakamies and Anneli Honko, 323–338. Helsinki: Suomalainen Tiedeakatemia.

Howe, Irving, and Eliezer Greenberg, eds. 1954. *A Treasury of Yiddish Stories*. New York: Viking.

Howe, Irving, and Eliezer Greenberg, eds. 1974. *Yiddish Stories, Old and New*. New York: Holiday House.

Howe, Irving, and Ruth Wisse, eds. 1979. *The Best of Sholom Aleichem*. New York: Washington Square.

Howells, William. 1962. *The Heathens: Primitive Man and His Religions*. New York: Doubleday.

Hunt Margaret, ed. 1884. *Grimm's Household Tales*. Translated by Margaret Hunt. 2 vols. London: George Bell.

Hurley, Dan. 2013. "Trait vs. Fate." *Discover* 40 (4): 48–55.

Hurley, Matthew M., Daniel C. Dennett, and Reginald B. Adams Jr. 2011. *Inside Jokes: Using Humor to Reverse-Engineer the Mind.* Cambridge, MA: MIT Press.

Hutcheson, Francis. 1750. *Reflections upon Laughter and Remarks on the Fable of the Bees.* Glasgow: R. Urie for Daniel Baxter.

Hyman, Stanley Edgar, 1957. "The Child Ballad in America." *Journal of American Folklore* 70 (277): 235–239.

Hymes, Dell. 1971. "The Contribution of Folklore to Sociolinguistic Research." *Journal of American Folklore* 84 (331): 42–50.

Hymes, Dell. 1975. "Folklore's Nature and the Sun's Myth." *Journal of American Folklore* 88 (350): 345–369.

Hymes, Dell. 1981a. "Comment." *Journal of the Folklore Institute* 18 (2/3): 144–150.

Hymes, Dell. 1981b. *In Vain I Tried to Tell You: Essays in Native American Ethnopoetics.* Philadelphia: University of Pennsylvania Press.

Ikeda, Hiroko. 1971. *A Type and Motif Index of Japanese Folktales.* FF Communications 209. Helsinki: Suomalainen Tiedeakatemia.

"Ivan Pavlov Salivates at the Idea." 2019. *Discover Magazine* 40 (7): 46.

Ivey, Bill. 2018. *Building an Enlightened Future: Folklorizing America.* Bloomington: Indiana University Press.

Jacobs, Joseph. 1893. "The Folk." *Folk-Lore* 4 (2): 233–238.

Jahoda, Gustav. 1971. *The Psychology of Superstition.* Middlesex, England: Pelican.

Jansen, William Hugh. 1957. "Classifying Performance in the Study of Verbal Folklore." In *Studies in Folklore,* ed. W. Edson Richmond, 110–118. Indiana University Publications Folklore Series No. 9. Bloomington: Indiana University Press.

Jarvie, I. C. 1968. "Limits to Functionalism and Alternatives to It in Anthropology." In *Theory in Anthropology: A Sourcebook,* ed. Robert A. Manners and David Kaplan, 196–203. Chicago: Aldine.

Järvinen, Irma-Riitta. 1985. *Contemporary Folklore and Culture Change.* Helsinki: Suomalaisen Kirjallisuuden Seura.

Jarvis, Peter. 1980. "Towards a Sociological Understanding of Superstition." *Social Compass* 27 (2/3): 285–295.

Jason, Heda. 1988. *Folktales of the Jews of Iraq: Tale-Types and Genres.* Babylonian Jewry Heritage Center. Or-Yehuda, Israel.

Javadi, Hasan, ed. 2008. *Obeyd-e Zakani: Ethics of the Aristocrats and Other Satirical Works.* Translated by Hasan Javadi. Washington, DC: Mage.

Jayanti, Vikram, dir. 2005. *Game Over: Kasparov and the Machine.* DVD. New York: THINKFilm and Alliance Atlantic.

Jeffreys, Mark. 2000. "The Meme Metaphor." *Perspectives in Biology and Medicine.* 43 (2): 227–242.

"Jesus Site." n.d. *Jesus Site.* Accessed October 24, 2022. http://www.jesussite.com/resources/clean-jokes/.

Jewish Virtual Library. n.d. "Tractate Hagiga: Chapter 1." *Jewish Virtual Library.* Accessed October 24, 2022. https://www.jewishvirtuallibrary.org/tractate-hagiga-chapter-1.

Jillette, Penn, and Paul Provenza. 2005. *The Aristocrats.* DVD. New York: THINKFilm and Mighty Cheese Production.

Johnson, A. E., trans. 1961. *Perrault's Complete Fairy Tales*. 2 vols. New York: Dodd, Mead, and Co.

Johnson, Robbie. 1973. "Folklore and Women: A Social Interactional Analysis of the Folklore of a Texas Madam." *Journal of American Folklore* 86 (341): 211–224.

"Jokes." n.d. Stewardship of Life Institute. Accessed October 24, 2022. http://www.stewardshipoflife .org/jokes/.

Jones, Michael Owen. 1971. "(PC + CB) x SD (R + I + E) = HERO." *New York Folklore Quarterly* 27 (3): 243–260.

Jones, Michael Owen. 2000. "What's Disgusting, Why, and What Does It Matter?" *Journal of Folklore Research* 37 (1): 53–71.

Kahneman, Daniel. 2011. *Thinking Fast and Slow*. New York: Farrar, Straus, and Giroux.

Kaivola-Bregenhøj, Annikki. 2000. "Varying Folklore." In *Thick Corpus, Organic Variation, and Textuality in Oral Tradition*, ed. Lauri Honko, 93–130. Studia Fennica Folkloristica 7. Helsinki: Finnish Literature Society.

"Kamehameha II." n.d. *Wikipedia*. Accessed September 9, 2013. http://en.wikipedia.org/wiki /Kamehameha_II.

Kantor, J. R. 1932. "Logic and Superstition." *The Journal of Philosophy* 29 (9): 232–236.

Kapferer, Jean-Noel. 1993. "The Persuasiveness of an Urban Legend: The Case of 'Mickey Mouse Acid.'" *Contemporary Legend* 3: 85–101.

Kaplan, Abraham. 1964. *The Conduct of Inquiry: Methodology for Behavioral Science*. San Francisco, CA: Chandler.

Keesing, Felix M. 1973 (1953). *Culture Change: An Analysis and Bibliography of Anthropological Sources to 1952*. New York: Octagon.

Keillor, Garrison. 2005. *A Prairie Home Companion's Pretty Good Joke Book*. New 4th ed. Minneapolis, MN: Highbridge.

Keith-Spiegel, Patricia. 1972. "Early Conceptions of Humor: Varieties and Issues." In *The Psychology of Humor: Theoretical Perspectives and Empirical Issues*, ed. Jeffrey H. Goldstein and Paul E. McGhee, 3–39. New York: Academic Press.

Kelley, Greg. 2020. *Unruly Audience: Folk Interventions in Popular Media*. Logan: Utah State University Press.

Kimball, James. 1999. *J. Golden Kimball Stories*. Salt Lake City: Whitehorse Press.

Kimball, James. 2002. *More J. Golden Kimball Stories*. Salt Lake City: Whitehorse Press.

Kirshenblatt-Gimblett, Barbara. 1998. "Folklore's Crisis." *Journal of American Folklore* 111 (441): 281–327.

Klein, Barbro, and Mats Widbom, eds. 1994. *Swedish Folk Art: All Tradition Is Change*. New York: Harry N. Abrams.

Kline, Paul. 1976. "The Psychoanalytic Theory of Humor and Laughter." In *It's a Funny Thing Humour*, ed. Anthony J. Chapman and Hugh C. Foot, 7–12. Oxford: Pergamon.

Koenig, Fred. 1985. *Rumor in the Marketplace: The Social Psychology of Commercial Hearsay*. Dover, MA: Auburn.

Koén-Sarano, Matilda, ed. 2003. *Folktales of Joha: Jewish Trickster*. Philadelphia: The Jewish Publication Society.

Kolatch, Alfred J. 1964. *Who's Who in the Talmud*. Middle Village, NY: Jonathan David.

Kramer, Thomas, and Lauren Block. 2011. "Non-Conscious Effects of Peculiar Belief on Consumer Psychology and Choice." *Journal of Consumer Psychology* 21 (1): 101–111.

Kravitz, Seth. 1977. "London Jokes and Ethnic Stereotypes." *Western Folklore* 36 (4): 275–301.

Kristol, Irivng. 1951. "Is Jewish Humor Dead?" *Commentary* 12 (November): 431–436.

Krohn, Kaarle. 1971 (1926). *Folklore Methodology Formulated by Julius Krohn and Expanded by Nordic Researchers*. Translated by Roger L. Welsch. Austin: University of Texas Press.

Kuipers, Giselinde. 2008. "The Sociology of Humor." In *The Primer of Humor Research*, ed. Victor Raskin, 361–398. Berlin: Mouton de Gruyter.

Kuper, Adam. 2000. "If Memes are the Answer, What Is the Question?" In *Darwinizing Culture: The Status of Memetics as a Science*, ed. Robert Aunger, 175–188. Oxford: Oxford University Press.

Kuznar, Lawrence A. 1997. *Reclaiming a Scientific Anthropology*. Walnut Creek, CA: Altamira.

Labrie-Bouthillier, Vivian. 1977. "Les éxperiences sur la transmission orale: d'une modèle individuel à un modèle collectif." *Fabula* 18 (1): 1–17.

Lang, Andrew. 1879. "Preface." *The Folk-Lore Record* 2: i–viii.

Lang, Andrew. 1884. "Introduction." In *Grimm's Household Tales*, ed. Hunt Margaret, xi–lxxv. London: George Bell.

Laws, G. Malcolm. 1957. *American Ballads from British Broadsides*. Philadelphia: The American Folklore Society.

Laws, G. Malcolm. 1964. *Native American Balladry*. Philadelphia: The American Folklore Society.

"Lay Advice." 2003. *World's Greatest Collection of Church Jokes*. Uhrichsville, OH: Barbour.

Leary, James P. 1980a. "Recreational Talk among White Adolescents." *Western Folklore* 39 (4): 284–299.

Leary, James P. 1980b. "White Ritual Insults." In *Play and Culture*, ed. Helen B. Schwartzman, 125–139. West Point, NY: Leisure.

Leary, James P. 1984. "The Favorite Jokes of Max Trebiatowski." *Western Folklore* 48 (1): 1–17.

Leary, James P. 2001. *So Ole Say to Lena: Folk Humor of the Upper Midwest*. 2nd ed. Madison: University of Wisconsin Press.

Lee, Hector H. 1964. *J. Golden Kimball Stories Together with Brother Petersen Yarns*. Folk-Legacy Records FTA-25.

Legman, G. 1968. *The Rationale of the Dirty Joke: First Series*. New York: Grove.

Legman, G. 1975. *The Rationale of the Dirty Joke: Second Series*. New York: Breaking Point.

Lesser, Alexander. 1931. "Superstition." *The Journal of Philosophy* 28 (5): 617–628.

Levenson, Thomas. 2016. *The Hunt for Vulcan*. New York: Random House.

Levitt, Eugene E. 1952. "Superstitions: Twenty-Five Years Ago and Today." *The American Journal of Psychology* 65 (3): 443–449.

Levitt, Steven D., and Stephen J. Dubner. 2005. *Freakonomics: A Rogue Economist Explores the Hidden Side of Everything*. New York: William Morrow.

Limón, José E. 1977. "Agringado Joking in Texas Mexican Society: Folklore and Differential Identity." *New Scholar* 6: 33–50.

Linton, Ralph. 1940. *Acculturation in Seven American Indian Tribes*. New York: Appleton-Century.

"Little Sister." n.d. *Emmitsburg*. Accessed October 24, 2022. http://www.emmitsburg.net/humor/archives/clean/clean_6.htm.

Livio, Mark. 2013. *Brilliant Blunders: From Darwin to Einstein—Colossal Mistakes by Great Scientists That Changed Our Understanding of Life and the Universe*. New York: Simon and Schuster.

Locke, John. 1798 (1690). *An Essay Concerning Human Understanding*. 3 vols. Collated with Desmaizeaux's edition. Edinburgh: J. Mundell.

Lord, Albert B. 1965 (1960). *The Singer of Tales*. New York: Athenaeum.

Lowthorp, Leah. 2020. "Kutiyattam, Heritage, and the Dynamics of Culture." *Asian Ethnology* 79 (1): 21–44.

Lubatov, Igor, and Hod Lipson. 2012. "Humor as Circuits in Semantic Networks." *Proceedings of the 50th Annual Meeting of the Association of Computational Linguistics*, 150–155. Jeju, Republic of Korea, July 8–14.

Lundell, Torberg. 1993. "An Experiential Exploration of Why Men and Women Laugh." *Humor: International Journal of Humor Research* 6 (3): 299–317.

Luomala, Katherine. 1980. "Folk Narrative 'Laws' Relating to Dramatis Personae in the Polynesian Māui Cycle." *Journal of the Polynesian Society* 89 (3): 367–371.

Lynch, Aaron. 1996. *Thought Contagion: How Belief Spreads through Society*. New York: Basic Books.

Lyons, John. 1977. *Semantics, Volume I*. Cambridge: Cambridge University Press.

Maier, Norman R. F. 1932. "A Gestalt Theory of Humor." *British Journal of Psychology* 23 (1): 69–74.

Malinowski, Bronislaw. 1937 (1931). "Culture." In *Encyclopedia of the Social Sciences*, ed. Edwin R. A. Seligman and Alvin Johnson, 15 vols., 621–646. New York: Macmillan.

Malinowski, Bronislaw. 1954 (1948). *Magic, Science, and Religion and Other Essays*. Garden City, NY: Doubleday Anchor.

Marret, R. R. 1920. *Psychology and Folklore*. London: Methuen.

Marsh, Moira. 2015. *Practically Joking*. Logan: Utah State University Press.

Martin, Rod A. 2007. *The Psychology of Humor: An Integrative Approach*. Burlington, MA: Elsevier Academic Press.

Marzolph, Ulrich. 1992. *Arabia Ridens: Die humoristische Kurzprosa der frühen adab-Literatur im internationalen Traditionsgeflect*. 2 vols. Frankfurt am Main: Vittorio Klostermann.

Mason, Jackie. 1988. *Jackie Mason on Broadway*. HBO Video. Vanoff Mason Productions.

Mayr, Ernst. 1986. "Review of *Natural Selection: The Philosopher and the Biologist* by Elliott Sober." *Paleobiology* 12 (2): 233–239.

McGee, W. J. 1898. "Piratical Acculturation." *American Anthropologist* 11 (8): 243–249.

McGraw, Peter, and Joel Warner. 2014. *The Humor Code: A Global Search for What Makes Things Funny*. New York: Simon & Schuster.

McNeil, Lynne S. 2009. "The End of the Internet." In *Folk Culture in the Digital Age: The Emergent Dynamics of Human Interaction*, ed. Trevor J. Blank, 80–97. Logan: Utah State University Press.

Mead, Margaret. 1956. *New Lives for Old: Cultural Transformation—Manus, 1928–1953*. New York: William Morrow.

Mechling, Jay. 1986. "Children's Folklore." In *Folk Groups and Folklore Genres: An Introduction*, ed. Elliott Oring, 91–120. Logan: Utah State University Press.

Medawar, Peter. 1977. "Pro Bono Publico." *The Spectator*. January 15, 1977.

Meir, Ofra. 1979. "Ha-nuskhaot ha-yehudiot shel tipus ha-sipuri AT 875" [The Jewish versions of AT 875]. *Yeda-Am* 19: 55–61.

Mendelsohn, S. Felix. 1935. *The Jew Laughs: Humorous Stories and Anecdotes*. Chicago: L. M. Stein.

Mendelsohn, S. Felix. 1941. *Let Laughter Ring*. Philadelphia: Jewish Publication Society of America.

Merten, Don E. 2005. "Transition and 'Trouble': Rites of Passage for Suburban Girls." *Anthropology and Education Quarterly* 36 (2): 132–148.

Miller, Tristan. 2020. "Reinhold Aman, 1936–2019." *Humor: International Journal of Humor Research* 23 (1): 1–5.

Mills, D. E. 1970. *A Collection of Tales from Uji: A Study and Translation of Uji Shui Monogatari.* Cambridge: Cambridge University Press.

Mills, Ladson F. III. 2019. *Abandoned Shipmate: The Destruction of Coast Guard Captain Ernie Blanchard.* Jefferson, NC: MacFarland.

Mills, Margaret A. 2020. "Introduction: Defining and Creating (A) New Critical Folklore Studies." *Journal of American Folklore* 133 (530): 383–391.

Mintzker, Yair. 2017. *The Many Deaths of Jew Süss: The Notorious Trial and Execution of an Eighteenth-Century Court Jew.* Princeton, NJ: Princeton University Press.

Mitchell, Carol A. 1976. "Some Differences between Male and Female Joke Telling as Exemplified in a College Community." 2 vols. PhD diss., Indiana University.

Mitchell, Carol. 1977. "The Sexual Perspective in the Appreciation and Interpretation of Jokes." *Western Folklore* 36 (4): 303–329.

Mitchell, Carol. 1978. "Hostility and Aggression Toward Males in Female Joke Telling." *Frontiers* 3 (3): 19–23.

Mitchell, Carol. 1985. "Some Differences in Male and Female Joke Telling." In *Women's Folklore, Women's Culture*, ed. Rosan A. Jordan and Susan J. Kalčik, 163–186. Philadelphia: University of Pennsylvania Press.

Monro, D. H. 1953. *The Argument of Laughter.* Melbourne: Melbourne University Press.

More, Douglas Mills, and Allyn F. Roberts. 1957. "Societal Variations in Humor Responses to Cartoons." *Journal of Social Psychology* 45 (2): 233–245.

"Morganking." n.d. *The Morgan King Company.* Accessed September 9, 2015. http://morganking .com/bkfinder/jokes.html.

Morin, Olivier. (2011) 2016. *How Traditions Live and Die.* Oxford: Oxford University Press.

Morreall, John, ed. 1987. *The Philosophy of Laughter and Humor.* Albany: State University of New York Press.

Morreall, John. 2008. "Philosophy and Religion." In *The Primer of Humor Research*, ed. Victor Raskin, 211–242. Berlin: Mouton de Gruyter.

Morrissey, Maureen. 1990. "Script Theory for the Analysis of Humorous Metaphors." In *Whimsy VII: Proceedings of the 1988 WHIM Conference*, ed. Shaun F. D. Hughes and Victor Raskin, 124–125. West Lafayette, IN, and Tempe, AZ: International Society for Humor Studies.

Mr. J., n.d. *Giant Book of Dirty Jokes.* N.p.: Castle.

Mr. P. 1984. *The World's Best Yiddish Dirty Jokes.* N.p.: Castle.

Mulkay, Michael. 1988. *On Humor: Its Nature and Its Place in Modern Society.* Cambridge, UK: Basil Blackwell.

Mullen, Patrick. 1969. "The Function of Magic Folk Belief among Texas Coastal Fishermen." *Journal of American Folklore* 88 (325): 214–225.

Mushabac, Jane. 2003. "Going Out on a Limb." *Midstream* 49 (5): 36–38.

Nadel, S. F. 1952. "Witchcraft in Four African Societies." *American Anthropologist* 54 (1): 18–29.

Nadis, Steve. 2013. "A Scientific Method to His Madness." *Discover*, April, 52–59.

Navon, David. 1981. "The Seemingly Appropriate but Virtually Inappropriate: Note about Characteristics of Jokes." *Center for the Study of Reading.* Technical Report 223. University of Illinois, Champaign Urbana. https://eric.ed.gov/?id=ED212989.

Navon, David. 1988. "The Seemingly Appropriate but Virtually Inappropriate: Note about Characteristics of Jokes." *Poetics* 17 (3): 207–219.

Nenola-Kallio, Aili. 1981. "Death of a Tradition." In *Adaptation, Change, and Decline in Oral Literature,* ed. Lauri Honko and Vilmos Voigt, 139–146. Studia Fennica 26. Helsinki: Suomalaisen Kirjallisuuden Seura.

Neulander, Judith S. 1998. "Jewish Oral Traditions." In *Teaching Oral Traditions,* ed. John Miles Foley, 225–238. New York: Modern Language Association.

Nevo, Ofra. 1991. "What's in a Jewish Joke?" *Humor: International Journal of Humor Research* 4 (2): 251–260.

Nevo, Ofra, and Brauch Nevo. 1983. "What Do You Do When Asked to Answer Humorously?" *Journal of Personality and Social Psychology* 44 (1): 188–194.

Newell, William Wells. 1963 (1903). *The Games and Songs of American Children.* New York: Dover.

Ng, Travis, Terence Chong, and Xin Du. 2010. "The Value of Superstitions." *Journal of Economic Psychology* 31 (3): 293–309.

Nichols, Shaun. 2002. "On the Genealogy of Norms: A Case for the Role of Emotion in Cultural Evolution." *Philosophy of Science* 69 (2): 235–255.

Nicolaisen, William F. H. 1990. "Variation and Creativity in Folk-Narrative." In *D'un Conte . . . à l'autre: La variabilité dans la littérature orale,* ed. Veronika Görög-Karady, 39–45. Paris: Centre Nationale de la Recherche Scientifique.

Novak, William, and Moshe Waldoks, eds. 1981. *The Big Book of Jewish Humor.* New York: Harper & Row.

Noy, Dov. 1962. "Ha-kayemet bedichat-am yehudit?" [Does the Jewish folk joke exist?]. *Machanayim* 67: 48–58.

Noy, Dov. 1971. "The Jewish Versions of the 'Animal Languages' Folktale (AT 670): A Typological Structural Study." *Scripta Hierosolymitana* 22: 171–209.

Noyes, Dorothy. 2009. "Tradition: Three Traditions." *Journal of Folklore Research* 46 (3): 233–268.

Noyes, Dorothy. 2019. " 'Incalculably Diffusive': Revisiting the Disciplinary Deficit." *Journal of American Folklore* 132 (524): 175–184.

Noyes, Dorothy, and Roger D. Abrahams. 1999. "From Calendar Custom to National Memory." In *Cultural Memory and the Construction of Identity,* ed. Dan Ben-Amos and Liliane Weissberg, 77–98. Detroit, MI: Wayne State University Press.

O'Connell, Walter E. 1960. "The Adaptive Functions of Wit and Humor." *Journal of Abnormal and Social Psychology* 61 (2): 263–270.

Ogden, C. K. 1967 [1932]. *Opposition.* Bloomington: Indiana University Press.

"Oil." n.d. *Make it Clear Ministries.* Accessed October 24, 2022. http://www.makeitclearnow.org /relhumor.html.

Olbrys, Stephen Gencarella. 2005. "Money Talks: Folklore in the Public Sphere." *Folklore* 116: 292–310.

Olrik, Axel. 1965 (1909). "Epic Laws of Folk Narrative." In *The Study of Folklore,* ed. Alan Dundes, 129–141. Englewood Cliffs, NJ: Prentice-Hall.

Olrik, Axel. 1992 (1921). *Principles for Oral Narrative Research.* Translated by Kirsten Wolf and Jody Jensen. Bloomington: Indiana University Press.

Opie, Iona, and Peter Opie. 1980. "Certain Laws of Folklore." In *Folklore Studies in the Twentieth Century: Proceedings of the Centenary Conference of the Folklore Society*, ed. Venetia J. Newall, 64–75. Suffolk, UK: D. S. Brewer, Rowman and Littlefield.

Oring, Elliott. 1971. "Whalemen and Their Songs: A Study of Folklore and Culture." *New York Folklore Quarterly* 27 (1): 130–152.

Oring, Elliott. 1973. "'Hey, You've Got No Character': Chizbat Humor and the Boundaries of Israeli Identity." *Journal of American Folklore* 86 (342): 358–366.

Oring, Elliott. 1975. "Everything is a Shade of Elephant: An Alternative to a Psychoanalysis of Humor." *New York Folklore* 1 (3/4): 149–159.

Oring, Elliott. 1976. "Three Functions of Folklore: Traditional Functionalism as Explanation in Folkloristics." *Journal of American Folklore* 89 (351): 67–80.

Oring, Elliott. 1977. "Review of *Rationale of the Dirty Joke: An Analysis of Sexual Humor, First Series* and *Rationale of the Dirty Joke: An Analysis of Sexual Humor, Second Series* by G. Legman." *Western Folklore* 36 (4): 365–371.

Oring, Elliott. 1978. "Transmission and Degeneration." *Fabula: Journal of Folktale Studies* 19 (3/4): 193–210.

Oring, Elliott. 1981. *Israeli Humor: The Content and Structure of the Chizbat of the Palmah*. Albany: State University of New York Press.

Oring, Elliott. 1984. "Dyadic Traditions." *Journal of Folklore Research* 21 (1): 19–28.

Oring, Elliott. 1987. "Jokes and the Discourse on Disaster." *Journal of American Folklore* 100 (397): 276–286.

Oring, Elliott. 1990. "Legend, Truth and News." *Southern Folklore* 47 (2): 163–177.

Oring, Elliott. 1992. *Jokes and Their Relations*. Lexington: University Press of Kentucky.

Oring, Elliott. 1995. "Appropriate Incongruities: Genuine and Spurious." *Humor: International Journal of Humor Research* 8 (3): 229–235.

Oring, Elliott. 1997. "On the Tradition and Mathematics of Counting-Out." *Western Folklore* 56 (2): 139–152.

Oring, Elliott. 1998. "Anti Anti-'Folklore.'" *Journal of American Folklore* 111 (441): 328–338.

Oring, Elliott. 2003. *Engaging Humor*. Urbana: University of Illinois Press.

Oring, Elliott. 2004. "Risky Business: Political Joking under Repressive Regimes." *Western Folklore* 63 (3): 209–236.

Oring, Elliott. 2006a. "Missing Theory." *Western Folklore* 65 (4): 455–465.

Oring, Elliott. 2006b. "Folk or Lore: The Stake in Dichotomies." *Journal of Folklore Research* 43 (3): 205–218.

Oring, Elliott. 2007. "Review of *The Aristocrats* by Penn Jillette and Paul Provenza." *Journal of American Folklore* 140 (478): 500–501.

Oring, Elliott. 2008. "Legendry and the Rhetoric of Truth." *Journal of American Folklore* 121 (480): 127–166.

Oring, Elliott. 2011a. "Contested Performance and Joke Aesthetics." In *The Individual and Tradition: Folkloristic Perspectives*, ed. Ray Cashman, Tom Mould, and Pravina Shukla, 265–285. Bloomington: Indiana University Press.

Oring, Elliott. 2011b. "Parsing the Joke: The General Theory of Verbal Humor and Appropriate Incongruity." *Humor: International Journal of Humor Research* 24 (2): 203–222.

Oring, Elliott. 2011c. "Still Further Thoughts on Logical Mechanisms: A Response to Christian F. Hempelmann and Salvatore Attardo." *Humor: International Journal of Humor Research* 24 (2): 151–158.

Oring, Elliott. 2012a. "Jokes on the Internet: Listing towards Lists." In *Folk Culture in the Digital Age*, ed. Trevor Blank, 98–118. Logan: Utah State University Press.

Oring, Elliott. 2012b. *Just Folklore: Analysis, Interpretation, Critique*. Los Angeles: Cantilever.

Oring, Elliott. 2013. "Thinking through Tradition." In *Tradition in the Twenty-First Century: Locating the Role of the Past in the Present*, ed. Trevor J. Blank and Robert Glenn Howard, 22–48. Logan: Utah State University Press.

Oring, Elliott. 2016. *Joking Asides: The Theory, Analysis, and Aesthetics of Humor*. Logan: Utah State University Press.

Oring, Elliott. 2019a. "Oppositions, Overlaps, and Ontologies: The General Theory of Verbal Humor Revisited." *Humor: International Journal of Humor Research* 32 (2): 151–170.

Oring, Elliott. 2019b. "Formalizing Humor: A Response to Christian Hempelmann and Julia Taylor Rayz." *Humor: International Journal of Humor Research* 32 (4): 537–543.

Oring, Elliott. 2019c. "Back to the Future: Questions for Theory in the Twenty-First Century." *Journal of American Folklore* 132 (524): 137–156.

Oriol, Carme, and Joseph M. Pujol. 2008. *Index of Catalan Folktales*. Folklore Fellows Communication No. 294. Helsinki: Suomalainen Tiedeakatemia.

Ortutay, Gyula. 1959. "Principles of Oral Transmission in Folk Culture." *Acta Ethnographica* 8: 175–221.

Ostrom, Hans, ed. 1991. *Lives and Moments: An Introduction to Short Fiction*. Fort Worth, TX: Holt, Rinehart, and Winston.

Ostrower, Chaya. 2014. *It Kept Us Alive: Humor in the Holocaust*. Jerusalem: Yad Vashem, The International Institute of Holocaust Research.

"Overslept Stupid Joke of the Night." 2005. *IGN Boards*. October 1, 2005. http://www.ign.com/boards/threads/overslept-stupid-joke-of-the-night.250311189/.

Palmer, Richard E. 1969. *Hermeneutics: Interpretation Theory in Schleiermacher, Dilthey, Heidegger, and Gadamer*. Evanston, IL: Northwestern University Press.

Paolillo, John C. 1998. "Gary Larson's Far Side: Nonsense? Nonsense!" *Humor: International Journal of Humor Research* 11 (3): 261–290.

Plato. 1998. *Cratylus*. Translated by C. D. E. Reeve. Indianapolis, IN: Hackett.

Pollio, Howard R. 1996. "Boundaries in Humor and Metaphor." In *Metaphor: Implications and Applications*, ed. Jeffrey Scott Mio and Albert N. Katz, 231–253. Mahwah, NJ: Lawrence Erlbaum Associates.

Pelto, Pertti J., and Gretel H. Pelto. 1978. *Anthropological Research: The Structure of Inquiry*. 2nd ed. London: Cambridge University Press.

Pentikäinen, Juha. 1979. "The Symbolism of Liminality." In *Religious Symbols and Their Functions*, ed. Haralds Beizais, 154–166. Stockholm: Almqvist and Wiksell.

Percy, Thomas. 1966 (1886, orig. 1765). *Reliques of Ancient English Poetry*, ed. Henry B. Wheatley. 3 vols. New York: Dover.

Piata, Anna. 2016. "When a Metaphor Becomes a Joke: Metaphor Journeys from Political Ads to Internet Memes." *Journal of Pragmatics*. 106: 39–56.

Piddington, Ralph. 1963. *The Psychology of Laughter: A Study in Social Adaptation*. New York: Gamut.

Pimple, Kenneth D. 1996. "The Meme-ing of Folklore." *Journal of Folklore Research* 33 (3): 236–240.

Plotkin, Henry. 2000. "Culture and Psychological Mechanisms." In *Darwinizing Culture: The Status of the Science of Memetics*, ed. Robert Aunger, 69–82. Oxford: Oxford University Press.

Poggie, John J. Jr., and Carl Gersuny. 1972. "Risk and Ritual: An Interpretation of Fishermen's Folklore in a New England Community." *Journal of American Folklore* 85 (335): 66–72.

Porter, James. 1976. "Jeannie Robertson's My Son Davis: A Conceptual Performance Model." *Journal of American Folklore* 89 (351): 7–26.

"Prairie Home." 1999. *Prairie Home*. http://www.prairiehome.publicradio.org/features/hodgepodge /19990410_jokeshow/jokes/0407_8.htm.

Propp, V[ladimir]. 1968. *The Morphology of the Folktale*. 2nd ed. Austin: University of Texas Press.

"Quotes of the Duke of Wellington." 1999–2017. *Napoleon Guide*. Accessed September 10, 2020. https://www.napoleonguide.com/aquotes_welli.htm.

Rabeeya, David. 2004. *1,001 Jokes about Rabbis and the Rest of the World*. Bloomington, IN: Xlibris.

Randolph, Vance. 1965. *Hot Springs and Hell and Other Folk Jests and Anecdotes from the Ozarks*. Hatboro, PA: Folklore Associates.

Randolph, Vance. 1976. *Pissing in the Snow and Other Ozark Folktales*. New York: Avon.

Raskin, Victor. 1985a. *Semantic Mechanisms of Humor*. Dordrecht, Holland: D. Reidel.

Raskin, Victor. 1985b. "Jokes." *Psychology Today* 19 (October): 34–39.

Raskin, Victor. 1996. "Computer Implementation of the General Theory of Verbal Humor." In *Automatic Interpretation and Generation of Humor*, ed. J. Hulstijn and A. Nijholt. Proceedings from the Twente Workshop on Language and Technology, 12: 9–19. Enschede: Netherlands.

Raskin, Victor. 2008. "Theory of Humor and Practice of Humor Research: Editor's Notes." In *The Primer of Humor Research*, ed. Victor Raskin, 1–15. Berlin: Mouton de Gruyter.

Raskin, Victor. 2011. "On Oring on GTVH." *Humor: International Journal of Humor Research* 24 (2): 223–231.

Raskin, Victor. 2017. "Humor Theory: What Is and What Is Not." In *Humorous Discourse*, ed. Waładisław Chłopicki and Dorota Brzozowska, 11–22. Berlin: Mouton de Gruyter.

Raskin, Victor, Christian F. Hempelmann, and Julia M. Taylor. 2009. "How to Understand and Assess a Theory: The Evolution of the SSTH into the GTVH and Now into the OSTH." *Journal of Literary Theory* 3 (2): 285–311.

Rayz, Julia Taylor. 2017. "Computational Humor and Christie Davies' Basis for Joke Comparison." *European Journal of Humour Research* 5 (4): 169–178.

"Read Your Bible." n.d. *The Jewish Magazine*. Accessed October 24, 2022. http://www.jewishmag .com/17mag/humor/humor.htm.

Redfield, Robert, Ralph Linton, and Melville J. Herskovits. 1935a. "A Memorandum for the Study of Acculturation." *Man* 35: 145–148.

Redfield, Robert, Ralph Linton, and Melville J. Herskovits. 1935b. "A Memorandum for the Study of Acculturation." *Oceania* 6 (2): 229–233.

Redfield, Robert, Ralph Linton, and Melville J. Herskovits. 1936. "A Memorandum for the Study of Acculturation." *American Anthropologist* 38 (1): 149–152.

Redlich, Fredrick C., Jacob Levine, and Theodore P. Sohler. 1951. "A Mirth Response Test: Preliminary Report on a Psychodiagnostic Technique Utilizing Dynamics of Humor." *American Journal of Orthopsychiatry* 21 (4): 717–734.

Richman, Jacob. 1952. *Jewish Wit and Wisdom*. New York: Pardes.

Richman, Jacob. 1954 (1926). *Laughs from Jewish Lore*. New York: Hebrew Publishing.

Ridley, Matt. 2000. *Genome: The Autobiography of a Species in 23 Chapters*. New York: Harper Perennial.

Ritchie, Graeme. 2002. "The Structure of Forced Reinterpretation Jokes." *April Fools' Day Workshop on Computational Humor*, ed. O. Stock, C. Strapparava, and A. Nijholt, 47–56. Enschede, Netherlands: University of Twente.

Ritchie, Graeme. 2004. *The Linguistic Analysis of Jokes*. New York: Routledge.

Ritchie, Graeme. 2009. "Variants of Incongruity Resolution." *Journal of Literary Theory* 3 (2): 1–20.

Ritchie, Graeme. 2014. "Logic and Reasoning in Jokes." *European Journal of Humour Research* 2 (1): 50–60.

Rogers, Everett M. 1995. *The Diffusion of Innovations*. New York: The Free Press.

Rosenwald, George C. 1964. "The Relation of Drive Discharge to the Enjoyment of Humor." *Journal of Personality* 32 (4): 682–698.

Roskies, David G. 2001. "Inside Sholem Shachnah's Hat." *Prooftexts* 21 (1): 39–56.

Rosten, Leo. 1968. *The Joys of Yiddish*. New York: McGraw Hill.

Roth, Cecil, ed. 1972. *Encyclopaedia Judaica*. 16 vols. Jerusalem: Keter.

Rothbart, Mary K. 1977. "Psychological Approaches to the Study of Humor." In *It's a Funny Thing Humour*, ed. Anthony J. Chapman and Hugh C. Foot, 87–94. Oxford: Pergamon.

Rubin, David C. 1995. *Memory in Oral Tradition: A Cognitive Psychology of Epic, Ballads, and Counting-out Rhymes*. New York: Oxford University Press.

Ruch, Willibald, and Franz-Josef Hehl. 1988. "Attitudes to Sex, Sexual Behaviour and Enjoyment of Humour." *Personality and Individual Differences* 9 (6): 983–994.

Rudski, Jeffrey M., and Ashleigh Edwards. 2007. "Malinowski Goes to College: Factors Influencing Students' Use of Ritual and Superstition." *The Journal of General Psychology* 134 (4): 389–403.

Rudy, Jill Terry. 2002. "Toward an Assessment of Verbal Art as Performance: A Cross-Disciplinary Citation Study with Rhetorical Analysis." *Journal of American Folklore* 115 (455): 5–27.

Ruiz, Juan. 1972 (1330). *Libro de Buen Amor*, Raymond S. White. Princeton, NJ: Princeton University Press.

Sacks, Harvey. 1974. "An Analysis of the Course of a Joke's Telling in Conversation." In *Explorations in the Ethnography of Speaking*, ed. Richard Bauman and Joel Sherzer, 337–353. Cambridge: Cambridge University Press.

Sacks, Harvey. 1978. "Some Technical Considerations of a Dirty Joke." In *Studies in the Organization of Conversational Interaction*, ed. J. Schenkein, 249–270. New York: Academic Press.

Sahlins, Marshall D., and Elman R. Service, eds. 1960. *Evolution and Culture*. Ann Arbor: The University of Michigan Press.

Salomonsson, Anders. 2000. "Documentation and Research." In *Thick Corpus, Organic Variation, and Textuality in Oral Tradition*, ed. Lauri Honko, 197–213. Studia Fennica Folkloristica 7. Helsinki: Finnish Literature Society.

Saucier, Jean-Francois. 1972. "Correlates of the Long Postpartum Taboo: A Cross-Cultural Study." *Current Anthropology* 13 (2): 238–249.

Schafer, R. 1970. "Requirements for a Critique of the Theory of Catharsis." *Journal of Consulting and Clinical Psychology* 35 (1): 13–17.

Scheibe, Karl E., and Theodore R. Sarbin. 1965. "Towards a Theoretical Conceptualisation of Superstition." *The British Journal for the Philosophy of Science* 16 (62): 143–158.

Schier, Kurt. 1955. "Praktische Untersuchungen zur mündlichen Weitergabe von Volkerzählungen." PhD diss., University of Munich.

Schiller, Paul. 1938. "A Configurational Theory of Jokes and Puzzles." *Journal of General Psychology* 18 (2): 217–234.

Schmidt, Sigrid. 2005. "Children in Nama and Damara Tales of Magic." *Folklore* 116 (2): 155–171.

Schrempp, Gregory. 1995. "On Aristotle's Metaphysics, Oring's Theory of Humor, and Other Appropriate Incongruities." *Humor: International Journal of Humor Research* 8 (3): 219–228.

Schrempp, Gregory. 2009. "Taking the Dawkins Challenge: The Dark Side of the Meme." *Journal of Folklore Research* 46 (1): 91–100.

Schwarzbaum, Haim. 1968. *Studies in Jewish and World Folklore*. Berlin: Walter de Gruyter.

Schweizer, Bernard, and Karl-Heinz Ott. 2016. "Faith and Laughter: Do Atheists and Practicing Christians Have Different Senses of Humor?" *Humor: International Journal of Humor Research* 29 (3): 413–438.

Scott, Sir Walter. 1803. *Minstrelsy of the Scottish Border*. 2nd ed. 3 vols. London: James Ballantyne.

Senft, Gunter. 1985. "How to Tell—and Understand—a Dirty Joke in Kilivila." *Journal of Pragmatics* 9 (6): 815–834.

Sharp, Cecil. 1907. *English Folksong: Some Conclusions*. London: Simpkin.

Sherman, Sharon. 2004. "Film and the Survival of Folklore Studies in the 21st Century." *Western Folklore* 63 (4): 291–318.

Sherzer, Joel. 1985. "Puns and Jokes." In *Handbook of Discourse Analysis*, 4 vols., ed. Teun A. Van Dijk, 3: 213–221. London: Academic Press.

Sholom Aleichem. 1956. *Selected Stories of Sholom Aleichem*. New York: Modern Library.

Simoons, Frederick J. 1994 (1961). *Eat Not This Flesh: Food Avoidances from Prehistory to the Present*. 2nd ed. Madison: University of Wisconsin Press.

Singer, David L. 1968. "Aggression Arousal, Hostile Humor, Catharsis." *Journal of Personality and Social Psychology* 8 (1, Pt 2): 1–15.

Siporin, Steve. 2013. "For Time and Eternity: BYU Coed Jokes and the Seriousness of Mormon Humor." In *Latter Day Lore: Mormon Folklore Studies*, ed. Eric Eliason and Tom Mould, 385–395. Salt Lake City: University of Utah Press.

Skinner, B. F. 1948. "'Superstition' in the Pigeon." *Journal of Experimental Psychology* 38 (2): 168–172.

Smith, John Maynard. 1982. "Genes and Memes." *The London Review of Books* 4 (2): 3–4.

Smith, Paul S. 1974. "Tradition—A Perspective: Part I, Introduction." *Lore and Language* 2 (1): 15–17.

Smith, Paul S. 1975. "Tradition—A Perspective: Part II. Transmission." *Lore and Language* 2 (3): 5–14.

Smith, Paul S. 1978. "Tradition—A Perspective: Part III. Information, Perception, and Performance." *Lore and Language* 2 (8): 1–10.

Smith, Paul S. 1986. "Tradition—A Perspective: Part IV. Variation on the Prospective Adopter's Access to Information." *Lore and Language* 5 (1): 3–38.

Šmits, Pēterīs. 1962–1970. *Laviesū Tautas Teikas un Pasakas* [Latvian Folk Legends and Fairy Tales]. 2nd ed. 15 vols. Waverly, IA: Latvju Gramata.

Sober, Elliott. 1984. *The Nature of Selection: Evolutionary Theory in Philosophical Focus*. Cambridge, MA: MIT Press.

Spalding, Henry D. 1969. *Encyclopedia of Jewish Humor: From Biblical Times to the Modern Age*. New York: Jonathan David.

Spencer, Herbert. 1860. "The Social Organism." *The Westminster Review*. New Series. 17: 90–121.

Sperber, Dan. 1996. *Explaining Culture: A Naturalistic Approach*. Oxford: Blackwell.

Sperber, Dan. 2000. "An Objection to the Memetic Approach to Culture." In *Darwinizing Culture: The Status of Memetics as a Science*, ed. Robert Aunger, 163–173. Oxford: Oxford University Press.

Spiro, Melford E. 1974. *Burmese Supernaturalism*. Philadelphia: Institute for the Study of Human Issues.

Stegner, Wallace. 2013. "Hierarch and Mule-Skinner: A Selection from Mormon Country." In *Latter Day Lore: Mormon Folklore Studies*, ed. Eric Eliason and Tom Mould, 396–401. Salt Lake City: University of Utah Press.

Stephens-Davidowitz, Seth. 2022. *Don't Trust Your Gut: Using Data to Get What You Really Want in Life*. New York: Dey St.

Stora-Sandor, Judith. 1991. "The Stylistic Metamorphosis of Jewish Humor." *Humor: International Journal of Humor Research* 4 (2): 211–222.

Strickland, John F. 1959. "The Effect of Motivation Arousal on Humor Preferences." *Journal of Abnormal and Social Psychology* 59 (2): 278–281.

Stross, Brian. 1971. "Serial Order in Nez Percé Myths." *Journal of American Folklore* 84 (331): 104–113.

Stubbersfield, Joseph M., Lewis G. Dean, Sana Sheikh, Kevin N. Laland, and Catherine P. Cross. 2019. "Social Transmission Favours the 'Morally Good' over the 'Merely Arousing.'" *Palgrave Communications: Humanities/Social Sciences/Business* 5 (70): 1–11.

Stubbersfield, Joseph, and Jamshid Tehrani. 2013. "Expect the Unexpected? Testing for Minimally Counterintuitive (MCI) Bias in the Transmission of Legends: A Computational Phylogenetic Approach." *Social Science Computer Review* 31 (1): 90–102.

Stubbersfield, Joseph M., Jamshid J. Tehrani, and Emma G. Flynn. 2015. "Serial Killers, Spiders, and Cybersex: Social and Information Bias in the Transmission of Urban Legends." *British Journal of Psychology* 106 (2): 288–307.

Stubbersfield, Joseph, Jamshid Tehrani, and Emma Flynn. 2018. "Faking the News: Intentional Guided Variation Reflects Cognitive Biases in Transmission Chains without Recall." *Cultural Science Journal* 10 (1): 54–65.

Suls, Jerry M. 1972. "A Two-Stage Model for the Appreciation of Jokes and Cartoons: An Information Processing Analysis." In *The Psychology of Humor: Theoretical Perspectives and Empirical Issues*, ed. Jeffrey H. Goldstein, and Paul E. McGhee, 81–100. New York: Academic Press.

Sykes, A. J. M. 1966. "Joking Relationships in an Industrial Setting." *American Anthropologist* 68 (1): 188–193.

Szpila, Grzegorz. 2017. "Polish Paremic Demotivators: Tradition in an Internet Genre." *Journal of American Folklore* 130 (517): 305–334.

Taylor, Archer. 1943. "The Riddle." *California Folklore Quarterly* 2 (2): 129–147.

Taylor, Julia. 2010. "Ontology-Based View of Natural Language Meaning: The Case of Humor Detection." *Journal of Ambient Intelligence and Humanized Computing* 1 (3): 221–234.

Telushkin, Joseph. 1992. *Jewish Humor: What the Best Jewish Jokes Say about the Jews.* New York: William Morrow.

Terrion, Jenepher Lennox, and Blake E. Ashforth. 2002. "From 'I' to 'We': The Role of Putdown Humor and Identity in the Development of a Temporary Group." *Human Relations* 55 (1): 55–88.

"This I Believe." 2007. https://www.google.com/search?tbm=bks&hl=en&q=Briskin+%22This+ I+Believe%22#q=Rabbi+Charles+K.+Briskin+%22This+I+Believe%22&start=10&hl=en.

Thompson, Mark. 1996. "A Political Suicide." *Time,* May 13, 1996, p. 44.

Thompson, Stith. 1955–1958. *Motif-Index of Folk-Literature.* Rev. ed. Bloomington: Indiana University Press.

Thompson, Stith. 1977. *The Folktale.* Berkeley: University of California Press.

Tindale, Christopher W. 2017. "Replicating Reason: Arguments, Memes, and the Cognitive Environment." *Philosophy & Rhetoric* 50 (4): 566–588.

Ting, Nai-Tung. 1978. *A Type Index of Chinese Folktales.* FF Communications No. 223. Helsinki: Suomalainen Tiedeakatemia.

"Titius-Bode Law." n.d. *Wikipedia.* Accessed January 18, 2019. https://en.wikipedia.org/wiki/Titius %E2%80%93Bode_law.

Titon, Jeff Todd. 1999. "'The Real Thing': Tourism, Authenticity, and Pilgrimage among the Old Regular Baptists at the 1997 Smithsonian Folklife Festival." *The World of Music* 41 (3): 115–139.

Titon, Jeff Todd. 2015. "Sustainability, Resilience, and Adaptive Management for Applied Ethnomusicology." In *The Oxford Handbook of Applied Musicology,* ed. Svanibor Pettan and Jeff Todd Titon, 157–195. Oxford: Oxford University Press.

Toelken, Barre. 1996. *The Dynamic of Folklore.* Rev. ed. Logan: Utah State University.

"Tokarska." n.d. *Tokarska Law Center.* Accessed September 5, 2015. http://www.sdbankrupt.com /Bankruptcy-Humor.html.

Tsang, Eric W. K. 2004. "Superstition and Decision-Making: Contradiction or Complement?" *The Academy of Management Executive* 18 (4): 92–104.

"Turkishclass." n.d. Message #541. *Turkish Class.* Accessed September 5, 2015. www.turkishclass .com/userMessages_barba_mama.

Trachtenberg, Joshua. 1961. *Jewish Magic and Superstition: A Study in Folk Religion.* Cleveland, OH, and New York: Meridian Books and the Jewish Publication Society of America.

Turner, Victor. 1969. *The Ritual Process: Structure and Anti-Structure.* Chicago: Aldine.

"Two Friends." n.d. *Inspirational Bible Devotionals & Prayer.* Accessed October 24, 2022. http:// storesonline.com/site/988791/page/942737.

"Two Headlines." May 15, 2018. "Qualcomm is Ready for Tesla, Inc. and its Biometric Upgrade" *Twitter.* https://twitter.com/twoheadlines.

"Two Headlines." May 15, 2018. "Weekly Poll: Meghan Markle—Hot or Not?" *Twitter.* https:// twitter.com/twoheadlines.

"Two Headlines." May 17, 2018. "US Ambassador to Donald Trump Defends Response to Gaza Protests." *Twitter.* https://twitter.com/twoheadlines.

Tylor, Edward Burnett. 1871. *Primitive Culture*. 2 vols. London: John Murray.

Tylor, Edward Burnett. 1873. *Primitive Culture*. 2 vols. London: John Murray.

uí Ógáin, Ríonach. 2000. "Aspects of Change in the Irish-Language Singing Tradition." In *Thick Corpus, Organic Variation, and Textuality in Oral Tradition*, ed. Lauri Honko, 537–555. Studia Fennica Folkloristica 7. Helsinki: Finnish Literature Society.

Upton, Dell. 1993. "The Tradition of Change." *Traditional Dwellings and Settlements Review* 5 (1): 9–15.

Uther, Hans-Jörg. 2011. *The Types of International Folktales: A Classification and Bibliography*. 3 vols. Helsinki: Suomalainen Tiedeakatemia.

Van Gennep, Arnold. 1960 (1909). *The Rites of Passage*. Chicago: University of Chicago Press.

Veale, Tony. 2012. *Exploding the Creativity Myth: The Computational Foundations of Linguistic Creativity*. London: Bloomsbury.

Veale, Tony. 2015. "The Humor of Exceptional Cases: Jokes as Compressed Thought Experiments." In *Cognitive Linguistics and Humor Research*, ed. Gert Brône, Kurt Feyaerts, and Tony Veale, 69–90. Berlin: Walter de Gruyter.

Veale, Tony. 2021. *Your Wit Is My Command: Building AIs with a Sense of Humor*. Cambridge, MA: The MIT Press.

Veatch, Thomas C. 1998. "A Theory of Humor." *Humor: International Journal of Humor Research* 11 (2): 161–215.

Vick, Karl. "No Laughing Matter." 1997. *Washington Post*. July 7, 1997.

Vlahos, James. 2019. "Talk to Me." *Discover Magazine* 40 (4): 59–63.

Vogt, Evon Z. 1952. "Water Witching: An Interpretation of a Ritual Pattern in a Rural American Community." *Scientific Monthly* 75 (3): 175–186.

Von Bernuth, Ruth. 2016. *How the Wise Men Got to Chelm*. New York: University Press.

Von Sydow, Carl. 1948. *Selected Papers on Folklore*. Copenhagen: Rosenkilde and Bagger.

Vyse, Stuart A. 1997. *Believing in Magic: The Psychology of Superstition*. Oxford: Oxford University Press.

Ward, Donald, ed. 1981 (1816–1818). *The German Legends of the Brothers Grimm*. Translated by Donald Ward. 2 vols. Philadelphia: Institute for the Study of Human Issues.

Weiner, Jonathan. 1995. *The Beak of the Finch: A Story of Evolution in Our Time*. New York: Vintage.

Weismann, August. 1893. *The Germ-Plasm: A Theory of Heredity*. Translated by W. Newton Parker and Harriet Rönnfeldt. New York: Scribner.

Wex, Michael. 2006. *Born to Kvetch: Yiddish Language and Culture in All Its Moods*. New York: Harper Perennial.

White, Leslie. 1949. *The Science of Culture*. New York: Grove.

"A Whole New World." 2019. *Discover* 40 (7): 12.

Wilson, David Sloan. 2001. "Evolutionary Biology: Struggling to Escape Exclusively Individual Selection." *The Quarterly Review of Biology* 76 (2): 199–205.

Wilson, Edward O. (1975) 2000. *Sociobiology: The New Synthesis*. Cambridge, MA: The Belknap Press for Harvard University.

Wilson, Edward O. 2017. *The Origins of Creativity*. New York: Liveright.

Wilson, William A. 1973. "Herder, Folklore, and Romantic Nationalism." *Journal of Popular Culture* 6 (4): 818–835.

Wilson, William A. 1977. "The Paradox of Mormon Folklore." *BYU Studies Quarterly* 7 (1): 40–58.

Wilson, William A. 2006a. "The Seriousness of Mormon Humor." In *The Marrow of Human Experience: Essays on Folklore*, ed. Jill Terry Rudy, 221–235. Logan: Utah State University Press.

Wilson, William A. 2006b. "On Being Human: The Folklore of Mormon Missionaries." In *The Marrow of Human Experience: Essays on Folklore*, ed. Jill Terry Rudy, 201–220. Logan: Utah State University Press.

Wisse, Ruth R. 2013. *No Joke: Making Jewish Humor*. Princeton, NJ: Princeton University Press.

"Woes." n.d. *Harry Leichter's Jewish Humor*. Accessed October 24, 2022. http://www.haruth.com /jhumor/jhumor62.htm#woes.

Wolfenstein, Martha. 1978 (1954). *Children's Humor: A Psychological Analysis*. Bloomington: Indiana University Press.

Wright, Thomas. 1879. "The Miller at the Professor's Examination." *The Folk-Lore Record* 2: 173–176.

Yassif, Eli. 1986. "From Jewish Oicotype to Israeli Oicotype: The Tale of 'The Man Who Never Swore an Oath.'" *Fabula: Journal of Folktale Studies* 27: 216–236.

Yassif, Eli. 2009. "Intertextuality in Folklore: Pagan Themes in Jewish Folktales from the Early Modern Era." *European Journal of Jewish Studies* 3 (1): 58–59.

"Yuksrus." n.d. *Yuksrus*. Accessed September 9, 2015. www.yuksrus.com/religion_priests.html.

Zane, Nicholas. 2006. "Feather & Hammer Drop on Moon." July 5, 2006. https://www.youtube .com/watch?v=5C5_dOEyAfk.

Zimmer, Carl. 2018. *"She Has Her Mother's Laugh": The Powers, Perversions, and Potential of Heredity*. New York: Dutton.

Zipes, Jack. 2006. *Why Fairy Tales Stick: The Evolution and Relevance of a Genre*. New York: Routledge.

Zipes, Jack. 2008. "What Makes a Repulsive Frog So Appealing: Memetics and the Fairy Tale." *Journal of Folklore Research* 45 (2): 109–143.

Zipes, Jack. 2009. *Relentless Progress: The Reconfiguration of Children's Literature, Fairy Tales, and Storytelling*. New York: Routledge.

Zipes, Jack. 2011. "The Meaning of Fairy Tale within the Evolution of Culture." *Marvels & Tales: Journal of Fairy-Tale Studies* 25 (2): 221–243.

Zipes, Jack. 2013. *The Irresistible Fairy Tale: The Cultural and Social History of a Genre*. Princeton, NJ: Princeton University Press.

Zipes, Jack, ed. 2014. *The Original Folk and Fairy Tales of the Brothers Grimm*. Translated by Jack Zipes. Princeton, NJ: Princeton University Press.

Ziv, Avner. 1984. *Personality and Sense of Humor*. New York: Springer.

Zumwalt, Rosemary Lévy. 1988. *The Enigma of Arnold van Gennep (1873–1957): Master of French Folklore and Hermit of Bourg-la-Reine*. FFC Communcations No, 241. Helsinki: Suomalainen Tiedakatemia.

Index

231

ALSO BY ELLIOTT ORING

Engaging Humor

Israeli Humor: The Content and Structure of the Chizbat of the Palmah

Jokes and Their Relations

The Jokes of Sigmund Freud: A Study in Humor and Jewish Identity

Joking Asides: The Analysis, Interpretation, and Aesthetics of Humor

Just Folklore: Analysis, Interpretation, Critique

EDITED BY ELLIOTT ORING

The First Book of Jewish Jokes: The Collection of L. M. Büschenthal

Folk Groups and Folklore Genres: An Introduction

Folk Groups and Folklore Genres: A Reader

Humor and the Individual

www.ingramcontent.com/pod-product-compliance
Lightning Source LLC
Chambersburg PA
CBHW031120020426
42333CB00012B/163